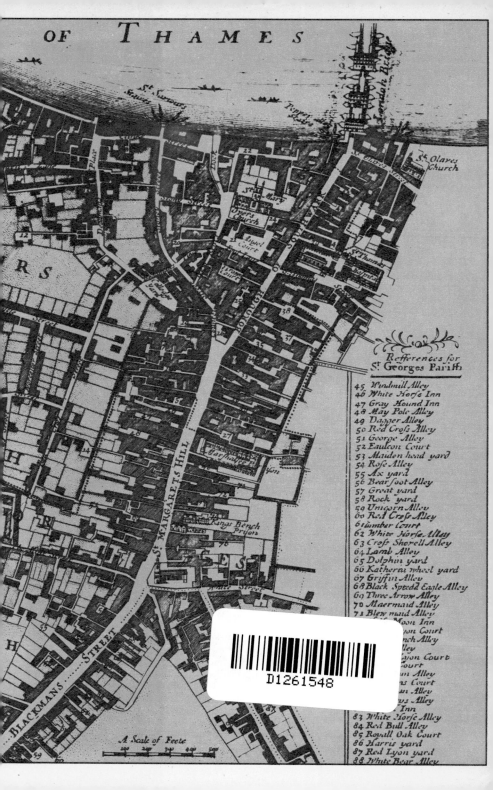

OF THAMES

St Olaves Church

Refferences for
St Georges Parish

45  Windmill Alley
46  White Horse Inn
47  Gray Hound Inn
48  May Pole Alley
49  Dagger Alley
50  Red Cross Alley
51  George Alley
52  Faulcon Court
53  Maiden head yard
54  Rose Alley
55  Ax yard
56  Bear foot Alley
57  Great yard
58  Rock yard
59  Unicorn Alley
60  Red Cross Alley
61  Lumber Court
62  White Horse Alley
63  Cross Sherell Alley
64  Lamb Alley
65  Dolphin yard
66  Katherin wheel yard
67  Griffin Alley
68  Black Spredd Eagle Alley
69  Three Arrow Alley
70  Maermaid Alley
71  Blew maid Alley
    Half Moon Inn
    Faulcon Court
    French Alley
    Alley
    Faulcon Court
    Court
    Swan Alley
    Thomas Court
    Davys Alley
    Inn
83  White Horse Alley
84  Red Bull Alley
85  Royall Oak Court
86  Harris yard
87  Red Lyon yard
88  White Bear Alley

St Margrets Hill

Kings Bench Prison

BLACKMANS STREET

A Scale of Feete

D1261548

# SOUTHWARK STORY

THE CATHEDRAL AND COLLEGIATE CHURCH OF ST. SAVIOUR AND
ST. MARY OVERIE, SOUTHWARK.

# SOUTHWARK STORY

By

## FLORENCE HIGHAM

With a foreword by
The Very Rev. H. E. Ashdown, M.A.
*Rector of St. Saviour with St. Peter, Southwark*
*Provost of Southwark Cathedral*

*To Pat, in remembrance
of our friendship and with love
to Texas and the U.S. of A.
Southwark 1975.*

*Come back soon!*

*Peter Delaney*

LONDON
## HODDER & STOUGHTON

*First printed 1955*

*Made and printed in Great Britain for Hodder and
Stoughton Limited by the Camelot Press Limited
London and Southampton*

TO

BERTRAM OUR BISHOP
(The Rt. Rev. Bertram Fitzgerald Simpson,
Fifth Bishop of Southwark)

WITH

AFFECTION AND RESPECT

# FOREWORD

THE occasion for which this story has been written is the celebration in 1955 of the golden jubilee of the foundation of the Diocese of Southwark and of the establishment of the parish church of St. Saviour and St. Mary Overie as its Cathedral. But this remarkable story needs no apology. It has not been told in full before, and it is time that it should be better known.

When Canon Thompson gave us *Southwark Cathedral, Its History and Antiquities* he planned it as a descriptive tour of the building. In spite of its digressions and the tantalising disorder into which it was thrown by later editions, it remains our guide book. Interpreted and supplemented by the work of Canon Stevens, it is an invaluable collection of notes and records to which we constantly refer; and we rarely turn in vain to Thompson's story of the stones of Southwark.

Here is the story of the people, and what a pageant of English history they present! They must not be forgotten, for to-day we owe so much to the conflicts and sufferings of the past. There has, of course, been the age-long effort to preserve our church, a struggle often sustained only by the few. More important were the battles for justice and the truth which are recorded here.

The publication of this book about the parish and church in which Lancelot Andrewes was to end his days and be buried, in the year of the four-hundredth anniversary of his birth, provides a modest recognition of our debt to a great scholar and saint. When we read how, in that same year 1555, the men who stood their trial in St. Saviour's Church were burnt alive in the name of God, believing that they died for the truth, we appreciate the deeper purpose of this book. It is not only to the labours of such as Andrewes and Nicholson that we owe the best in our Anglican inheritance. It is also to the sufferings of such men as Hooper and Gardiner that we owe our freedom to serve the truth.

7

To tell the story of 1300 years in a single parish in 300 pages is not an easy task—when that parish lies near London Bridge and in the very path of so much of English history. For the range of the story I admit myself responsible. The willingness of the author to undertake such a work is the initial reason for my admiring gratitude. In a life already full, Mrs. Higham has laid aside other important, if not more congenial, work to give us the benefit of her experience in handling original sources and all the time needed for the collecting of material, for the details of production, as well as for the writing of the book itself. My very real gratitude to her for all she has given us, and to her family for their constant help and forbearance, will most certainly be shared by all who look to the Cathedral as their own, and, I am sure, by many beyond the borders of the Diocese.

We have enjoyed the most sympathetic co-operation of the publishers, and their work will commend itself. The Friends of Southwark Cathedral may now add *Southwark Story* to the growing list of their achievements, for without their encouragement and generosity this book could not have been made. May this story help to further the purpose of their fellowship, the strengthening of the bond of mutual service between the Diocese and the Mother Church.

H. E. ASHDOWN.

# ACKNOWLEDGEMENTS

AN author has no more pleasant task than that of saying thank you and I record my gratitude to those who have helped me in writing this book with a very real appreciation of how much I owe to many whose knowledge of Southwark is deeper and of longer standing than my own. I would first thank the Corporation of Wardens of St. Saviour for permission to print excerpts from the parish records and Mr. S. Bentley, their clerk, for his help and advice. I would also acknowledge the courtesy and assistance received from the staff of the London County Record Office and of the Southwark Central library. My thanks are due to Dr. R. C. Carrington, headmaster of St. Olave's and St. Saviour's Grammar School and Miss D. A. Southwell of the Newcomen Technical School for the friendly help they have given me, and above all to Mr. George Young, secretary to the council of the Friends of Southwark Cathedral, whose devotion to St. Saviour's is so deep and so well-grounded in knowledge. I am indebted to Canon T. P. Stevens, Professor M. Deanesly and Miss K. Downham for reading parts of the manuscript and giving me their expert criticism. I must also thank Miss Benedicta Whistler for her cheerful and unfailing assistance. In choosing the illustrations and maps I have been guided by the advice of the Provost of Southwark, the Very Rev. H. E. Ashdown, Canon Laurence Brown and Canon Colin Cuttell, and I am indebted to Mrs. Freda Wallis for compiling the index. I would in conclusion record my appreciation of the help and encouragement given me at every stage by the Provost, whose faith in the project has meant so much to me.

# CONTENTS

| Chap. | | Page |
|---|---|---|
| | FOREWORD *by the Provost of Southwark* | 7 |
| I | INTRODUCTORY | 15 |
| II | BEFORE THE CONQUEST | 18 |
| III | THE CHURCH OF THE THREE WILLIAMS | 27 |
| IV | PETER OF THE ROCKS | 39 |
| V | SOUTHWARK IN ITS HEY-DAY | 52 |
| VI | WILLIAM OF WYKEHAM | 62 |
| VII | YORK AND LANCASTER | 78 |
| VIII | CHANGING TIMES | 95 |
| IX | TRAGIC DILEMMA | 110 |
| X | NEW BEGINNINGS | 122 |
| XI | ON BANKSIDE | 142 |
| XII | PARISH POLITICS | 152 |
| XIII | THE TRANQUIL YEARS | 166 |
| XIV | INTERREGNUM | 184 |
| XV | THE LATER STUARTS | 202 |
| XVI | LAISSEZ-FAIRE | 222 |
| XVII | CHANGES AND CHANCES | 246 |
| XVIII | THE CATHEDRAL | 267 |
| XIX | POSTSCRIPT | 283 |
| | NOTE ON THE CATHEDRAL WINDOWS | 293 |
| | NOTE ON SOURCES | 295 |
| | INDEX | 297 |

# LIST OF ILLUSTRATIONS

*Facing page*

The Cathedral and Collegiate Church of St. Saviour and St. Mary Overie, Southwark       *Frontispiece*
*(Photograph by Noel Warner)*

View of Southwark, *c.* 1558, by A. van den Wyngaerde     48

View of Winchester House and Gardens, *c.* 1644, by Wenceslaus Hollar     49
*(By permission of I. A. Williams)*

View of London Bridge showing St. Saviour's Church and Montague Close (temp. seventeenth century)     96
*(From* Old London Illustrated, *ed. H. A. Cox,* pub. The Builder)

The Lady Chapel To-day     97
*(Photograph by Gilbert Benham)*

The Sanctuary     112
*(Photograph by A. W. Kerr, F.I.B.P., F.R.P.S.)*

The Trehearne Monument, 1618     113
*(Photograph by S. Essex Camera Club)*

The Candelabrum given by Dorothy Applebee in 1680     113
*(Photograph by Gilbert Benham)*

The Nave of the Cathedral Church looking West     168
*(Photograph by T. S. Mobey)*

London and Southwark, *c.* 1600, by C. V. Visscher     *between*
*(By permission of the London County Council's Library)*     168 *and* 169

Lancelot Andrewes, Bishop of Winchester, 1619-26     169
*(By permission of the Bodleian Library, Oxford)*

William Austin of Lincoln's Inn (d. 1634), from the frontispiece to his collected works (pub. 1635)     169
*(By permission of the Trustees of the British Museum)*

*Facing page*

St. Mary Overie's Dock to-day     240
*(Photograph by A. W. Kerr, F.I.B.P., F.R.P.S.)*

The Yard of the old Tabard Inn     241

St. Thomas's Church, now the Chapter House     241
*(Hanslip Fletcher drawing by permission of* Sunday Times*)*

Guy's Hospital looking over the bombed site of Great Maze Pond     256
*(Photograph by E. P. Miles)*

Bankside Boys: the Parishioners of the future     257
*(Photograph by J. H. Shelton, F.R.I.C.)*

Map of the Diocese of Southwark     *page* 281

### Front endpaper

*The Eighteenth-century Map.* This Map of the Parishes of St. Saviour's and St. George's was printed in 1720 for Strype's edition of Stow's *Survey of London*
*(Reproduced by permission of the London County Council's Library)*

### Back endpaper

*The Modern Map* has been drawn to show the ancient roads and lanes which survive and the modern roads and railways which have transformed the area. The churches and schools mentioned in the book are marked

# INTRODUCTORY

THE Cathedral Church of Southwark stands at the Surrey end of London Bridge, hemmed in by wharves and warehouses, the Borough Market on the southern side and a great brewery nearby. No gracious buildings, no green close surround it, fit for the successors of Trollope's clerical dignitaries, only between the market and church lies a narrow strip of garden, well-loved and well-tended, a welcome resting place for tired worker or for tramp. From the viaduct above, the thunder of the trains challenges the indomitable ardour of the bells. The passer-by, looking over the parapet from the roadway, notes, on a level with his eye, the fine tracery of the four windows of the Lady Chapel, the strength and dignity of the ancient square tower. Curious to see more, he may walk down the steps and through the quiet garden and so enter the cathedral and collegiate church of St. Saviour and St. Mary Overie.

The nave of Southwark is a modern copy of a thirteenth-century original. The stalwart columns and groined roof lead the eye onward and upward to the lovely choir and the fine Tudor altar-screen. Behind is the retro-choir, Southwark's particular jewel, known incorrectly but lovingly as the Lady Chapel. All this is basically thirteenth-century work and the whole forms a unity that makes it one of the finest medieval buildings left in London, marked though it is by much and careful restoration. This evidence of continued care is as it should be for Southwark is no dead historical monument but a living church. True there have been errors of taste and judgment; had our predecessors in the early nineteenth century been both richer and more enlightened, the original nave need not have perished in decay; had their predecessors of Tudor and Stuart times not been blinded by their zeal, the old glass and the old records of the medieval church might have survived. To the shortcomings of men have been added the assaults of nature, and fire, more than once, has done grave damage to the fabric. But neither the chance of circumstance nor their own mistakes have broken the spirit of those who loved this place. Somehow or other, beauty has been preserved; come well, come ill, the worship of God has continued.

That is the secret of the appeal of Southwark Cathedral. No sooner is one within its walls than one knows that here is holy ground, a place where people have prayed. It may be empty except for a few sight-seers, it may be full for one of its great services, men of the Borough on a national occasion, elderly people at a service for the aged, boys and girls from the schools of the diocese, or a motley congregation from Reigate and Rother-hithe, Camberwell and Kingston bringing their parish contributions to the work of the church in South London. But whether the place be full or empty, the feeling of prayer lingers in its very stones. On every side are the memorials to those who once have worshipped here, a crusader, a poet, an eminent London citizen, a bishop, more than one. But in the main they were simple folk. Let St. Paul's and the Abbey claim their heroic dead. St. Saviour's, Southwark, was a parish church (as it still is to-day) for some three hundred and sixty years before it became a Cathedral in 1905. With a few glorious exceptions, those remembered here are not the illustrious great but the men and women who lived and worked and died on Bankside and along the Borough High Street in the years when Shakespeare acted at the Globe, when Goldsmith as a young doctor tended the Southwark poor, when Dickens wrote Little Dorrit and described for all time the infamous Marshalsea. And behind these years as the parish church of St. Saviour, there stretch another seven centuries during which, at first as a college of priests and then as a great Augustinian priory, the church of St. Mary Overie witnessed to the things of the spirit at the southern end of London Bridge.

The worship of God and the service of their fellows, such was the rule of St. Augustine to which the Canons vowed obedience, who came to St. Mary Overie's during the twelfth century. One of the first recorded acts in the history of the Priory was the foundation of a hospital dedicated to St. Thomas, to succour the wounded and the needy wayfarers passing to and fro across the bridge. The new capitalists of the Borough in Tudor and Stuart

times turned much of their money to good account in the provision of almshouses and schools, and Edward Alleyn, rich through
the profits of theatres and bear-baiting, gave to posterity God's
Gift of Dulwich College. With other years come other problems.
To-day, the Cathedral stands as the headquarters in the fight to
save South London from the frustration and despair that come
from too long a disregard of things eternal. There is no need to
regret the serenity of the Close. It is well for the church whose
concern is with the puzzling, challenging life of to-day that it
should stand as it does among the wharves and warehouses with
the trains thundering by overhead. Alert to the needs of the community which it serves and proclaiming day by day the worship
of the risen Lord, it opens its doors to all who labour in this place,
that some at least may pause and turn aside and pray, and feel
across the centuries their unity with those who loved the Borough
and Bankside in former years.

# II

# BEFORE THE CONQUEST

IN the days of the Roman occupation there were people living in the place which is now Southwark, though the archæologists dispute with vigour as to the nature and extent of the settlement and the lie of the great roads approaching the river from the south. A spit of gravel among the surrounding swamps made it possible to build at this point just as a similar deposit on the north bank formed the foundation of the thriving trading centre that became Londinium. In all probability, Londinium was linked with the settlement across the river by a bridge, at this the lowest point of the Thames where there were "firm and fordable" places, and upon this crossing, a little to the eastward of the present London Bridge, there converged (so most of the authorities agree) the two great roads of Watling Street, running inland from Dover, and the Stane Street which came by way of Chichester and Dorking over the Leatherhead downs. In A.D. 62 while the Roman commander-in-chief was absent subduing Anglesey, the triumphant Boadicea swept down upon London slaughtering, ravaging and burning. At the first threat of her approach, many of the more prudent traders crossed the river while others escaped in the panic of the onslaught, and it was probably from this date that a colony of prosperous citizens developed on the south bank. The tessellated pavement discovered in 1832 in the churchyard of St. Saviour's is one indication among others that citizens of wealth and standing lived here in the later Roman period.

Five centuries later came the Saxon invasions, the withdrawal of Rome and darkness over the land. No sign of a bridge remained when the invaders sailed up the Thames, settling along its shores or prospecting in their tiny boats up the Wandle to establish themselves at Mitcham and Beddington and elsewhere. To this area was given in due course the name of Suthrige, the

South region, which became the Surrey of later times. Lying between the kingdoms of Kent and Wessex, it was a remote isolated area, characterised even then by the double loyalty that continued throughout Southwark's history, to the settlements along the river dominated by London and to the hinterland southward which looked towards Winchester.

In 597, Augustine landed in Kent and pin-points of light began to shew in the darkness. The first missionaries to England were so perturbed, it is said, by the rumours they heard at Aix-en-Provence that they wrote back to Rome suggesting that the project be cancelled. St. Gregory replied that it were better never to begin a good work than, after it was once begun, to go from it again and the mission proceeded without serious mishap, "save only," wrote Fuller in his *Church History*, "at the village of Saye in Anjou, where some giggling housewives (light leaves will be wagged with little wind) causelessly fell a-flouting at them." Shortly after Augustine had established himself at Canterbury the Pope sent him reinforcements and among the newcomers were Mellitus, Justus and Paulinus, learned and distinguished natives of Italy who gave up all that they knew of civilised living for this odyssey to England.

Mellitus became the first Bishop of London in 604 and the founder of St. Paul's. At the same time, Justus was made Bishop of Rochester, the first of the long line of Fathers-in-God who have cherished the Christian people of the south bank. It is fitting that a place should have been found for him in the restored altar screen in the Cathedral to-day as Paulinus, the third holder of the See, was commemorated in one of the baptistery windows. There were many vicissitudes in these years when Christianity was firmly planted in this country and we know next to nothing of the men who preached the faith. Paulinus had gone as chaplain with King Ethelbert's daughter when she married Edwin of Northumbria, and up and down the dales of Yorkshire had taught the gospel of Christ, baptising in that land of running water, where no churches were, all who came in hope and longing to find an answer to the mystery of life in this new compelling faith. When Justus had become Archbishop and his successor at Rochester had been drowned on his way back to Rome, Paulinus accepted the see, for in Fuller's pithy words, "he minded not whether he went up or down hill whilst he went on straight in his calling to glorify God and edify others."

The Saxons took to Christianity somewhat slowly, the people following their chiefs' example both in conversion and relapse. It was Erconwald, a Saxon thegn and a Bishop of London, who in 666 founded at Chertsey the first known minster in Surrey. Some four years later he established at Barking in Essex a nunnery, dedicated to St. Hilda. It is to these years that legend attributes another house of sisters on the south bank, and the fact of the nunnery at Barking shows that there is no inherent reason why the legend may not have been true. If so, it was this second house of sisters dedicated to St. Mary Overie, that stood on the site of the later priory and marks the beginning of the unbroken tradition of worship which is still upheld in the Cathedral of Southwark to-day.

In the Close of the dissolved Priory, during the disturbed years of the mid-sixteenth century, Linsted the last prior lived out his days in peace. Here John Stow discovered him, when he crossed the river to Southwark to find out what he could about the beginnings of London Bridge, and from him he heard the story of the fair church called St. Mary-over-the-Rie. It was "of old time long before the conquest a house of sisters founded by a maiden named Mary, unto the which house and sisters, she left (as was left to her by her parents) the oversight and profits of a cross ferry, or traverse ferry over the Thames, there kept before that any bridge was builded." Others were less restrained than Stow in telling the story. The maiden's name, they said, was Mary Overs and her father, the ferryman, old John Overs, was so miserly a creature that he pretended death to ensure that at least for one day his friends would fast. "The true history" of his life and sudden death was published at "the Looking Glass on London Bridge" in 1744, wherein one may read of the tragic result of this macabre trick, for hearing sounds of revelry at his funeral feast the outraged "corpse" leapt up and entered the room whereupon one of the company, thinking he saw a ghost, struck him a fatal blow. His daughter Mary, beautiful and pious according to the legend, had a lover who fell from his horse and was killed as he hastened to her side, and the young woman, left desolate, devoted the ferryman's fortune to the foundation of the house of sisters by whom the ferry was maintained.

Divested of its unlikely if attractive trimmings, the story of the ferry and its connection with an early nunnery is not improbable. But the dedication of the church on the south bank was undoubtedly to the Virgin Mary. Indeed, in the majority of records prior to the fifteenth century the church is called simply St. Mary's, Southwark. The "overie" used in common parlance, which persisted long after the Priory was dissolved, signified simply, as at Dartford and elsewhere, "across the river," "on the bank" or "over the ferry." According to Stow's report the house of sisters was later converted into a college of priests, "who in place of the ferry built a bridge of timber and from time to time kept the place in good reparations. . . ." It was St. Swithun, Bishop of Winchester in 852, who probably made the change, perhaps because of the Danish invasions and the vulnerable nature of the site by the river. St. Swithun was a great bridge-builder himself and the care of the river-crossings was one of the many practical works of mercy in which the church was concerned, but although the existence of the college of priests is reasonably certain, one does not know whether they did indeed build a wooden bridge or merely maintained the ferry. Colleges of secular priests appeared in increasing numbers in Saxon England after Alfred's reign. Their members lived a corporate life without taking the monastic vows, and had for their two-fold aim the worship of God in their church and the care of the people among whom they dwelt. Nothing is known of the priests in Southwark, but during the next two centuries of growing intercourse with Europe, there would be much coming and going along the roads that led to the sea, much traffic between the city and the suburb, now known as Sudwerke, which was the southern defence work of London. And though not proven it is probable that already near to the crossing stood St. Mary Overie's, whose priests ministered to all and sundry in perils of fire and sickness and sudden death, and whose quiet precincts were a symbol of eternity in the midst of stridency and change.

St. Swithun, who like Justus of Rochester looks down from the Cathedral's altar-screen, was Bishop of Winchester for ten years in the reign of King Alfred's father, and from his day until

1877, Southwark remained within the Winchester diocese.
Swithun himself, one of the finest of the Saxon churchmen, pos-
sessing an equal measure of learning and humility, consorted with
kings and when he died asked to be buried on the northern side
of the churchyard, where the common folk lay and sun and rain
fell on all alike. When he was canonised and men tried to flout his
wishes by removing his body to a costly tomb within the church
at Winchester, a great storm broke over them, so the story went,
and for forty days and nights it rained without ceasing.

> St. Swithun's day, gif ye do rain
> For forty days it will remain.
> St. Swithun's day, an ye be fair
> For forty days, 'twill rain no mair.

Alfred's strong rule checked for a while the menace of the
Danes, but in the last years of the tenth century, fresh waves of
marauding invaders swept up the Thames from Scandinavia.
Although in 993 Olaf Tryggvason sailed as far as Staines without
obstruction, London seems to have been regarded as a barrier
and there was probably a bridge of sorts during most of these
stormy days. In 1009, according to the Anglo-Saxon Chronicle,
the Danes at the close of a successful campaign "took up winter
quarters on the Thames. . . . They made frequent attacks on the
borough of London but praise be to God she still stands safe and
sound." Three years later, however, London surrendered to
Sweyn, and in 1014 Olaf of Norway came as the ally of Ethelred
the Unready to help him regain his kingdom. It is at this point
that Southwark and London Bridge emerge in the forefront of
the story as recorded in the thirteenth century in the Icelandic
sagas of Snorre Sturlason. "A great trading place which is called
Suthvirki" lay opposite to London, and this the Danes had fortified with large ditches and a bulwark of stone, timber and turf.
Between it and the capital "there was a bridge so broad that two
waggons could pass each other upon it" and this also had been
well barricaded. The bridge was supported by piles embedded in
the river. When Ethelred and Olaf advanced they found it impossible to dislodge the enemy either from Southwark or the
bridge, whereupon Olaf and his men tore down old houses and

built wooden rafts, roofed to protect them from the stones that came hurling down. Making their way beneath the bridge they fastened strong ropes around the piles, and then with all their might they rowed down stream. As the cables tautened the whole structure groaned and shuddered and mightily collapsed.

> London Bridge is broken down,
> Gold is won and bright renown,
> Shields resounding,
> War horns sounding
> Hildur shouting in the din;
> Arrows singing,
> Mailcoats ringing
> Odin makes our Olaf win!

Thereafter Southwark was stormed and taken. Olaf himself had recently been baptised, but Saint or Viking, Odin's man or Christ's, it made little difference to those who suffered in the onslaught. He took back with him to Norway Saxon priests to help him to unify and convert his country, but in 1030 his people rose against him and he was slain in battle, and at the southern end of London Bridge, where once he had encamped, they built in the next century, as elsewhere in London, a church dedicated to the memory of the soldier saint. St. Olave's parish lay eastward of the bridge, and developed into a district peopled increasingly by traders and artisans of every kind, many of foreign extraction and closely connected with the traffic of the Thames. With the parish west of the High Street later to become St. Saviour's, its fortunes were interlocked; a seventeenth century communion cup belonging to St. Olave's is among the oldest pieces of Cathedral plate and in their joint schools the names of the two churches are honourably linked. But of Olaf himself, third figure on the altarscreen, one knows little more than of the myriad others who during these years were hammering England into shape. The picture of Southwark, however, is gradually emerging, in times of war the outwork of defence, the prosperous market in days of peace, on the spit of gravel opposite to London with swamps all about it to prevent a wider growth. Through these swamps Canute cut a canal in 1016 and brought his fleet by that means to attack London from the south-west side. Only once is there a hint of the priests' more immediate concerns. When peace was restored and Canute was established King of England he made one great act of restitution. In 1012 Aelfheah, the saintly Archbishop of Canterbury, had been murdered by Danish soldiers when he had attempted to restrain them; eleven years later his body was exhumed at St. Paul's and "the illustrious king, the archbishop, diocesan bishops, earls and very many others, both clergy and laity, conveyed his holy body by ship over the Thames to Southwark," thence, "with a distinguished following and happy jubilation," the body was carried to Rochester and thereafter to Canterbury, "to the eternal salvation of all those who daily resort there to his holy body with devout heart and in all humility." Of such strange contrasts is the story of Saxon England compounded.

During the comparatively tranquil reigns of Canute and Edward the Confessor, Southwark was in the possession of Godwin, the great Saxon Earl, who united under his leadership, in opposition to Edward's French advisers, the national aspirations of the Anglo-Saxon people. There is no reference to the College of priests in the annals of these years when in turn Godwin and his son Harold were banished and returned triumphant, confident that when they and their men sailed up the Thames the bank on the Surrey side would be crowded with eager friends. Yet in all these stresses of war and calamity the priests alone could heal and succour; in times of peace they alone had learning to teach the children or to counsel kings. In Southwark, when Edward the Confessor died, there existed according to the Domesday Book one minster (*monasterium*) held of the King and one tide-way (*aque fluctum*) or wharf "where ships used to come alongside," the dues being divided between the King who took two parts and Godwin who took a third. How far the College had survived the Danish wars, how far it was still an effective force is doubtful. There was much decay and disintegration in the religious life in every part of the country, so much so that though something was lost in the process, the discipline and reorganisation of the Norman régime were necessary if the Church were to survive. That unwelcome yet perhaps salutary change was now imminent. When William the Conqueror advanced after Hastings, he found barring his way to the capital, the sullen hatred of Southwark, staunchly loyal to Godwin's sons. He did not challenge it but, turning up-stream, crossed the Thames at Wallingford and approached London from the west. He left Southwark in flames behind him, and his duty as a soldier, to allow no active enemy to threaten his rear, consorted well with his inclination to ravage Harold's patrimony.

Thus stormily amid the clash of swords and the menace of fire, the Borough came to birth. After 1066, Godwin's lands passed to the Conqueror's half-brother, Odo of Bayeux, who during his tenure of the vil gave the church and the profits of the wharf to one Adelold in exchange for a house. This involved him in a quarrel with the Sheriff of Surrey who declared that he had not received the King's precept or seal regarding this transaction. A dispute about the tolls followed, only the first of the many conflicts of jurisdiction between lord of the manor and the King's officers, between the City and the county, which were to continue right down to the nineteenth century. In this as in most of the other disputes the result was indecisive. The Sheriff withdrew from the suit on the ground that it was not being conducted "justly to the King's advantage" from which it would seem that the balance of power rested with the lord of the vil. Certainly the feudal lord played a large part in the Southwark story in the years ahead. When Odo of Bayeux forfeited his lands through rebellion the manor was granted to William de Warenne, one of the Conqueror's most trusted advisers, who had set out with him from Normandy to carve out his fortunes by the power of a strong right arm. And so for the next two hundred years it was the family of de Warenne who were the lords of Southwark, and who enriched the church with their benefactions and came in person to the Borough when they rode in from their wide estates to attend the Councils of the King.

## Note on Sources

For Roman Southwark see *Victoria County History*, London, I, 30–43, 82; Historic Manuscripts Commission: *Inventory of*

*Historic Monuments in London,* pp. 12, 14, 32, 51 *seq.*, and Taylor, *Annals of St. Mary Overy*, pp. 7, 15. Stow's *Survey of London* (Ed. Kingsford) II, 56, gives the legend of the House of Sisters, and other early references occur in the *Anglo-Saxon Chronicle* (trans. and edited by G. N. Garmonsway in the Everyman's library No. 624). Gordon Home quotes the Icelandic sagas in *Old London Bridge* (1931), pp. 11-13.

# III

# THE CHURCH OF THE THREE WILLIAMS

WILLIAM DE WARENNE, who was known before his death as Earl of Surrey, had not been disappointed in the good fortune that his loyalty and his might had won for him in England. In 1086 at the time of the Domesday survey he owned land in twelve counties and at least three castles, of which Lewes in Sussex was his favourite. His loyalty was unimpeachable and he was a not unworthy representative of the feudal baron playing his part in an ordered society in which each man knew his status, whether warrior, priest or peasant, and the violence and cruelty which were the hard facts of existence were redeemed by the disciplined living alike of soldier and of monk. It was a conception not easily realised in a disordered world, as the violent struggles between Pope and Emperor all too clearly showed, but William I had set out from Normandy with the Pope's blessing on his expedition and in an attempt to achieve a measure of order and unity in church and state, had called to be his Archbishop, Lanfranc, the Prior of Bec, an abbey which followed the Cluniac observance. During the eleventh century a genuine movement of reform had been initiated at Cluny; learning had been encouraged, piety deepened and cells were established throughout Europe, all owing allegiance to the abbey from which they had sprung and sending out trained and disciplined men to play their part in the council of kings and the service of the Church.

De Warenne and his wife, who had stayed at Cluny on a pilgrimage to Rome, founded at Lewes the first Cluniac cell in England. In 1082, five years later, a London merchant called Alwyn Child built a church among the Southwark marshes on an island of higher ground, known as Bermondsey. With Lanfranc's approval he invited four monks from the Cluniac priory of La Charité sur Loire to come and serve his church. After some delay they arrived, and when in 1094 William Rufus endowed the small community with the Manor of Bermondsey, in return for hospitality whenever required, the future of this off-shoot of Cluny was assured. Endowments flowed in and though most of their land in Southwark was in St. Olave's parish, there was one stretch that lay to the west of the decayed college, whose priests probably looked with no good grace on these Frenchmen of the Loire thrust into their midst. They themselves, however, did not remain unaffected by the reforming zeal of the period. In 1106 two Norman knights, William Dauncey and William Pont de l'Arche, assisted after 1107 by William Giffard, Bishop of Winchester, refounded the college, which became a priory of canons, and set about to build a new and worthy church.

Of the church of the three Williams nothing is left in the Cathedral to-day beyond a few traces of Norman work in the north transept and nave, a recess at the western end of the north aisle and the outline of the doorway by which the canons went in and out of the cloisters. Further to the east is the Prior's entrance, at one time a fine and elaborate piece of work, which was discovered in a mutilated state when the nave was rebuilt in the nineteenth century. Only the jambs on which it rested now survive. Traces of Saxon workmanship discovered in a shaft in the outer wall of St. John's Chapel, now restored as the Harvard Chapel, probably indicate that this was the site of a Saxon church whose stones would be embodied in the Norman building. The conventual buildings of the Priory lay, contrary to usual custom, on the northern side between the church and the river, but any who seek to-day for traces of them find themselves in an intricate maze of wharf and warehouse where they are more likely to be entangled with cranes and lorries than to meet the ghost of any Austin Canon.

William Pont de l'Arche was a member of the royal household and had for a while been the King's Treasurer. He took his name from a town in Normandy, famous for its bridge of twenty-two arches, and went frequently between Normandy and England in the entourage of the Conqueror's sons, William Rufus and Henry I; he was one of the small band of knights and clerics concerned with the daily administration of the household and of England. William Giffard was another of those whom the King trusted. He had been Chancellor to Rufus and soon after Henry I's succession was Bishop-designate of Winchester. King Henry put him in possession of the temporalties of the see and Archbishop Anselm invested him with the pastoral staff, but before he was consecrated he was caught up in the quarrel between the King and his Archbishop, which was part of the long difficulty of reconciling church and state.

The dispute turned on the question of lay investiture. Anselm, with that quiet obstinacy which so often marks the saint, refused to consecrate any further bishops until the King ceased to demand homage from them as for their spiritual office. Rather than submit, he withdrew to Europe. Henry at once required the Archbishop of York to consecrate Giffard and another bishop-elect at a great service at St. Paul's. A King's orders were not lightly to be disregarded and preparations for the ceremony were put in hand. The day came and a great congregation assembled, the bishops knelt, the service began. Then, and only then, something greater than himself impelled William Giffard to resist. To the consternation of the assembly he rose, protesting that he could not with a good conscience receive his consecration from any other than his lawful primate. The service ended precipitately and Giffard did not linger. He withdrew speedily to the Continent where he stayed for some three years heartened by Anselm's gratitude and friendship. He probably came back to England in 1105, shortly before a compromise settlement of the points at issue enabled the Archbishop also to return. In 1107 Anselm consecrated Giffard, who, now in full possession of his see, assisted his two friends in building the nave of St. Mary Overie's and prepared to erect for himself a town house near to the new church.

Southwark, if developed properly, was an ideal spot for an ecclesiastical residence. The Prior of Lewes already had a house close to that of his patron, the second William de Warenne. Other dignitaries were soon to follow suit. The roads running south in all directions were sufficiently good for journeys to and from Winchester or Dover not to be over-arduous; it was easy to get by boat to Westminster for meetings of the Great Council, or to cross into the City to visit the King in the Tower. On the western side of St. Mary Overie's there was only a scattering of houses along the river, and here Bishop Giffard decided to build, renting from Bermondsey a hide of land that ran inland some little way from the river and stretched upstream as far as the Wydfleete or Pudding Mill, which within a few years was leased to the Knights Templars.

Thus the face of Southwark changed. It was no longer merely the busy mart, the first stage on the journey, though this it always was and has remained. It became also, as the twelfth century progressed, the home of great prelates, whose comings and goings with their numerous retainers gave life and business to the borough. And with all the new buildings Winchester House could brook comparison, with its great hall and fine rose window and lovely park. As the magnificent church arose beside it, Bishop Giffard with twenty years of growing wealth and power before him looked with satisfaction on his handiwork. His piety was genuine though it is not easy to apprehend that mixture of piety with worldly astuteness which was the Norman churchman. Giffard was a man of determined character as his temerity at St. Paul's indicated, *vir nobilissimus* a contemporary chronicler calls him. All too often in those twenty years the Holy Spirit of God, that had seemed so near to him on that fatal day when he went into exile, appeared to have withdrawn. Arrogance, ill-temper, worldliness, of all these sins at times he was guilty, and after Anselm's death no firm and gentle friend was there to guide him. But at the end he caught again a glimpse of the heavenly vision and spent his last days among his monks at Winchester, wearing their dress, taking his place among the novices and going thence to the infirmary to die.

The church of the Three Williams prospered, richly endowed by the King himself and by the Earl of Surrey of the day, the second William de Warenne. A reckless young man whose earlier record of loyalty had not been as unspotted as his father's, he had become one of King Henry's closest friends and his companion on the battlefields of Normandy. When the Priory was founded at St. Mary Overie's he granted it sixty acres called Wadeland at Footscray in Kent and the advowsons of various Surrey churches. It was the custom of the feudal age in which the symbol played so large a part, for such endowments to be marked by the exchange of a piece of personal property and the first formal ceremony to be noted in the annals of the Priory was on the occasion of Earl William's gift of Kirkesfeld, or Crechesfeld, the church at Reigate where his Surrey castle stood. With due solemnity, he placed on the altar of St. Mary Overie's his small dagger (*cultellum*) which lay there through the night, to be retrieved next morning by the Prior. In the same year Hugh de Stokes and his wife gave to the Priory the church of Stoke Poges and the quiet spot that a poet was to make immortal made its first appearance in history when Hugh's brother, Reginald, laid down his dagger in Bishop Giffard's presence on St. Mary's altar.

From Banstead, Wendover, Tooting and even as far afield as Hokering in Norfolk the endowments came. Henry II bestowed upon the canons the neighbouring parish church of St. Margaret which stood in the highway a little to the southward. The Earls of Surrey continued to befriend it. The second Earl's son, another William, died in 1148 on a crusade in which he had accompanied his kinsman, St. Louis of France. But his younger brother, Reginald was buried in St. Mary Overie's and he and his sister Beatrice made it many benefactions. The third Earl had left one daughter to whom his estates passed and by his marriage with this rich heiress, Hamelin, a natural brother of Henry II, acquired the name and fortune of the Warennes. He did not forget the duty he owed to the church, and the Priory received from him the advowsons of Newdigate and Mitcham and five city churches, St. Benet Sherehog, St. Mary Abchurch, St. Mildred Bread Street, St. Mildred Poultry and Trinity the Less. A more humble donor, William de Rose, gave the hermitage of Plumstead "with three acres of land in the marshes and a certain wood," to provide for the upkeep of a chaplain.

The temporalties also grew in number. King Stephen, whose brother Henry of Blois became Bishop of Winchester after Giffard's death, endowed St. Mary's with a tithe of his farm in Southwark and confirmed the grant of a house in Dowgate which had belonged to Pont de l'Arche. From an Earl of Pembroke, who intermarried with the Warennes, came a "mansion at Easinges with the garden and ten acres of meadow-land." The family of Scales in Cambridgeshire were constant benefactors, little guessing that beneath the shadow of St. Mary Overie's one of their family would meet a violent end. From the Fitzgeralds at Kingston Lisle in Berkshire came "two weighs of cheese" as well as the land at Walton which belonged to Alexander Fitzgerald: he willed also that "if he died in those parts" he should be buried in the Priory. And in return for all these gifts, in gratitude and to the glory of God, the Canons said their masses and prayed as in duty bound for the souls of the faithful departed, while beyond the Close, up and down the High Street and over London Bridge the life of the world outside went its tumultuous way.

The Priors of St. Mary's, Southwark, in this first century of its existence are little more than names; Aldgod, the first of them, whose figure appears on the altar-screen, may well have been of Saxon origin and one of the superseded priests who joined the new foundation after 1106. He lived till 1130, long enough to see the Priory well established. Many of his successors, also, held office for a number of years, for example Valerianus, from 1163 to 1189, and William of Oxford from that year till 1203. It boded well for the peace and stability of the Priory, and stability was a precious quality in those turbulent days. It owed its fortunate state very largely to the patronage of the good neighbour at Winchester House next door; Richard Toclyve, for instance, Bishop from 1174 to 1188, took St. Mary's and all its possessions under his special care, confirming the canons in the quiet enjoyment of their various properties and calling down maledictions upon any who interfered. No picture of the medieval Priory is complete if one does not in imagination place beside it the prelate-statesmen of Winchester House, who throughout the Middle Ages in so many different capacities played a leading part in the evolution of England.

From that outer world the canons of St. Mary's were not entirely remote. Certainly the sacrist, who was in charge of the services at St. Margaret's, would be well-acquainted with the traffic of the streets. It was not by chance that the three Williams had chosen to found a community of canons, not just another monastery. A characteristic of the monks proper was their separateness, a feature stressed in the new Cistercian order who sited their abbeys in distant spots where the monks could work and worship and yet remain unspotted from the world. Such was the site of Waverley among the Surrey pines, the Cistercian house which Bishop Giffard founded. Canons were not separate in quite the same way. They were priests, living in a religious community but continuing to fulfil their priestly duties, serving their bishop in his cathedral or taking charge of a parish or teaching or tending the sick. Thus an attempt was made to solve the problem that increased daily with the growth of trade and the market towns, of great centres of population inadequately served by secular clergy who were sometimes devoted, often ignorant, and frequently guilty of moral slackness, which the reforming popes of the eleventh century too easily identified with the tendency to marry, a practice they were as ready to condemn as the other prevalent habit of living with a concubine. It was to improve the standards of the clergy in the towns and to make better provision for the people that the conception of priests living under a rule of poverty, obedience and above all of chastity, was developed in the first quarter of the century, with the same fervour that had been expended earlier on the cells of Cluny.

Prior to 1106 such bodies of canons as existed in England had been established to meet a special purpose, to serve a hospital, to provide as at Huntingdon a song school, to minister to a number of scattered churches as originally at Barnwell in Cambridgeshire. After that date, their numbers rapidly increased. They were established at St. Hilda's, Aldgate, in 1108, and in the same year Gilbert of Merton invited a small group from Huntingdon to set up on his land on the Stane Street, some eight miles south of London, a Priory which grew all too quickly in power and riches. Sometimes as at Southwark a decayed college of secular priests was infused with new life and reconstituted on the monastic basis, and in 1123 Rahere, the King's jester, recuperating in Rome after a dangerous illness, was impelled by a vision to return to London to found at Smithfield an Augustinian Priory dedicated to St. Bartholomew and the care of the sick and needy. Before fashion changed in favour of the more rigorous Cistercians, some two hundred houses of Canons Regular had been set up in England.

In spite of its comparatively late development on monastic lines, the order could look back for its beginning to the years that followed the break-up of the Roman Empire when for the sake of security as well as training, the clergy whom a bishop gathered round him came to depend upon a common purse and shared a common life. It was for such a community that St. Augustine of Hippo first laid down his rule. There had been later variants; in the eighth century, Chrodegang, Bishop of Metz, had drawn up a rule based on the communal apostolic life, and in Lanfranc's time Ivo of Chartres had produced another, but gradually, the majority of canons professed themselves followers of the rule of St. Augustine, with its wise admixture of discipline and sound spiritual counsel, later summed up in the words, "Before all things, dearest brethren, let God be loved and then your neighbour." As Augustine's detailed precepts had proved too stringent for general adoption, the rule was usually supplemented in each priory by a set of Observances by which every-day behaviour was ordered and which often varied from place to place in immaterial points. The Observances in use in the priory of Barnwell in Cambridgeshire still survive and enable one to obtain a vivid picture of the canons' daily life.

St. Augustine's rule, as eventually adopted, was not as strict as that of the other monastic orders. A thirteenth-century writer, Guyot de Provence, described it as "more courteous than that of Benedict" and added "among them one is well-shod, well clothed and well fed. They go out when they like, mix with the world and talk at table." In the Barnwell Observances the canons were reminded that Augustine "had no wish to confine his disciples within an iron fence beyond what they could bear, but by the help of a less severe rule to induce them to enter the harbour of salvation as lovers of spiritual beauty." The Observances in use at Southwark may have differed considerably from those of Barnwell in points of detail. But the shape of the twenty-four hours was probably the same, with worship in the church as the framework in which the days were set, and so it is possible to reconstruct their pattern. At some hour between midnight and the dawn the main service of matins and lauds took place; it was then customary for the canons to return to their dormitories and sleep until another bell summoned them to prime. The day was divided into hours, that varied in length with the seasons and were measured by the sun not by the clock. Every third "hour" there was a service in the church. Between prime and terce the daily Chapter was held at which the Prior appeared in his full authority to order alike the temporal affairs and the spiritual well-being of his flock. Here the brethren daily confessed their faults and if necessary were punished, in which decisions the Prior depended greatly on the shrewd advice of the sub-prior, generally chosen for just those qualities which would enable him to mediate between his superior and the convent. At the Chapter, matters of general policy were discussed, the younger members usually keeping silence but "should the spirit of wisdom . . . which gives intelligence to babes sometimes touch their hearts, let them state their reasons with modesty and reverence in the spirit of humility."

When there was time to spare between the services the canons worked in the cloister and were allowed to talk in seemly fashion. In Southwark, they had also certain pastoral duties outside the Priory. After terce, High Mass was celebrated, followed by sext the service of the sixth hour. Then, and only then, dinner was served and the brothers broke their fast. Here the Observances left no opening for slovenly behaviour. "It is the duty of the fraterer to lay the table-cloths at proper times . . . to set clean salt on each table in clean salt-cellars and if it should have got damp to serve it out for use in the kitchen." He had also to be particularly careful that the bread had not been gnawed by mice and that the hatch was kept clean so that "dishes dirty on the under side may not be set before the brethren." After dinner, during which a canon read aloud, there was a period of rest in the dorter until the hour of none, when the brethren went again to the church. There followed a drink and the washing of the hands, an act which had about it a certain symbolic character, a making clean of the outer man to match the inner purity for which they were striving. With an hour in the cloister and with evensong the canons' day came quietly to an end, and when they had supped and said the sweet office of compline, the brothers went in tranquillity to bed.

No, there was little of hardship in the life of the brethren, once their bodies were accustomed to the long fast and the broken rest. There was however a complete lack of privacy that must have been extremely galling. In the service of the choir, every detail of the liturgy, the very movements of the body were carefully ordered; no over-zealous spirit was to spoil the perfection of the tune, "and do not sing anything except that which you have read to be sung." This discipline was only relaxed when the canons withdrew periodically, for blood-letting, when for a few days they were released from all duties and "living free from care" were encouraged to walk in the priory garden, "telling each other the secrets of the heart." Did their steps lead them at St. Mary Overie's to the northern edge of the precincts where they could watch from their quiet sanctuary the traffic of the Thames and the gay panorama of roofs and towers and battlements upon the City shore?

In practice some scope was provided for brethren of strong character, for the running of the priory depended on the "obedientiaries," and any who possessed marked ability or personality were usually entrusted with a specific task. At the apex was the Prior, with the sub-prior as his adjutant, the former requiring deep gifts of humility if he were not to be corrupted by his complete authority, the latter needing to combine great administrative skill with a shrewd understanding of human nature if he were to settle aright the petty differences and the day-to-day crises of their circumscribed existence. The church services were in the care of the precentor, who was often also the librarian. The Observances urged him to walk so humbly and sing so sweetly and with such devotion that he should be worthy of an office "which is a source of delight and pleasure to God, the Angels and mankind." Upon the sacrist and his subordinate depended the care of the church buildings and the time keeping that was all important: it was the subsacrist who rang the bell for the services at night. The most important official in charge of the Priory's temporal affairs was the cellarer, who not only kept an eye on the kitchen but was responsible for the rents and upkeep of the outside properties. A man of thrift and prudence should be chosen for his post, noted the Observances, while the fermerer who looked after the sick among the brethren should be a mixture of efficiency and compassion. "It should rarely or never happen that he has not ginger, cinnamon, peony and the like ready in his cupboard. . . ." The fermerer also watched over the "stationaries," those who had "quit themselves like men in the vineyard of the Lord" and who now grew old in peace. The latter were advised to abjure temporal affairs, "nor ought they to repeat silly tales of old days with foolish hilarity or laughter, after the fashion of secular old men." One would have liked to have thought of them sitting in the sunshine recalling with the kindly tolerance of old age the follies of their youth. Perhaps, in spite of the Observances they did!

Finally there was the almoner, whose concern was with the poor of the neighbourhood, and who was warned never to be without "a stock of socks, linen and woollen clothes . . . so that if by chance Christ himself should at some time appear in the guise of a naked or poor man, He need not go away empty without a gift." At St. Mary Overie's this work of healing played from the beginning a very important part and the canons opened a hospital at the Priory gates to supply the needs of the poor way-farers and wounded soldiers who passed in a broken relentless stream on their way to London.

For more than four centuries with greater or less success the twenty or more brethren of St. Mary Overie's worked and wor-shipped according to this rule of St. Augustine. And at the heart of it all, giving it value and meaning, was the church. Whatever happened in the streets outside—and how much did happen—the worship of the church continued. Over London Bridge, kings came and went, their armies in array behind them; pestilence raged, rebels attacked and faltered; the turbulent world beat upon the Priory gates; and, within these gates, the brethren rose for matins, every day the Mass was solemnised, every evening they gathered together for compline. The offering of liturgical prayer led them safely on the road to the Holy City, whereas, in the words of the rule, "so many run hither and thither over the fields, they leap over hedges, they walk where there is no way . . . and . . . when night comes on they cannot reach the city." But it was for the world's sake not only for their own that they prayed. For prayer was potent, by prayer miracles could be accomplished, and so long as this conviction remained, all the sacrifice of personal comfort, of private ambition, the tedium of the days, the restless-ness of the flesh, the overmastering temptation to be spiteful or mean or dull, all these were obstacles readily to be met and resolutely to be countered in the service of the Lord.

## Note on Sources

A life of William Giffard is included in S. H. Cassan's *Lives of the Bishops of Winchester* (1827) and cf. the article in the *Dictionary of National Biography*. A description of the existing remains of the Norman church is in G. Worley's excellent brief account of *Southwark, the Cathedral and See*, pp. 52–60. See David Knowles: *The Religious Orders in England* (1950) for a general survey of monasticism, and Knowles and Hadcock: *Medieval Religious Houses: England and Wales* (1953), p. 153, for the suggestion that the Austin Canons came to Southwark at a later date than 1106. The *Observances at use in Barnwell Abbey*, ed. J. W. Clark (1897), are quoted in reference to the Augustinian rule and further details are found in W. H. Frere's article: *Early History of Canons Regular* in *Fasciculus, J. W. Clark dicatus* (1909), pp. 106–217. For the Priory's endowments, cf. *V. C. H. Surrey*, II, 107, Manning and Bray, *History of Surrey*, III, 562–5, and Dugdale's *Monasticon Anglorum*, II, 69. An illustrated article on *Winchester House, Southwark*, by Sidney Toy is included in *Surrey Archeological Collections*, XIX, 75–81.

# IV

## PETER OF THE ROCKS

LONDON BRIDGE had fallen down more than once since the days of St. Olaf, as the onslaughts of wind and tide, of fire and hurricane battered the wooden structures that were built and rebuilt in the uncertain years between the reign of Canute and the coming of the Plantagenets. In 1176 Peter, the priest architect of St. Mary Colechurch, began the first stone bridge which was thirty-three years in building. It stretched upon nineteen arches between the City and Southwark, guarded by two great gates, of which the one at the City end was defended by a drawbridge. The houses with which the old prints have made us so familiar were not built upon it until a later stage, but towards the centre a chapel dedicated to St. Thomas of Canterbury jutted out over the eastern parapet and added not a little to the congestion as traffic increased.

Some years previously as a young man, Peter had rebuilt the old bridge in elm, and the new magnificent venture in stone was begun in the same year as the great bridge over the Rhone at Avignon. This and other of the Rhone bridges were constructed by the famous order of Pontist brothers, who not only built the bridges but housed and looked after the wayfarers wherever they might find them. Peter may have belonged to an English guild of bridge-builders but, whether or not the Saxon priests had cared for the crossing in earlier times, there is no legend of the canons being similarly concerned. Peter's bridge, a little to the westward of the previous one, came nearer to their gate than it had done though still some yards further downstream than the London Bridge of to-day.

Peter did not live to see the finishing of his great work. Every few years another arch was laboriously completed and a new generation of children grew up to watch the men at their work and to sing the old nursery rhyme. In 1205 Peter the architect, who surely deserved to be remembered more widely than the caprice of fame has allowed, died ripe in years and was buried in the chapel of St. Thomas on the bridge. Five years later in 1209 the last arch was joined and the work was done, paid for by a mixture of voluntary subscriptions and taxation, not without the usual amount of grumbling. Within a few years a terrible calamity bade fair to undo the labour of three decades.

It was on St. Benet's day (July 10th) in the year 1212 or 1213, that fire broke out in the neighbourhood of the Priory. The Londoners, as ready then as now for any excitement, poured on to the bridge to watch the terrible yet fascinating spectacle. The flames advanced and, driven by heat and the first tremors of fear, those in the van attempted to withdraw. But the sparks borne by a strong wind had by this time set fire to the wooden parts of the bridge and even to houses on the City side and the crowd was trapped, unable to retreat or to go forward. In the panic that ensued some were burnt, many were crushed to death and the boats that dashed out from the shore, to rescue whom they could, were in many cases swamped by the wretches that leapt down from above. Many hundreds of people were said to have perished. When the desperate night was over and the flames were quenched, and only irrevocable death remained, Peter's stone bridge stood firm but smoke was still rising from the charred ruins of St. Mary Overie.

Somehow in this hour of crisis, the canons carried on their duties. The hospital at their gate had never been needed more. It had grown of recent years, encouraged among other things by the interest of Thomas Becket, who had visited the Priory shortly before his death when he stayed the night at Winchester House but was not allowed to enter London. When he was murdered, the brothers, remembering the visit and eager to acclaim the new English Saint, dedicated their hospital to St. Thomas, as Peter had dedicated his chapel on the bridge. At the time of the fire, the hospital was staffed by four of the canons and by two professed sisters, with their own master, the keeper of the poor within the precincts.

There was a small chapel attached to the hospital and here the services of the Priory were held in the years after the fire, for the church of the three Williams had been completely gutted. As time passed the first exhilaration of rising to an emergency gave way to the inevitable reaction, and the inadequate quarters and shortage of water added to the day-to-day difficulties of those who tended the sick. As Martin the Prior looked out on the contemporary scene his heart must have ached for the ruined house of God, which he could not hope to rebuild in an England rent by rebellion and civil strife. For it was a distracted time. King John, absolute, ruthless, unbridled in his appetites and passions, had quarrelled with the Pope and the land lay under an interdict. The church doors were shut, no masses were said in public and the dead were buried in unconsecrated ground. Most of the bishops had fled and only two remained loyal to John, de Gray of Norwich and Peter des Roches of Winchester. For five years, from 1208 to 1213, the wrath of Holy Church lay like a blight upon England, until the King suddenly changed his tactics and made friends with the Pope to strengthen himself against his recalcitrant barons. In the years after the fire, as the Priory was trying in vain to regain its lost tranquillity, in England the great drama was played out that ended at Runnymede with the issue of Magna Carta. During those two years the Bishop of Winchester was the King's chief adviser and, while John was absent in Poitou, Justiciar of England. Yet he found time to help the Priory in its hour of need.

Peter des Roches, Peter of the Rocks, was as hard as his name, able, cultured, unscrupulous, knighted for valour by Richard Coeur de Lion and always more ready to wield the sword than the crozier. He had served Richard I and John in every branch of administration and been rewarded by the latter with rich livings at first in Poitou and then in England. His election as Bishop of Winchester in 1205 had been disputed but he had gone to Rome to prove his claim and been successful, so that the jealousy and hatred, which had been roused by his foreign blood and the ability with which he implemented John's arbitrary schemes, was deepened by his possession of the richest see in England with five fair castles, eighty knight's-fees and a diocese stretching from Surrey to Somerset. More zealous in accounting than in evangelising, said the satirist, and it was this lack of spiritual qualities, so marked as to be a positive characteristic, this consummate secularism which offended even his contemporaries, accustomed though they were to the conception of the church as the recruiting ground for the civil service.

And yet—listen to the words with which he began his appeal for funds to remove the Priory's hospital to better quarters. The church had received a mandate from Christ: "I was an hungered and ye gave Me to eat, I was thirsty and ye gave Me to drink. I was a stranger and ye took Me in; I was naked and ye clothed Me; I was sick and ye visited Me, in prison and ye came to Me." Then the Bishop continued: "Behold, at Southwark an ancient spital, built of old to entertain the poor, has been entirely reduced to cinders and ashes by a lamentable fire". Moreover the place wherein the old hospital had been founded was less suitable, the Bishop continued, "less appropriate for entertainment and habitation both by reason of the straitness of the place and by reason of the lack of water and of many other conveniences; according to the advice of us, and of wise men, it is transferred and transplanted to another more commodious site, where the air is more pure and calm and the supply of water more plentiful." Those who contributed to the "many and manifold outlays," entailed by this removal, were upon confession of their sins to be let off twenty days of the penance enjoined upon them. Money was also raised by St. Mary Overie's and Prior Martin asked for contributions, "in return for the right to participate in all masses, psalms, vigils, prayers, alms, fasts, disciplines and genuflexions of worshippers at the priory."

A new site for the hospital had been found a little further from the river on the opposite side of the highway. The Priory of Bermondsey had already set up in the neighbourhood, if not on the actual site, a small almshouse also dedicated to St. Thomas and intended for the use of "indigent children and necessitous proselytes," and Peter des Roches now combined the almshouse and the hospital and gave it an establishment of its own following the Augustinian rule but with a separate master directly under the Bishop's supervision and entirely independent of St. Mary Overie's. As most of the Southwark property with which it was endowed belonged to Bermondsey its connection with the Cluniacs became closer as that with St. Mary's lapsed. Martin gave up the right to hold a market at the Priory Gate which had been the custom when it was also the entrance to the hospital, and he undertook not to establish another infirmary on the same site. Thus the earlier ties were severed, in Peter des Roches' usual arbitrary manner, though he could not rob St. Mary Overie's of her proud distinction as the first home of that place of healing which would one day grow into St. Thomas's of world renown.

Before more could be done to rehabilitate the burnt-out priory the country was again plunged into the distractions of war. Within a few months of the issue of Magna Carta John had gone back on his word, the barons were again in arms and at their invitation the Dauphin of France had launched an invasion. One morning in June in 1216 the people of Southwark watched with mingled feelings a French army march over London Bridge. The drawbridge was down and the invaders were welcomed by the City, but the canons knew that the Pope had not countenanced the venture and that Peter des Roches was loyal to the King and fighting by his side in the west of England. He remained stubbornly loyal when even William de Warenne (Hamelin's son) had refused to defend Reigate and made his peace with Louis, the Dauphin. But the tide had began to turn even before John's death in October, and when Peter des Roches crowned and anointed the infant king at Winchester the claims of loyalty manifested themselves anew. After a brisk campaign in which the Bishop fought vigorously, Louis made peace and left the country, and until Henry III tired of his tutelage, Peter des Roches remained the strongest man in England. Until his death in 1238 he won and lost in turn the young King's confidence, struggled for power with Hubert de Burgh, his rival, went on crusade and moved, a suave and compelling figure, at the court of foreign kings, and in his full life of intrigue and battle, statecraft and administration, kept his diocese in excellent order and did much for the welfare of St. Mary's, Southwark.

During the century before the fire it had been the custom for the people of the immediate neighbourhood to attend the services of the Priory, watching from the nave the worship of the brethren in the choir. In the restricted quarters after 1212 this was impossible, and to remedy this the Bishop built a small chapel for use as a parish church which he dedicated to St. Mary Magdalene. It stood at the eastern end of the priory church against the southern wall of the choir and like St. Margaret's was in the charge of the sacrist. The scattered houses along Bankside and beyond the park of Winchester House came within St. Margaret's parish and St. Mary Magdalene was specifically for the use of laymen living within the precincts and in the Priory's immediate propinquity.

The great priory church itself was already in process of rebuilding when St. Mary Magdalene's was consecrated. There is no way of ascertaining exactly how much was accomplished before Peter des Roches died in 1238, and the passion for quick returns in our own day makes it easy to forget how many generations of loving toil went to the making of our ancient churches. But the Bishop's vigour and ability no less than the architectural style of the whole indicate that a great deal of the work was done before money ran out and the original impetus dwindled. The nave was attempted first and the stalwart pillars of the Norman church were encased in Caen stone and the new type of pointed arch tentatively introduced. The experiment was so successful that the King's craftsmen, at work on the Abbey, are said to have come over from Westminster to examine and admire St. Mary Overie's. In the choir the new methods were used more boldly first on the south and then on the northern side, while behind the altar there was built at the same period a Lady Chapel or retro-choir of outstanding grace and delicacy, claimed to be among the best examples of early English architecture in the country. The elegance of the groined roof and the four eastern bays is an inheritance to remind us that the ruthless and worldly Peter was also a man of taste. Before Bishop Fox built his altar-screen, there were two arches which opened a vista from the retro-choir on to the high altar, so that the elderly and infirm among the brethren, incapable of the exacting drill of the choir, could sit in greater comfort and share in the Priory's worship.

After Bishop Peter's death the clerestory with its delicate arcading was added to the nave, the roof of the choir was adorned and the lower levels of the tower were built. The transepts were added later and were much restored at the beginning of the fifteenth century after further damage by fire. Thus St.

Mary Overie's came into being, fortified by a Bishop's munificence and the gifts of devout men and women. In size and grandeur it is not to be compared with the great cathedrals of the country and its fabric was to suffer through the centuries as much from the hands of its friends as its enemies. Yet it stands almost alone in London as a lovely product of the years which saw the full flowering of the England that had grown out of the intermingling of the previous centuries. The coming of the Friars, refreshing and challenging the established monasticism, the emergence of Oxford to take pride of place with Paris and Bologna and Padua as one of the great Universities of the world, the steady growth of the wool trade, encouraging the citizens of London and Norwich to stand up to baron or to priest alike, all combined to make the mid-thirteenth century a period of vitality and growth of which the builders caught an echo in their harmonies of stone. To these years St. Mary Overie's belongs, evoking comparison with the cathedrals at Salisbury and Chichester built at a like date. The qualities that have endeared it to countless generations are the serene graciousness with which it stands amid the discordant clatter of the neighbouring streets, and a sense, fostered by the unity of its style, of continuity in worship flowing down the years in essentially the same pattern through all the changes of time and circumstance.

In the political and ecclesiastical sphere, the deepened sense of Englishry clashed with the personal preferences of the pious but unstable King and with his liking for his foreign friends and relatives. Upon Peter des Roches' death the see of Winchester became one of the bones of contention. The King insisted on the election of his wife's uncle, William of Savoy, and when the latter died a year later, refused to accept a Devonshire man, William de Ralegh, whom the monks of Winchester had chosen to succeed him. The dispute went on for some years and at one stage, in 1244, Ralegh was so afraid of the King's anger that he withdrew from Winchester House and took sanctuary in St. Mary Overie's until he could escape by boat to France. When he died in 1250, Henry nominated his half-brother, Aymer de Valence, an ignorant youth who became the most-hated of the King's Poitevin kindred.

His only ally among the English earls was John de Warenne, who had married his sister Alice. For eight years as Bishop-elect, for the Pope refused to consecrate him, Aymer enjoyed the revenues of the see and the possession of Winchester House, where, so rumour said, at a great feast he once tried to poison his opponents. By 1258, an empty treasury, and the distress of the people laid low by plague and famine, forced the King to summon his barons and submit to their reforms. Aymer and his relatives were driven from the country. In due course the monks at Winchester elected an Englishman, Henry de Wengham, in his place, but the Pope was now of a different mind and at once consecrated the exiled Aymer. Henry de Wengham was compensated with the see of London and, probably because he was already in residence at Winchester House, he was consecrated in St. Mary's, Southwark, by the Archbishop of Canterbury in February 1260. The King's brother Richard, the recently elected King of the Germans, was present at this, the greatest occasion that had as yet occurred in the history of the Priory, and the new church must have looked its loveliest, the magnificence of silver and gold and the multi-coloured vestments enhanced by the light of the candles and the lofty grace of the stone.

For Southwark and England in the immediate future lay the disturbed years of the baronial wars. Aymer died on his journey home to claim his see but John de Warenne, true to the tradition of his family, fought loyally on the King's side. The Priory's days were uneventful although in 1273 there were signs of financial strain, due perhaps to an effort to build the transepts but possibly caused by the recurrent floods. Whatever the cause of the emergency, in that year the Archbishop of York, Walter Giffard, who as a kinsman of the first William Giffard was interested and concerned, ordered that thirty days' indulgence should be given to all who contributed to the upkeep of the fabric of St. Mary Overie's. Ten years later immediately after the appointment of William Wallys as prior, Archbishop Pecham conducted a personal visitation of the Priory. Pecham was a brilliant Franciscan scholar, recalled against his will from his studies at Rome to the see of Canterbury. He combined a scholar's zeal for the truth with defects of manner characteristic of the don and he caused considerable offence by his fussy and somewhat domineering ways and his habit of conducting visitations in his bishops' territory in an attempt to find out the true state of affairs. But he was shrewd and kindly at heart and entirely honest, and the advice he gave to St. Mary Overie's was very sound. It looks as if the sub-prior had been making himself unpopular and Pecham urged him to "study the dignity of religion, but also the bonds of charity, and to correct the faults of the brethren with due gentleness." The cellarer and chamberlain, on the other hand, were to be removed from office and also William de Cristehall who had been both almoner and fermerer, a combination of office which was forbidden in the future but which had, perhaps, grown up naturally when the separation of the hospital removed "the keeper of the poor within the precincts." Pecham ordered a general tightening up of routine; silence was to be more strictly enjoined in cloister and refectory and on no account was any canon to go out into Southwark unaccompanied. Only on formal occasions in company with other ecclesiastics were they to eat or drink in the town. Along Bankside, under the very shelter of the Bishop of Winchester's wall, were the taverns and the houses of ill-fame which an unworthy brother could reach so easily, slipping out after darkfall with a servant's connivance. On the whole, the Priory was free from any great scandal and the dangers that Pecham foresaw were rather those of worldliness, and the impingement upon the canons of the buying and selling that went on at their very gates up and down the High Street. The brethren were strictly warned by their Archbishop that the possession of private property was a "detestable crime" for men dedicated to "holy Poverty."

In 1303, while Wallys was still prior, there is another glimpse of the state of the Priory in a letter of his to King Edward I. The latter had asked, according to the custom of the time, that lodgings and a pension should be granted to one William Fisher a retired member of the royal household. Wallys replied that the Priory could not afford it, and that if the King insisted, it would be necessary to turn out one of the brethren already in residence (their numbers are given as twenty in the succeeding year). To soften his refusal, the Prior referred to the state of the church which, he said, "for thirty years last past (oh shame) has been a ruin we have laboured our utmost about the repairs of." How often that word

repairs is to occur in the history of the next seven hundred years!
Wallys blamed "the violence of the river Thames on whose bank
our little house [domuscula] is situated." He concluded by exhort-
ing the King to write to some "rich, great and super-abounding
manor," to support his aged servant, not to "the issues and petty
cells of brethren which have been founded from the simple
generosity of good men out of their small portions." The medieval
prior had usually his full share of the serpents' guile and it may
well be that all this amounts to is that Prior Wallys did not like
Mr. Fisher, but Edward was too shrewd a King to be easily hood-
winked and Wallys' reference to thirty years back, which was
exactly the date of Giffard's Indulgence, makes it probable
that the Priory had suffered from some mishap at that time
and that Pecham's visitation came when its fortunes were at
a low ebb.

The armies of Edward I marched more often north and west
than over London Bridge but in his grandson's reign, in the
earlier years of the French wars, the specious prosperity they
engendered in the Borough was reflected in the material well-being
of the Priory. The value of its property in the City and in Southwark steadily increased and the scattered references in the Papal
registers make it clear that the prior of St. Mary's, Southwark, was
used not infrequently by the Pope as his agent in providing
clerics to vacant English benefices or as assessor in appeals,
made to the papal courts to avoid an obligation or to escape
the "intricacies and convolutions . . . of the common law." The
spiritual well-being of the Priory is more difficult to compute. The
very vagueness of the Augustinian rule as now observed made
it difficult to impose reforms where requisite. Every now and
again the various houses of Canons Regular scattered up and down
England met in a general Chapter to consider the welfare of the
order. Between 1220 and 1340, the north and the south met
separately, after the latter date there were again joint meetings at
Leicester. There were genuine attempts to prevent scandals and
to initiate reforms but the fact that each priory had its own set of
Observances with "manifold minute differences" made it well-
nigh impossible to impose discipline from without. Even more
than in the stricter monastic orders, everything depended on the
character of the prior. Too many of the Priors of St. Mary's,

VIEW OF SOUTHWARK, *c.* 1558, BY ANTHONIE VAN DEN WYNGAERDE.

This shows Long Southwark and St. Margaret's Hill, with Southwark Place formerly Suffolk House on the left in the foreground. St. Thomas's and St. Saviour's are shown, but St. Margaret's Church is already demolished. Van den Wyngaerde was a Fleming who worked as a topographical artist in Brussels and Antwerp, and travelled in England between 1558-62. His English drawings are in the Sutherland collection at the Ashmolean, Oxford. A facsimile of this view of Southwark was issued by the London Topographical Society (see A. M. Hind, *Engravings in England*, p. 30 and note).

VIEW OF WINCHESTER HOUSE AND GARDENS, *c.* 1644, BY WENCESLAUS
HOLLAR.

This is a portion of an unpublished drawing by Hollar, now in the
possession of Mr. I. A. Williams, by whose permission it is reproduced.
Hollar was born in Prague in 1607, and as a youth was a pupil of the
engraver Matthaeus Merian in Frankfurt, and thence made his way
across Germany, meeting the Earl of Arundel at Cologne. Hollar
travelled under his patronage to Vienna and England (1637). He was
presented at court where he made an engraving of the Queen's mother,
Marie de Medici. He fled to Antwerp in 1644 and there etched his
*Long View of London*, which was published in Amsterdam in 1647.
The portion of the drawing reproduced above is one of the original
drawings made on the spot, from which he later worked up his etching.
It contains details which do not appear in the etching (cf. A. M.
Hind, *Wenceslaus Hollar and His Views of London*, pp. 44 *et seq.*).

Southwark, remain names on a lifeless list. There were some exceptions. Martin at the time of the fire, William Wallys and Henry Collingbourne in the reigns of Edward I and Edward III, Robert Weston who was Gower's friend, and Henry Werkworth, an upright man, who succeeded him in 1414: these were all persons of character and ability. Henry de Burton worked his rebus into the wooden roof of Edward IV's reign; Bartholomew Linsted, a gentle priest, was in office when Thomas Cromwell struck. For the rest, they sleep in the peace of oblivion: may God have mercy on their souls.

In the Cathedral to-day there are three memorials of these distant years, the first an old stone coffin which may have contained the body of one of the Priors. In the floor of the Lady Chapel on the southern side is a slab inscribed with the name of the M.P. for Southwark in the reign of Edward III, and in the north choir aisle there lies the recumbent effigy of a crusader. Priest, burgher, knight, it is a fitting triology of those who moulded the life of England during these formative years. The crusader, wearing armour of the time of Edward I, is reputed to have been a de Warenne. Earl John did go on crusade like so many of his family, subjugating their reckless and domineering temper in the service of the Cross. But John like his forebears was buried at Lewes, the last of the great de Warennes, protesting when King Edward sent out his writ of *Quo Warranto*. "My ancestors who came with William the Bastard conquered these lands with the sword and with the sword will I defend them." But no bold words of his could out-wit destiny, and with the troubled and disordered life of his grandson, the second John, his line came to an end. The earldom of Surrey passed to the FitzAlans, already earls of Arundel, one of whom appears briefly in the story of St. Mary Overie's, demanding lodgings in the Priory on his visits to London on the strength of the de Warenne benefactions.

The Member of Parliament was Aleyn Ferthing who represented Southwark five times in the middle of the thirteenth century. From the days of the Model Parliament of 1295 Southwark sent members to Parliament by prescriptive right, but only those who lived in the Borough could shout at the hustings and the dwellers in the Clink Liberty and Paris Garden could not poll.

Ferthing died in 1348 and was buried in St. Margaret's, the merchants' church in the High Street. The stone inscribed with his name and the date of his death was found in 1833, on the site of the old church, and was moved to its present resting place in the Cathedral's Lady Chapel, the sole memento of one who is little more than a name.

Once only was there an irruption into violent action in which he was concerned. Unlike the Austin Canons who seem to have got on well, perhaps too well, with their neighbours, Bermondsey was constantly embroiled. Until its sequestration in 1371 and its subsequent refounding as an abbey it was still an alien priory and the anti-French feeling of Edward III's reign no doubt had its effect on the position. The immediate cause of the disputes between the monks and the residents was usually connected with the drainage works and the repair of embankments necessitated by Bermondsey's low-lying site and on one occasion those who refused their labour and molested the monks in protest were no vagabonds but respectable folk led by Aleyn Ferthing himself. It is a reminder of the turbulent, teeming life of Southwark in the midst of which the religious houses were oases of quiet. As yet there was little overt criticism of their separateness and Professor Knowles, the authority on English monasticism, describes their state between 1300 and 1350 as that of a society "untroubled by regrets and undisturbed by reforms . . . as a tree no longer white as a bride with April blossom, but not unduly cumbering the ground." Two years after Aleyn Ferthing died, the Black Death swept over Europe into England and put an end to the facile prosperity of the earlier period. It were as well to pause, therefore, at this point and envisage more clearly the shape of Southwark during these years when Wallys' "domuscula" looked out not unhappily over the Thames and his successors caught a glimpse of King Edward's armies marching over London Bridge to Crecy and Poitiers.

## Note on Sources

For the early history of London Bridge see Gordon Home *op. cit.*, pp. 18–41, and for the hospital, F. G. Parsons, *History of St. Thomas's Hospital*, vol. I (1932), and Charles Graves, *The Story of*

*St. Thomas's, 1106–1947* (1947). For Peter des Roches, see, in addition to Cassan *op. cit.*, a booklet published by Warren & Son Ltd., Winchester: *Peter de Rupibus* by Madeline de Havilland (1936). Cf. also S. Painter, *The Reign of King John* (1949); Clarence Ellis, *Hubert de Burgh* (1952). An account of Archbishop Pecham's visitation is in the printed volumes of his *Episcopal registers*, II, 1, 2.

# V

# SOUTHWARK IN ITS HEY–DAY

IN the course of his domestic broils, the last John de Warenne had forfeited his estates and so the original "gildable" manor of Southwark passed into the possession of the Crown. It formed however only a small part of the Borough of later times. Much of the land in St. Olave's parish east of the bridge, belonged to the Abbey of Bermondsey and was known as the Great Liberty, while a large stretch of land to the south was held by the Archbishop of Canterbury. The meadow and pasture land that lay about Winchester House and St. Mary Overie's gave place to the westward to low-lying marshy ground, intersected by numerous streams and planted with willow-trees, and here was the land held in turn by the Knights Templars and Hospitallers, and later called Paris Garden. The Bishop's park and the surrounding district was protected from the river by Bankside, an artificial embankment upon which the Thames had made its silent assault since Roman times. This region to the west of St. Mary Overie's was known as the Clink Liberty, from the name of the Bishop's prison which lay under his very walls in a narrow alley leading to Bankside. In these three Liberties, the Archbishop's, the Great Liberty and that of the Clink, the ordinary course of law did not run, all being subjected to the jurisdiction of the church. In addition near the southern end of the High Street, stood the Marshalsea, for the custody of persons arrested by the King's Marshal, and not far away was the prison of the King's Bench.

It was little wonder that this region of conflicting rules and jurisdictions became a haunt of rogues and vagabonds, and the ease with which one could slip over London Bridge commended it in particular to those who wished to avoid the strict victualling laws enforced by the City. In an attempt to improve matters, the citizens petitioned the Crown in 1327 for a lease of the manor and this was granted them for the additional yearly rent of £10, but though it may have enabled them to obtain some control over malefactors who went no further than Long Southwark and attempted to do unlicensed trading in the High Street, it had no effect on the problem of the Liberties. Moreover it added a new cause of friction, in the continuous disputes as to their respective fields of authority between the City magistrates and the Surrey Justices of the Peace, a perennial source of annoyance of which an echo survives in John Donne's lines:

> There we will scorn his household policies
> As th'inhabitants of Thames right side
> Do London's mayor.

Of all the Liberties that of the Clink was the most disreputable, in part because of the paucity of inhabited houses and the remoteness of the area, and also because along Bankside there were already a number of brothels, known locally as the stews and interspersed with numerous alehouses, which presented a constant source of temptation not only to the men of Southwark but to the citizens of London, who slipped over so easily after nightfall, and to the watermen who thronged the area between St. Mary's Dock and Paris Garden Stairs.

The existence of the brothels was regarded by the authorities as inevitable, some of the land on which they stood belonged to the Bishop, and periodical attempts were made to regulate them, the most elaborate as early as 1162, though it is difficult to see any guiding principle behind the rules beyond the avoidance of open scandal and the necessity of safeguarding the rights of husbands. The stew-holders were not to admit a married woman or a nun, and at a later stage the wretched "single women" were made to wear a distinctive badge and to be buried in the unconsecrated single woman's burial ground which lay just to the south of the Bishop's Park. The stew-holders of the fourteenth century were generally Flemish women, detested even by those members of the populace who profited from their vicious practices. They were not allowed to serve food or drink on the premises, but what was lacking in this respect in the stews was richly provided in the Borough as a whole. All along Bankside were the taverns, the Spur, the Unicorn, the Cardinal's Cap, while along the High

Street, the more reputable inns, the Grapes, the King's Head, the George, the Tabard, stretched from London Bridge as far as St. George's Church. The latter church, appropriated to Bermondsey in the twelfth century, stood then as now where Long Lane ran out of the High Street and where the road into Kent began. The prisons of the King's Bench and the Marshalsea came within the bounds of St. George's parish, its chief problem through the centuries, as the large proportion of foreign merchants was the peculiar concern of St. Olave's, and as the stews and the undesirables of the Clink Liberty fell to the share of St. Margaret's and St. Mary Magdalene's.

The great high street, known as Long Southwark between the Bridge and St. Margaret's and as St. Margaret's Hill between that church and St. George's, was then as now the heart of the Borough. It was peopled already by reputable merchants mostly connected with the wayfaring and victualling trades. For Southwark was far from being only a rendezvous for the less respectable. Its geographical position at least as much as the conflict in jurisdiction conditioned its development. As the gateway to the coast and so to Europe, and as the only approach to the city from the south until in the eighteenth century other bridges were built, it was from the earliest times a great thoroughfare, a place of arrival and departure. Of the "fair inns for receipt of passengers" that Stow described, none remain; only the timbered courtyard of the George, a seventeenth century building, makes the past a little less remote, while the barrow boys on the slopes of the station approach remind one of the street markets that have continued in these parts for centuries past, on the bridge itself, till forbidden in 1276, in St. Margaret's churchyard till that also was stopped and up and down Long Southwark. There were butcher's stands at the entrance to St. Thomas's, a meal market in Fowle Lane close to the Priory and saddlers and leather sellers in the shadow of St. Margaret's. There were brewers in abundance and signs of the beginnings of industry in the manufacture of vinegar and the gradual appearance of soap yards in the neighbourhood of Winchester Park. Already the unhappy future was foreshadowed by a petition made in 1368 by certain prelates and magnates who had come up to London and Southwark to attend a session of Parliament and who complained of the increasing use of sea-coal whereby "an intolerable stench" diffused itself in the neighbourhood. The coal was brought round from Newcastle by water and the men of the coal ships were not the least unruly among the many sojourners on Bankside who frequented the watermen's haunts and were all too ready to embroil themselves in whatever excitement was on foot.

Changed with the years but still recognisable, the vagabonds, the travellers, the merchants have persisted through the centuries, but the prelates and magnates seldom visited Southwark after medieval days. Their coming and going gave the suburb, in the thirteenth and fourteenth centuries, a character all its own, for not only did their retinues require feeding and servicing, not only were watermen continually in demand for the journey to and from Westminster and the Tower, but their fine palaces gave to South-wark a peculiar beauty and distinction. Winchester House was only the first among many; a little further from the river was a house dedicated to St. Swithun and belonging to the monks of Winchester, which passed at the Reformation to the Bishops of Rochester by whose name it was then known. On this side of Long Southwark in close propinquity to the Priory, was the town house of the Abbot of Waverley, another of Giffard's founda-tions. Below the Bridge near to St. Olave's church was "one great house builded of stone with arched gates (which) pertained to the Prior of Lewes in Sussex," whose connection with the de Warennes brought him thither as naturally as the group linked with Winchester encircled St. Mary Overie's. The Earl's manor house was just beyond the Prior of Lewes' inn, "a great house of stone and timber" probably one of the oldest buildings on the south side of the river. In 1281 the Earl leased it to the Abbot of St. Augustine's of Canterbury. The abbot of Battle's Inn stood also on the banks of the Thames; the Abbot of Hyde on the other hand had lodgings at the Tabard Inn and obtained special leave to set up a chapel within its walls. It is easy to imagine how the residence of so many important people, occasional though it was, must have increased the status and prosperity of Southwark.

In the reign of the third Edward when Aleyn Ferthing was M.P. for the Borough, a new growth in population and prosperity came to it during the French wars, with the constant passage of

soldiery and the need for equipment of every kind. These were
the years of Southwark's hey-day, with the High Street alive with
buying and selling, thronged with wayfarers, pilgrims, pedlars,
men of great estate, soldiers going to the wars and soldiers returning wounded to the shelter of St. Thomas's. Tragedy and comedy
jostled each other in the crowded streets. A criminal taking sanctuary within the precincts, forced to put on the white sheet of a
penitent and abjure the realm, might on his way to the boat, which
was to bear him down river, be set upon and man-handled by a
hostile crowd. A scold set in the ducking stool or a vagrant in the
stocks endured the jeers and torments of the passers-by or a cavalcade of horsemen jangled by St. Margaret's causing the sacrist
to press back against the wall lest he be trampled underfoot. And
every few yards there was the gateway of an inn, and the bustle of
arrival or departure. It was this day-by-day activity which has significance in the story of the church, which was then St. Mary
Overie's and is now Southwark Cathedral, for its neighbours
to-day as in every stage of its long history still remain men at
work.

As one wanders through the streets of modern Southwark it is
all but impossible to recover a sense of the buried past. The modern Cathedral Street follows the lie of the old lane, which ran
diagonally out of Long Southwark and curved northward to the
west end of the Priory church, but the lorries and offices of the
Borough Market stand where once was Rochester House, and of
Winchester House only a few traces remain in the relics of broken
arch and window, embedded in the walls of the modern warehouses. The Priory buildings have vanished completely though
the ruins of the fine refectory were still in existence at the end of
the eighteenth century when Concanen and Morgan wrote their
history and described the vaulted oak roof with its carved angels,
its lantern light in the centre and a great window at the end.
The refectory was apparently divided into seven divisions and had
two aisles with a central range of columns, a room of distinction
and character even in those days of fine buildings. The Prior's
house stood near the river on the northern side of the cloisters,
and between this site and that of Winchester House the survival
of St. Mary Overie's dock reminds one that hereabouts, so many
centuries ago, the ferry made its start. Upstream along Bankside

the ghosts still linger. Clink Street and Cardinal's Cap, Rose Alley, and Bear Garden, the names are laden with the years; but Bankside ends where the colossus of the new power station raises its arrogant height opposite St. Paul's and again the past is banished. But in Bermondsey, east of the Borough High Street, a turning off Tooley Street leads to Abbey Wharf, on the site of the great town house of Battle Abbey. At this point one may see across the Thames the strong white keep of the Tower of London, and for a moment the past catches up with the present, for the rest of modern London is obscured by the walls of the shed and one sees only the great medieval fortress and the foreshore and the river between. This was how it looked when the Tower was the home of the Kings of England and when a similar line of river front, between the Tower and St. Paul's, lay in view of the men of Southwark, the spires and towers of innumerable churches, the bastions of the city-walls, the trees and gardens of palace and monastery, the huddle of mean houses and the tangle of roofs that lay along the streets of merchandise. Between that sky-line and St. Mary Overie's there passed the constant traffic of the Thames and as prelates and potentates, kings and commoners went on their lawful occasions, the canons looked out from their river-side priory and murmured a paternoster for the souls of wayfaring men.

The Bridge itself, some yards further down-stream than its modern successor, was by now ornamented, or hampered as the case might be, by a number of houses built upon it and peopled in the main by haberdashers and stationers and other small traders. This added not a little to the traffic congestion, sometimes with tragic results. On one occasion at the end of the century, when Richard II returned with his child bride from France and rode with great pomp from Southwark to the Tower of London, the multitudes thronged the bridge with such relentless pressure that nine persons were crowded to death, of whom the Prior of Tiptree in Essex was one and a worshipful matron of Cornhill another. Like the unfortunate Prior of Tiptree, the Austin Canons no doubt ventured forth to watch more closely the fine processions that passed so near to them. The greatest of them all occurred in 1357 when the Black Prince returned in triumph after Poitiers and rode through Southwark streets with the King of France, his royal prisoner, beside him. Such hours of rejoicing are to be set beside the other grimmer pictures, that come before and after, of Simon de Montfort storming the bridge and capturing London or the rebels marching down from Blackheath in the train of Wat Tyler or Jack Cade.

Yet these great days of history were after all rare if unforgettable experiences. More often the excitements that brought the Canons into the street, or the people of Southwark into the southern precincts of the Priory, where the churchyard lay and the church of Mary Magdalene, were concerns of a more local colour. There is an unexpected glimpse of the Priory at one such moment when in 1369 Joan, Lady Cobham, was buried in the churchyard. She belonged to a family long connected with Southwark and she herself was one of that long line of devout women who have loved the church, linking Mary Overs with Dorothy Applebee and Elizabeth Newcomen and with the deaconesses who face the challenge of to-day. Lady Cobham's husband, who had predeceased her, owned the Green Dragon, immediately to the south of the Priory Close. In her will Joan laid down that it should be sold to pay his debts and provide masses for the soul of his forebears in the Kent village whence the family came. If her son had already built a church for that purpose the house was to go to him, "to endow two priests for ever." But she herself would rest in the place where she had lived through the grey and golden years. She asked for her body to be buried in the churchyard of St. Mary Overie's in Southwark before the church door "where the image of the blessed Mary sitteth on high over that door," and at her funeral twelve poor persons in black gown and hoods were to carry twelve torches to light her to her grave. The great door, of which all traces have long since disappeared, stood on the southern side at the western end of the church where the main entrance to the Cathedral is still to be found to-day. The proximity of the houses clustering round St. Mary Overie's dock made the more usual western position unsuitable for the great processions so dear to the hearts of the men of the Middle Ages. The great welcoming door, a fine example of thirteenth-century Gothic work, was much more effective where it stood, the Virgin above its portals looking out on all who passed through the church-yard on their way from the Borough to the Clink, and greeting alike the brides who paused on its threshold and the dead who came to rest beneath the church's benignant shade.

Out of the great south door upon which Peter des Roches' craftsmen had expended so much care and skill there passed at times other processions going out into the streets to bring to the wayfarers a reminder of things eternal. There was always some holy day to be celebrated and how the folk of the Borough and Bankside must have loved the children's festival which began on December 6th, St. Nicholas' day, and lasted till the feast of the Holy Innocents. Then it was the custom of the Priory, serving the parishes of St. Margaret and St. Mary Magdalene, to choose a boy Bishop, as elsewhere in England. For three weeks the lad held rule, visiting with his train of cherub-faced urchins all the houses in the neighbourhood, sharing with boyish gusto in the frolics and party-fare with which they were greeted and collecting, as they went, for the great feast with which the celebrations ended. On one occasion the boy Bishop of St. Mary's was warned not to go too far afield so as to trespass on the territory of his colleagues of St. Olave's and St. George's, and incidents on the parish boundaries must have been hard to avoid. On December 28th, in full canonicals, the "bishop" preached a sermon and recited a special liturgy and then his brief reign over became again a scrubby schoolboy.

Candlemas, on February 2nd, was a feast of early origin, of which a Saxon commentator wrote: "we on this day bear our lights to church and let them there be blessed, and that we should go afterwards with the light among God's houses and sing the hymn that is thereto appointed. Though some men cannot sing they can nevertheless bear the light in their hands for on this day was Christ the true light borne to the temple."

The customs of Easter, the blessing of the Palms on Palm Sunday, the washing of the poor men's feet on Maundy Thursday, the lighting of the Paschal candle and the solemn joyous festival of Easter day are still, thank God, familiar in the modern world. But there was one procession which in particular must have stirred the passer-by in Southwark streets. On Corpus Christi day, from every Priory and Abbey and parish church the dedicated men of God walked through the streets, intoning their liturgies and medieval chants, and the busy world rested for a few

moments silent. The young faces of the novices, often as yet un-
formed, with every now and again that of a fanatic or a born
mystic standing out clearly among them, the muttered *ora pro
nobis* of the old men of the infirmary, sounding like the dull surge
of the ocean battering for mercy on the rock of God's righteousness, the quiet benign beauty of a priest who had made his peace
with Christ, and the proud eager diffidence of the little boys
swinging the censers—all passed in turn till at the end came the
Host itself, lifted high above the crowds, and men uncovered and
bent their knees and even the veriest scoundrel of them all felt
for a moment the imminence of God.

This then was the Southwark of the fourteenth century, of
Prior Wallys and John de Warenne, of Aleyn Ferthing and Lady
Cobham, of prelates and prostitutes, vintners and saddlers and
the market women in the High Street and of "mine host" at the
Tabard inn of whom Chaucer was soon to write:

> A large man he was with eyen steep,
> A fairer burgess is there none in Chepe.
> Bold of his speche and wise and wel y taught
> And of manhood him lacked righte naught.

This was the world to whom the Austin canons of St. Mary
Overie's belonged; and the society for whom they made intercession as the crowds passed to and fro each on their own affairs
and England's history went its allotted course. Yet close as their
concern remained with the life on their perimeter and the Southwark at their gates, the circumference of their interests and loyalties stretched afar to the confines of the holy Catholic church and
the Pope in his supreme judgment seat. They had relations also
with the other houses of their order, notably the sister Priories,
over the river, of St. Hilda's, Aldgate, and St. Bartholomew's in
Smithfield, whose hospital like St. Thomas's witnessed to the
practical aspect of St. Augustine's rule. At St. Mary Overie's, the
special circumstance of the propinquity of Winchester House provided yet another strain in the complex harmony of the Priory's
life and gave it an unexpected measure of prosperity in the hundred years that followed the Black Death. For it chanced that at
this time there were in possession of the see of Winchester men of

outstanding influence and ability, and so to no small degree, as their bishops moulded the future of England, the story of St. Mary Overie's is linked again with the fortunes of great men.


## Note on Sources

W. Rendle's *Old Southwark* (1878) includes a mass of valuable detail both as regards people and places and reproduces a plan of the district (*c.* 1542), preserved in the Public Record Office. Manning and Bray's account of the Borough (Vol. III, 545 *seq.*) can be supplemented by the *Victoria County History* IV, 125–62, including a description of the relations between Borough and City. The *Survey of London: Bankside*, pp. 1–8, contains a useful summary of the involved jurisdictions. Stow's survey (1st edition 1598) is of assistance, the face of the Borough changing little until the 17th century.

# VI

# WILLIAM OF WYKEHAM

G K. CHESTERTON describes as the worst result of the Black Death, "which turned Christendom into a house of mourning," the consequent scarcity of priests and, he adds, "bad priests had so easily become priests that the whole Christian philosophy and morality was brought into contempt." The anti-clericalism of these years and the turmoil of thought which led by way of the Lollards to the English Reformation was deeply rooted in many different sources of which the deterioration in personnel was certainly predominant. The worldliness of such of the prelates who had ability and influence and the slackness of some of the monasteries and priories combined with the social and economic upheaval to foster the discontent, which Chaucer and Piers Plowman voiced alike, and which the intellectuals who sympathised with Wycliffe and the peasants who rose with Wat Tyler shared in common.

Yet in spite of its many defects there was at least one respect in which the Church, as an organisation, still deserved well of the people. It was in a feudal society the one truly democratic institution, providing a means whereby the "poor scholar" could rise to the height of his ability; its doors were open to men of spiritual insight or intellectual power whatever their rank or station. No better example of this can be found than that of William of Wykeham who was Bishop of Winchester from 1367 to 1404. He was a man of humble parentage, born in the Hampshire village of Wykeham. His father was known as John Long, though it is uncertain whether the second name was surname or soubriquet; the son certainly was a man of exceptional height. William was befriended by the local squire and sent to the choir school at Winchester where he shewed an aptitude for the exact sciences and in particular for geometry. Otherwise his scholarship was not outstanding and he had no special bent towards theology, but it is probable that he received the first tonsure at an early date for the very reason that the clerical career alone offered prospects to a young man without wealth or family prestige.

He had good luck as well as ability. He entered the service of William Edington, the then Bishop of Winchester, and was in attendance when King Edward visited the Bishop after the Crecy campaign. The King took a liking to the young man and he was transferred to the royal household at Windsor where Edward was engaged on extensive building operations. The King had recently founded the Order of the Garter in an attempt to bind in loyalty to himself the flower of chivalry in England. The Castle at Windsor was in process of being enlarged and remodelled to make a fitting college for the knights of the new Order, and after he had proved his faithfulness and circumspection, William of Wykeham, "a prudent and discreet man," was appointed a clerk of the works in 1356. Thereafter preferments were showered upon him mostly in the form of prebends and benefices although as yet he was not an ordained priest. He liked the good things of life and his appreciation of riches, both for their own sake and as a badge of his success, was symptomatic of his peasant stock to which the prudent care that made him so excellent an administrator also bore witness. Arrogant he never was, not even in the hour of his greatest success, but withal kindly, generous, humble and devoted to the details of his job, as he advanced steadily in power and prestige. In 1360 he assisted in France at the conclusion of the short-lived Peace of Bretigny and in 1362 he was ordained at Southwark in the chapel of Winchester House. To such an extent did the King come to rely upon him that when he was keeper of the Privy Seal two years later, Froissart went so far as to say that "by him everything was done, and without him they did nothing." The pluralities he continued to acquire offended even the Pope's sense of what was fitting, especially as he saw in William of Wykeham, an English ecclesiastic who encouraged the King in his policy of resisting papal encroachments. When William was elected bishop of Winchester in succession to Edington, it was nearly a year before the Pope agreed to his consecration, though he referred very politely to his "knowledge of literature, uprightness of life and habits, prudence in spiritual and guardedness in temporal matters." At length, after some of the pluralities had been resigned, in October 1367, one month after becoming Chancellor of England, William of Wykeham was consecrated Bishop. His first acts shewed that he was no charlatan, nor merely an ambitious statesman. He subjected himself to a severe self-examination, that he might "redeem the time," and remitted to his poorer tenants, at the cost of some £500 to himself, the feudal dues he had a right to exact in acknowledgement of his lordship.

He had achieved the supreme office of state at a most unfortunate time. Even before the peace of Bretigny the French wars had begun to go awry, as the enemy learnt to avoid pitched battles and their fleets swept down on Sandwich and Winchelsea burning and pillaging and bringing to peaceful homesteads tragic evidence of the realities of war. When hostilities were renewed, the English failed to achieve a victory in the field to revitalise their flagging enthusiasm and in 1371 the return of the Black Prince, a wreck of a man coming home to die, underlined for all the ineluctable fact of failure. It was natural that the burden of blame should fall on the circle of clerical advisers upon whom the King had depended in his middle years. Their removal consorted well with the plans of Edward's younger son, the ambitious and rather problematical John of Gaunt, who saw his opportunity in the Black Prince's collapse. William of Wykeham was driven from office with the rest, and in March 1371 resigned the Great Seal. For the first time, during the next five years, he was able to expend his talents for organisation upon the welfare of his diocese and the maintenance of his wealthy see, and to begin his plans for establishing a college of poor scholars at Winchester to be companioned by another for higher learning at Oxford.

In 1376 there was another stormy incursion into politics. There had been no improvement in public affairs; the malcontents found that they had merely replaced King Log by King Stork, for John of Gaunt and Alice Perrers, the greedy mistress of Edward's old age, combined to dominate the scene in their own interests. Eventually the "good parliament," to a large extent guided by William of Wykeham, attacked the corruption and tyranny of Gaunt's officials and appointed nine councillors, including Wykeham, to guide and advise the King. But no sooner was Parliament

64

dissolved than John of Gaunt seized power again, his hands strengthened by the death of the Black Prince at Kennington. Perhaps for some personal reason, he now regarded the Bishop of Winchester with an implacable hostility, and charges of malversation were preferred against Wykeham, who was forbidden to come within twenty miles of the court while his case was pending. He had in consequence to leave Winchester House and retired to Merton Abbey where the full fury of the storm followed him. He was, so the contemporary chroniclers write, "hunted from place to place, both by letters and by writs, so that no man could succour him throughout his diocese neither could he nor durst he rest in any place." His temporalties were seized and he bade the scholars of his new foundation to disperse, going himself for shelter in turn to Woking and Waverley Abbey. Then the news came that the old King was dying. Three days before the end William of Wykeham received back his temporalties, promising in return to fit out for three months three ships each furnished with fifty archers and fifty men of war. It was rumoured that Wykeham had bribed Alice Perrers with the gift of a manor, and he would have counted that a small price to pay for a chance to say farewell to the King who had befriended him for thirty years. On the other hand their approaching change of fortunes made John of Gaunt and Alice equally anxious to improve their relationships with their powerful opponents. Whatever actually occurred, the Bishop was fortunate in that he remained during the new reign in favour but in the background, Chancellor again for a brief period when Richard II's personal rule began but never taking a prominent part and urging always the moderation the King so tragically cast aside.

Early in the new reign a great wave of discontent swept over England. The evil effects of war and pestilence had riddled the country and no consistent attempt had been made to oppose to them a constructive economic policy. The old feudal customs and conceptions were still upheld though the system was manifestly breaking down. Wages were tied, though prices were rising and the free movement of labour was prohibited. In the towns the closed shop policy of the craft gilds put the brake on industrial development. A harsh poll-tax that bore hardly on the poorer

E

classes proved the match which lit the flame of revolt and the insurrection, which began in Essex in the early summer of 1381 and spread into Kent, found at Maidstone a leader in Wat Tyler who knew how to discipline men sufficiently to turn the rebels into a dangerous force. John Ball preached to them at Blackheath:

> When Adam delved and Eve span,
> Who was then a gentleman?

and they marched on to Southwark, demanding admission to the City and to the King. Of all the anxious hours that the canons of St. Mary's spent in those turbulent times, none can have equalled in terror the Wednesday night in June when Wat Tyler and his men burnt down the Marshalsea and added to their numbers released criminals who had nothing to gain from the restoration of order.

Coming yet nearer to the Priory, the rebels attacked and destroyed the stews and swept on to Lambeth to burn the palace of Archbishop Sudbury, the gentle but too compliant Chancellor who had taken refuge in the Tower. As they went their way, Wat Tyler's army, fanatics, ruffians, honest desperate men, challenged all and sundry and legend says that any suspect as foreigners were ordered to pronounce the shibboleth, "bread and cheese." There were many such in the narrow streets of Southwark, Flemish weavers, Lombards from south of the Alps; if their tongues faltered over the phrase they were butchered on the spot. That night, at St. Mary Overie's, as the canons passed from the cloisters to the church, they saw the flames lighting up the western sky and listened to the uproar of the mob.

Next morning through a mixture of fear and treachery the drawbridge was lowered and the rebels swept across London Bridge. For three days and nights they wrought havoc in the city as the lawless elements gradually gained control. Archbishop Sudbury and the Treasurer Hales were dragged from sanctuary in the chapel of the Tower and summarily executed on Tower Hill. From the south bank the people saw the heads impaled on the gate of London Bridge. But two days later the ghastly trophies were replaced by another: the head of Wat Tyler himself, killed at Smithfield at the end of a parley with the King. It was the Lord

Mayor Walworth who struck Tyler down and personal anger at the destruction of his property on Bankside may well have added venom to the blow. The rebels dispersed upon promise of reforms which were never put into effect; not by the path of insurrection was John Ball's dream of equality to be fulfilled. But the memory of those terror-laden days are deeply embedded in Southwark's history, a sudden incursion of violence into the pattern of ordinary living.

From September 1360 to June 1395, for most of the time that William of Wykeham was Bishop of Winchester, Henry Collingbourne was Prior of St. Mary Overie's, a period of thirty-four years, nine months and two days as the records proudly state. His name recurs not infrequently as an owner of corporate property and in the Papal registers as one in whom the Popes trusted. For more than twenty-five years he and Wykeham were neighbours, for the Bishop was constantly at Winchester House until the last few years of his life, and though there is more of conjecture than one could wish in any account of his relationship with the Priory, he must have known every inch of the pleasant close, which the wharves and warehouses have swallowed up, and a measure of neighbourly interest and intercourse can be taken for granted. It was probably with the Bishop's help that Collingbourne completed the building of the transepts of the Priory church, making some use of the new perpendicular style which Wykeham, a magnificent builder to the last, had introduced at Winchester in his reconstruction of the Norman nave. No doubt the Bishop helped with money as well as advice for he was prodigiously rich and generous by nature. At some point in Richard II's reign the work at St. Mary Overie's received a sudden check, when a fire only less disastrous than its predecessor destroyed a considerable part of the southern transept. It was not till the next century, after a few rather unsettled years in the Priory's domestic history, that the necessary repairs were undertaken and the work of reconstruction, begun by Peter des Roches, completed in its entirety.

Wykeham's interest in St. Mary's was not restricted to the enriching of its outer form. He was intensely concerned with an improvement in the calibre of his clergy for only by this means did he think it possible to combat the ills of the contemporary world. To increase the number and ability of the clerical militia had been his prime objective in founding his colleges at Winchester and Oxford, which were provided for the use of young scholars who had received the first tonsure and were to become priests. Perhaps regretting his own lack of learning he staked the future upon the ennobling effect of the search for truth, "in the firm hope that men steeped in learning and different sciences will keep God before their eyes and thus will look more clearly than others at his Will. . . ." In the year after the collapse of the Peasants' Revolt the charters of the two colleges were sealed at Winchester House in Southwark. Each of the foundations was dedicated to St. Mary though the one at Oxford stubbornly persisted in calling itself New College. The Bishop, who has been described by his biographer as "no theologian but a man with a clear head and a large heart," allowed the scholars at Winchester to be leavened each year with the addition of "ten sons of noble and capable persons," and gave them as their motto, "Manners Makyth Man."

The Bishop's registers also shew that so far as his powers and pressure of time allowed he and his suffragans kept a strict eye upon the parochial clergy by means of regular visitations, "to correct the erring, to extirpate the thorns of vices and to establish in the paths of justice the upright and them that walk the way of the Lord." St. Mary's, Southwark, is mentioned in 1390 when the altars were dedicated and reconciled after the second fire, and again a year later after "pollution by bloodshed." There is no record of the cause of the latter trouble, perhaps a street fight or a murder in the Priory Close where the populace had wrought rough justice on a criminal taking sanctuary. On the whole the Priory and its churches had, while Collingbourne ruled, a better record than their neighbours, for at St. Thomas's at one juncture a prior absconded while, at Bermondsey, there were not only the disputes with the local inhabitants but at least one affray between the monks and the secular clergy of the neighbourhood.

After Collingbourne's death, however, there was trouble at St. Mary's. His successor John Kyngeston proved quite unequal to his task. His grave infirmities led to a complete break-down of discipline and to an open scandal. In 1396 Wykeham sent two officials to the priory to investigate. The cause of the trouble proved to be the same sin that Pecham had rebuked a hundred years before. The Austin Canons found it only too easy to be on good terms with their neighbours, and slipped out, without legitimate cause, to wander *per vicos et plateas*, through the narrow alleys and broad highway of Southwark, "to the great danger of their souls." Financial affairs also appeared to be in some confusion. The custody of the Priory was therefore taken out of Kyngeston's hands and was entrusted to the sub-prior and a certain John Stacy, one of the brethren. No canon was to leave the precincts without grave cause and then armed with a special pass from the custodians. The great gate by which lay-folk came in and out of St. Mary Overie's was to remain shut, unless there were good reasons to the contrary. The accounts were to be submitted in detail, with particulars of rents received from churches, manors, farms and bailliwicks and all money was to be placed, "honestly and faithfully," into a safe in the sacristy, of which safe the treasurer had one key and the Bishop's representative another. Finally, there had apparently been some jobbing in the matter of repairs and it was laid down that all plumbing and other similar work was to be under the counsel and direction of Simon Hoke, stoneman, and Stephen Carpenter, experts in their craft and devoted to the welfare of the Priory.

The only other letters concerned with St. Mary Overie's were directed to Prior Weston who succeeded Kyngeston in 1398. He was given permission to let out various parsonages, provided none of them were used as taverns, or for illicit or dishonest trade. He was however reprimanded by the Bishop soon afterwards for alienating some of the Priory's property, always a temptation when one was short of ready money. As by this date, the fire of Richard II's reign had occurred and the prospect of much rebuilding loomed ahead, one can sympathise with the Prior.

In 1399 Wykeham visited Southwark for the last time in the uneasy days before Henry of Lancaster usurped the throne. Thereafter as his health failed he dwelt mostly at Bishop Waltham where he died in 1404, a great and typical figure of his time and one who, despite his worldly wisdom, did perform honestly and well the duties of his see nor entirely forgot that he was in the service of a greater King than any Plantagenet.

If the chapter ended thus one could not claim for St. Mary Overie's any distinguished part in these dramatic years at the end of the 14th century. But this was not all. During the very years that Wat Tyler marched on London, that John Ball preached and William of Wykeham built, English poetry was born. A man walked along the Borough High Street, drank at the Tabard "the nappy ale of Southwark" and, as he watched the Pilgrims gathering on their journey to Canterbury, envisaged a masterpiece. And close by in St. Mary Overie's, a poet of established reputation, living in lodgings in the Priory in his latter years, had turned aside from writing French and Latin to try his hand at English verse. A great age had passed its prime: in England King Richard was deposed and murdered; abroad the authority of Holy Church was shattered by the Great Schism; yet in these calamitous years, Chaucer wrote poetry full of vigour and hope and Prior Weston's companion in the Close was John Gower, the first of the men of letters whose names have been linked with Southwark.

John Gower, born about 1330, came from Kent; so much, in spite of conflicting Welsh and Yorkshire claims, the authorities agree. He was a man of substance, who owned land in East Anglia, and of considerable education and standing. The known facts of his life are extremely meagre, even more so than in the case of his younger contemporary Geoffrey Chaucer. Chaucer's background was of the City and his father and grandfather were wine-merchants, but his own life had been full of varied interests, much more so it would seem than that of Gower. Chaucer had done military service in France, entered the household of Lionel, Duke of Clarence, and subsequently that of the King and been on at least two visits to Italy, the Italy of the Visconti, of Petrarch and the first hints of the dawning Renaissance. The first visit in 1373 affected him deeply, stirring his imagination into vivid life and bringing his genius to flower. In the years between it and the second journey of 1380, he rented a house at Aldgate and obtained the post of comptroller of the customs; he was also engaged on various royal missions, associating himself with the party of John of Gaunt, whose mistress Catherine Swynford was sister to his wife. But he also found time to write and to talk with other writers, and on his second Italian journey he left his power of attorney with John Gower, with whom he would seem at this time to have been intimate. He returned from a further experience of Petrarch's influence and Italy's potent magic to write *Troilus and Chresyde*, and he dedicated it to his friends, "Moral Gower and Philosophic Strode."

The epitaph of moral affixed itself firmly to Gower and indicated a reliability of character and a sober piety which made him a good friend to whom to entrust the care of one's property. But it was a quality not without its drawbacks to a poet, and though Gower tells us that he had written love songs in his youth and though in later years he mellowed sufficiently to compose some ballads in French of no mean quality and to include in his English poem some scurrilous tales worthy of Chaucer's Wife of Bath, his desire to edify and improve his readers too often led him astray from the true paths of poetry. His first work, written in Norman French about the end of Edward III's reign and entitled *Speculum Meditantis*, or *Mirour de l'homme*, was an ambitious attempt to "set forth the purposes of Providence in dealing with Man" and to give an account of the shortcomings of the individual and of society. Chaucer was content to use the weapon of satire in attacking the corruption of the times and lightens his canvas with the compensating portrait of the parish priest; Gower slates the church, the law, the physicians alike; it was perhaps because as a Southwark man he knew them best that the merchants were on the whole most gently treated. His writing was serious and didactic in tone and though not devoid of poetic imagery, the most romantic thing about the *Mirour de l'homme* was its subsequent history. For no copy seemed to have survived and it was lost for centuries. Then a librarian of Cambridge bought a bundle of old papers at a sale, and in 1895 G. C. Macaulay discovered among them the missing manuscript of Gower's first full-length poem.

The *Vox Clamantis*, the second of Gower's three works, was written, in Latin, soon after the Peasants' Revolt while the fears and emotions roused by the 1381 rebellion were still hot in the minds and hearts of author and readers alike. Gower was moved to unwonted vigour and depth of feeling, and the opening of the poem is in some ways reminiscent of the beginning of *Pilgrim's*

*Progress.* "Methought I went out upon a Tuesday to gather flowers, and I saw people in bands going abroad over the fields. Suddenly the curse of God fell like lightening upon them and they were changed into the forms of beasts . . . ." One band became asses, wishing they were horses, another were oxen, proud of their dragon's tails and spurning the yoke; a third were changed into swine feasting in the city, a fourth into dogs barking at the heels of men. Gower, remembering the pillage and the slaughter of that night in June, did not spare the rebels but he also flayed the society which had produced them, the worldliness of the church, the unscrupulous lawyers, the greedy lords.

During the years that Chaucer was writing *The Canterbury Tales*, Gower was busy with his third book, in English, the *Confessio Amantis*. The poem owed its inception to a chance meeting with King Richard.

"As it befell upon a tide," so Gower himself wrote of the incident,

> As I by boate came rowing,
> So as fortune her time set
> My liege lord perchance I met,
> And so befel as I came nigh
> Out of my boat when he me sigh
> He bade me come into his barge,
> And when I was with him at large
> Among other thinges said
> He hath this charge upon me laid
> And bade me do my business,
> That to his high worthiness
> Some new thinge I should book
> That he himself it might look
> After the form of my writing.

So Gower wrote his new book in English, and he wrote in the dialect which Chaucer also used and which was destined to survive, the English of the East Midlands, of the lawyers and of the court. Like Chaucer he was concerned with a series of tales, the prototypes of the fiction of a later age, but whereas Chaucer's backcloth was the crowded English scene all along the road from the

Tabard to Canterbury, as brimful of life and human idiosyncrasies as were Long Southwark and St. Margaret's Hill, Gower puts his stories in a conventional framework. In the *Confessio Amantis*, a lover sought advice from a Father-confessor, who regaled him with tales to illustrate the theme of love. The stories were sufficiently popular at the time and for two centuries to come for Shakespeare and his collaborators to make use of one of them in the play of *Pericles* and to bring Gower on to the stage to introduce it, in the certainty that his name would be known to the groundlings. If they lack the human sympathy and virility and humour of Chaucer, they have in large measure Gower's own qualities of clarity and technical skill, purity and simplicity of language and honest, straightforward story-telling. The tales are drawn from diverse sources, from Ovid and the Greek legends, from the Bible and the romances of the troubadours, and they were an immediate success for the book ran into many editions and was translated into Spanish and Portuguese. The sixteenth-century critics hailed Gower and Chaucer as joint-founders of English poetry and Skelton described Gower as he that first garnished English and Chaucer as he that "nobly enterprised how that English might freshly be." Thereafter Gower's reputation faded, for he suffered unduly from comparison with his greater contemporary, but he made his own contribution, in his careful hammering out of English as a literary medium, and rightly shares with Chaucer the honour of fashioning the language that was to flow in yet nobler cadences from the pens of Shakespeare and Milton and in the pages of the English Bible.

One would like to be sure that Chaucer, riding over the bridge towards the Tabard and noting the various types who passed him on his way, turned aside into the precincts to have a friendly gossip with his old friend John Gower. But there is no proof that Gower was at the Priory during the years that Chaucer lived in Aldgate; the first and only definite reference to his sojourn there is in January 1397-8, only a short time before Chaucer provided lodgings for himself in Westminster Abbey, where he died in 1400. Also Gower's intimacy with Chaucer seems to have lessened as time passed and there may have been a coolness between them owing to a criticism that Chaucer made of one of the tales in the *Confessio*. But much is conjecture and all that survives for certain are the great poems themselves and the knowledge that, as England stood on the verge of revolution and the hour of a new dynasty drew near, Gower lived and wrote in Southwark, an honoured and respected figure, and Chaucer also passed that way, catching more truly than any other the shape and colour of medieval England to hold it captive for posterity.

The political calamities of Richard's reign disturbed Gower less than Chaucer, who was so closely associated with John of Gaunt. Gower's admiration and respect for young Henry of Lancaster did not seem, in the earlier years of Richard's manhood, inconsistent with loyalty to the King and Gower's own position as a recognised and favoured poet. The *Vox Clamantis* included laudatory passages to both the royal cousins. Only by degrees did Gower, like the majority of his countrymen, accept the fact that Richard himself and not his advisers was responsible for the evils of his reign, and it was not as time-server but as one convinced against his will that he deleted his dedication to Richard in the new edition of *Vox Clamantis* and sent forth the *Confessio* dedicated to his country not to his king. There was a personal tie with Lancaster, for in 1393 Henry's wardrobe accounts note the purchase of a new collar to replace the one given to John Gower, Esquire. This collar Gower proudly wore in later years and it bore then the badge of a swan which the House of Lancaster adopted as a sign of loyalty and remembrance. According to the domestic accounts the collar was an inexpensive one (in spite of Stow's claim that it was made of gold) but it was little wonder that the poet treasured the gift for whatever cause, a wager, a debt, a token of friendship, it had first been given him. In that year while Richard's thoughts still ran on peaceful projects, while his first wife still lived and there was room for poetry in the world, there was no disloyalty in a subject treasuring a gift from the King's cousin. But within a short time, after the Queen's death and Henry's exile, the King's own character disintegrated, the hour of crisis came with ruthless speed and Henry returned as avenger to seize the throne. Gower added to his next edition a salutation of the new House of Lancaster and perhaps he did not know, or refused to think, of what had happened at Pontefract to the anointed King who once had greeted him on the Thames.

Gower's own circumstances had changed meanwhile. In 1398

74

William of Wykeham, an old man now who came no more to Southwark, issued a special licence to the curate of St. Mary Magdalene to marry John Gower and Alice Groundolf in the private chapel attached to Gower's lodgings within the Close. Precious as the information is it is most provoking in what it fails to disclose. Had Gower been married before, as some references in his poems would seem to indicate? Was it an old man's fancy (he was nearing seventy) or the need for a nurse and companion as his eyesight failed, which impelled him to this drastic action? Is there any significance in the fact that the licence permits the wedding to take place without the issue of further banns and elsewhere than in their parish church of St. Mary Magdalene? We only know that William, the curate, married them in Gower's private chapel, and that the poet lived on within the precincts finding, one trusts, in the care and affection of the wife of his old age and in the friendship of Prior Weston and the canons a foretaste of that divine love, which he had invoked in the closing lines of the *Confessio*.

> Such love is goodly for to have,
> Such love may the body save,
> Such love may the soul amend,
> The high God such love us send.

During his remaining years he shared at St. Mary's the fortunes of the day. There was a large amount of rebuilding about 1400, particularly in the south transept, to which he made a liberal contribution. He erected a chantry chapel, which unfortunately has not survived, within the chapel of St. John in the north-eastern corner of the church. But it is from the terms of his will that one can best comprehend how closely he was involved in the life of the Priory. He made careful provision for the welfare of his own soul, for special prayers to be said daily in the chantry with a yearly *obit* on the Friday after the feast of St. Gregory; he even obtained an indulgence of 1,500 days for all who knelt to pray beside his tomb. Then he turned his attention to a number of small legacies. There were forty shillings for the prior and twenty shillings for the sub-prior, thirteen shillings and fourpence to each canon in holy orders and to every novice six and eightpence.

There were two shillings for each valet within the gates and twelve pence to every serving boy. The priest at St. Mary Magdalene's received ten shillings for his prayers and there were forty shillings assigned for lights and ornaments. At St. Thomas's the priest received six shillings, the sisters three and fourpence, the nurses twenty pence and every patient a shilling. Not even the lepers in Lock Street were forgotten. With all these provisions made and his wife provided for from the rents of his manors, he died in peace in 1408.

His tomb stands in the Cathedral still. It has had many vicissitudes and in the course of the removals, the allegorical figures of Charity, Mercy and Pity which once adorned it and the Latin lines which the poet himself may have written, have been destroyed or entirely defaced. It is to-day in process of being restored and the effigy remains of John Gower, the swan collar round his neck, a long robe buttoned to his feet, his dark hair falling to his shoulders and somewhat incongruously a wreath of red roses on his brow. The features are stern; they do not fit ill the conception of a sober thoughtful man, though it is an idealised portrait of what he was in his prime, not of the old blind man of seventy.

> Thro' thee the Father's only Son
> Be safe who lies beneath this stone;
> Thy mercy O Good Jesus shew
> The soul whose body lies below;
> For pity's sake O Jesus keep
> The soul of him who here does sleep.

So the French lines have been translated that were inscribed on the scrolls of Charity, Mercy and Pity and, though the promise of 1,500 days' indulgence may no longer entice the passer-by in 1955, he might well in the names of Charity, Mercy and Pity pause for a moment to pray by the tomb of an English poet.

## Note on Sources

In addition to the standard works on the history of the period, see Cassan *op. cit.*, for William de Wykeham and for his officials' visits to the Priory: *Wykeham's Register,* ed: T. F. Kirby (2 vol. 1899).

For Gower and Chaucer, see G. C. Macaulay, *The Works of John Gower,* 4 volumes, of which Vol. IV [the Latin works] contains a biographical introduction; and ed. F. N. Robinson, *The Poetical works of Chaucer* with introductory life, pp. XV–XXIV. The Calendars of entries in *Papal registers relating to Great Britain and Ireland,* 1198–1304, 1305–42, and 1362–1404 contain scattered references to the Priory of St. Mary, Southwark, mainly of a formal nature. Gower's collar is described by Thompson *op. cit.,* pp. 202–3.

# VII

## YORK AND LANCASTER

HENRY BEAUFORT, second of the four children whom Catherine Swynford bore to John of Gaunt, became Bishop of Winchester in 1404. In 1396 his father in his old age had married the woman who for more than twenty years had been his acknowledged mistress, and a year later King Richard issued letters patent legitimating the Beauforts. The way was thus opened for preferment in the church for Henry, the ablest of the brood, who became in turn Dean of Wells, Bishop of Lincoln and for a short time Chancellor of the University of Oxford. He was still a mere lad, according to the chroniclers, in all probability a man in the early twenties, who had supplemented his English education by the study of civil and canon law at Aachen. When his half-brother became Henry IV, the loyalty of the Beauforts was very precious to the King in the loneliness of his usurped throne and Henry Beaufort was for two years his Chancellor, resigning the office only a fortnight before he became Bishop of Winchester. Intellectually able, ambitious, cosmopolitan, he was better qualified for the King's council chamber than for the cure of souls and, in so far as he strove to fulfil adequately the episcopal position, it was not by means of the careful supervision of manners and morals nor the desire to root out scandals among those committed to his charge, but by playing his part, as a skilled legalist and an influential statesman, in the counsels of the church at home and abroad. For Beaufort was pre-eminently a man of the world. It was not the worldliness of the wastrel or the dilettante; although in his youth he had had a liaison with the Earl of Arundel's daughter there were no further hints of immorality or licentiousness and both in his private life and his financial transactions he had a reputation for honourable dealing. Nor could one call him irreligious for he was staunchly orthodox, but there was little natural piety in him and he was arrogant and careless of the things of the spirit. In this sense he was of the world, as in the better sense that his whole outlook and interests were the reverse of insular. He was entirely different both in his virtues and vices from his very English predecessor, William of Wykeham, whose imagination was limited while his heart was kind. Beaufort was too forcible a character to make friends easily but he was interested in every corner of Europe and devoted his immense wealth not to founding colleges but to subsidising the King, endeavouring thereby to mould the destinies of England and of the world.

The part that the Bishop played in his country's history was no immediate concern of St. Mary Overie's but, during the forty years of his episcopate, the life of the Priory could not fail to reflect the fact that quasi-royalty lived next door and that Winchester House was the headquarters of one who was three times Lord Chancellor and, as Henry IV's half-brother, Henry V's close personal friend and a chief councillor to the young King Henry VI, deeply influenced the policy of the crown.

On two occasions during his episcopate the Priory church was the scene of a royal wedding, and at the first in 1406 King Henry IV was present. In outward form, the church was much as it is to-day, except that the tower was half its present height and the little chapel of Mary Magdalene lay in the shelter of choir and southern transept. About it, instead of asphalt and railway bridges were meadows and pasture-land, the fair proportions of Winchester House and St. Swithun's and the tangle of small houses that lay between the east front and the highway. Within, it glowed with the radiant beauty of the many embellishments, of which the Reformation robbed it, and there were candled shrines and coloured tiles upon the floor, gleaming silver and the glorious blue and gold of the vestments on the day that Edmund Earl of Kent married Lucia of Milan. The bride was one of the nineteen children of Bernabo, Duke of Milan, who had been deposed and imprisoned by his nephew, the able and ruthless Gian Galeazzo. Thirteen years before, Henry Bolingbroke, still a frank and friendly young man untrammelled by thoughts of kingship, had visited Galeazzo, and Lucia who was then a young girl of fifteen had fallen in love, so it was said, with the handsome stranger and later had flatly refused to marry a German princeling. At length, a woman of mature years, she came to the England of which she had dreamed as a girl, to marry another. King Henry attended the wedding at St. Mary Overie's to add lustre by his presence to one of the many foreign alliances by which he endeavoured to strengthen himself in Europe. According to the custom of the time he gave the bride away at the entrance to the church, within the great porch which the Virgin adorned, where Joan de Cobham's body once had lain, and Lucia, turning away forever from the dreams of girlhood, went forward to plight her troth to Edmund Holland, the Earl of Kent.

The bridegroom was a man of valour and tried loyalty, the grandson of that Joan of Kent who after her first husband's death had married the Black Prince. He was thus a close kinsman of the deposed Richard whose cause his father and brothers had upheld, dying on the scaffold at Cirencester in the first year of Henry's troubled reign. But Edmund had remained loyal to Henry and had received back the Earldom his father had forfeited. Among the congregation who watched the wedding ceremony was his former mistress Constance le Despenser, but what she thought and whether the Earl of Kent was solaced by the promised dowry of 70,000 florins we cannot tell, any more than we know whether on that day it was misty and damp by the Thames or whether the sweetness of an English spring comforted the young woman who had left behind for ever the passionate life and sharp contrasts of her native Italy. All we know is the sad ending of the story. Next year the Earl of Kent was made an Admiral and sailed out in command of a fleet to attack an island off the coast of Brittany. Not a penny of the promised dowry had been paid, for under the vicious rule of Gian Galeazzo's son the power of Milan was rapidly disintegrating. The Earl of Kent, in order to raise the £200 necessary to finance his expedition, had to pledge his spoons and forks and goblets and his silver gilt basins inlaid with the arms of Kent and Milan. Then he set sail in June 1408, stormed the island with success but was mortally wounded and died in mid-September. His widow remained in England, and though some authorities say she married again she is referred to as Countess of Kent at the coronation of Queen Catherine in 1421. She died in London in 1424 and left, among many charitable bequests, 1,000 crowns to the new Cathedral in Milan, thus linked so unexpectedly with the Priory church of Southwark.

Before the next great occasion, much had changed. Beaufort had grown in stature, and in spite of his hard nature, his lack of spiritual concern in matters either national or episcopal, his possible greed, his certain lack of political scruple, he had deserved well of England by his devotion of time and energy and pocket, by the sound statesmanship whereby he steered the Lancastrian parliaments in their first essays in constitutional rule and by his genuine interest, so rare in an Englishman, in the wider issues of European policy. In the latter years of Henry IV's reign, his close friendship with the Prince of Wales and the hostility of Archbishop Arundel led to bitter faction and an unseemly struggle for political power between two leading prelates, who should have been brothers in Christ. Only in crushing Lollardry and burning a wretched tailor, who persisted in his error, were they in accord. Henry V's accession meant Beaufort in the ascendant and in that brief and glorious interlude he was the King's mouthpiece and managed affairs at home while Henry rode out upon the campaign that was to end at Agincourt. There was no wisdom, as it proved, in reopening old wounds and fighting France again, yet as the royal army passed over London Bridge in the autumn of 1414 the canons speeded it with their intercessions with as little doubt of the Lord's favour as the followers of St. Joan were to feel a few years later. The royal cavalcade paused at St. George's for the King to say his prayers and went thence to Southampton, where the discovery of a plot on the eve of embarkation struck a chill through the hearts of thinking men till Henry's own courage and military genius put reason out of court. When the news of Agincourt came to London at Easter time, a great procession made its way to Westminster from the City amid an outburst of rejoicing. The next great procession that delighted the dwellers of the Borough and Bankside escorted Catherine of France to London for her crowning. Yet within a few more years Henry V was dead, the war lingered on, and at home, the proud nobles intrigued for power at the court of an infant King who bore in his blood the taint of Catherine's father, the mad King of France. The personal rivalry between the King's uncle, Humphrey, the popular but erratic Duke of Gloucester, and Henry Beaufort, "the proud prelate," rose in these years to the height of scandal depicted so vividly though at times inaccurately in the first two parts of Shakespeare's *Henry VI*.

One of the charges that Gloucester later made against the Bishop concerned the marriage of the latter's niece to James I, the young King of Scotland who eighteen years before on a journey to France had been captured by the English and kept prisoner ever since. Henry IV had thus secured a hostage for Scotland's good behaviour and, though his action was a blatant illegality, he quietened his conscience by bringing up the boy with his own sons and giving him as good an education as the England of the day could supply. James had fought in France in the train of Henry V, who when he died was planning to liberate him, and a treaty to this effect was concluded with Scotland in November 1423. It also stipulated that James should take an English bride, and a few months later he was married to Joan Beaufort at St. Mary Overie's probably by the Bishop himself. From the young King's point of view, it was all rather a miracle. He related in the *King's Quair* how he looked out at Windsor, from the window of his lodgings, and espied:

> walking under the tower,
> Full secretly, new coming her to plain
> The fairest and the freshest yonge flower
> That ever I saw, methought, before that hour.

It was of course Joan Beaufort.

> Onely through letting of mine eyen fall,
> That suddenly, my heart became her thrall
> For ever of free will, for of menace
> There was no token in her sweete face.

The idyll prospered, for the Bishop approved. It gave him just the security he needed for the future good relations of England and Scotland and the prospect of immediate aggrandisement for the Beaufort family. No one was more of an adept than he in identifying his own and his country's welfare. Gloucester charged him with engineering the whole affair but James' verse and his young Queen's devotion gave the lie to such aspersions and there were no carping critics at the ceremony that morning in South-wark. Henry Beaufort, proud, powerful and since Henry V's death so very lonely, can have seldom had a more satisfying day than that of his niece's wedding. After the marriage there was a great feast at Winchester House, and when the young Queen went north with her husband she took with her in-numerable rich presents from her family, of gold and plate and jewels and "a suit of hangings in which the labours of Hercules were most curiously wrought." But not all the riches of the Beauforts nor the love of her husband could suffice to ward off advancing destiny. Scotland was a grim and turbulent land, and James was too eager to mould it to a southern pattern. In 1437, some members of his household conspired against him and forced their way one evening into the Queen's apartments, where they knew him to be. In vain she placed herself between James and his assailants, twice she was wounded and thrust aside until at length the King was cut down and slain. Thus tragedy wrote finis to the story and only the *King's Quair* remained to tell of a young man's love.

In October 1425 the rivalry between Beaufort and Gloucester threatened to break out into open flame. The Bishop's enlightened encouragement of foreign merchants and craftsmen made him unpopular in the City and, in one of the periodic manifestations of hostility to aliens, threatening placards were affixed by the mob to the gates of Winchester House and other episcopal residences. Beaufort replied by garrisoning the Tower to prevent the spread of disorder, while Gloucester stirred up the Londoners against him and each watched the other, lest by violence he should seize the person of the young King who was not far away at Eltham. The Bishop collected a troop of archers about him in Southwark and Gloucester encouraged the spread of panic by bidding the new Lord Mayor; "keep well the city that night and make good watch." Next morning the shops were shut and the citizens swarmed to defend the bridge against Beaufort's forces, who had attempted to cross into the City and who now withdrew to the southern side and barricaded the way into Long Southwark. The Archbishop and one of the peers hastened to the scene and during that anxious day went eight times to and fro until at length the proud protagonists consented to go in peace.

It was shortly after this crisis that Beaufort made his greatest error of judgment, so far as his influence in England was concerned. The Pope, for the second time, offered him the position of Cardinal, which on the first occasion Henry V had dissuaded him from accepting. Now a growing sense of frustration in home affairs impelled him to look, for the satisfaction of his ambition and the exercise of his marked ability, to the wider problems of Christendom and he accepted the new honour. His investiture took place at Calais in the spring of 1427, when he was robed in a habit of scarlet and the Cardinal's hat placed upon his head. When the craftsmen of St. Mary Overie's completed at long last the South transept, thanks to the help of Beaufort's benefactions, they worked into the eastern wall a copy of the hat, which can still be seen to-day, its strings intertwined about his coat of arms.

For the last twenty years of his life Beaufort tried in vain to reconcile a dual loyalty. Immediately after his investiture, the Pope entrusted him with a new commission as Legate in Germany, Bohemia and Hungary to organise a crusade against the Hussites, those Bohemian heretics who were inspired by a like spirit to the Lollards and were as indomitable as they in their new and dangerous beliefs. With a thousand men drawn from the French forces, Beaufort joined the vast German army which advanced into Bohemia, and was met and cut to pieces by the heretics at Tachau. A vivid picture remains of the Cardinal-Legate attempting to rally his contingent by holding a crucifix before them, tearing the imperial flag in pieces in a rage as he failed to check the rout and, only at the very last, himself retreating. This was a brave man, and one to whom the Church was becoming increasingly dear, but it was the rigid, arrogant church of the Roman curia to which he gave allegiance, alien in spirit to the religion of the men of Thames-side among whom his English home was set. When he returned to England in the summer of 1428 the conflict of loyalties increased. Gloucester and the Council looked askance at his new dignity, and questioned his right to retain his bishopric while commissioned as Legate. He was not permitted to preside as Bishop of Winchester at the forthcoming Chapter of the Order of the Garter at Windsor. The Council agreed, however, to the organisation of a new crusade, which had the advantage of again removing Beaufort from the country, though in view of the need of English manpower in the French wars the numbers were limited to 250 spears and 2,500 bowmen. There were indulgences available for all who contributed, even for the women who could only fast and pray, and perhaps at the gate of the Priory, as at most of the principal churches, there was, in the new year of 1429, a collecting box marked with a cross and labelled, "This chest is for the crusade."

Yet even this proved nugatory. The Cardinal marched out with his little force from Southwark but at Rochester he was faced with a cruel choice. The emergence of Joan of Arc had changed the whole temper of the scene in France and the Regent, the King's elder uncle, the Duke of Bedford, was in a critical position. Beaufort agreed to deflect his forces, volunteers for the crusade, to fight for six months for the English in France. When the Pope heard what had occurred he withdrew the Legantine commission. Whether or not the Cardinal hoped to be free within six months to proceed on the crusade, his decision ruined his chance of supreme influence in the counsels of the Papacy, as his acceptance of the office of Cardinal undermined his influence at home in a church increasingly conscious of its Englishry.

For another eighteen years Beaufort played an active part in his country's chequered history, supporting the Regent in the French adventure while a chance of success remained and sharing in the guilt of the martyrdom of Jeanne d'Arc. After Bedford's death he became the leader of the peace party and the bitter struggle with Gloucester continued, for the latter was the mouthpiece of those who clamoured for victories in the field. As the political see-saw swung hither and thither, each dominated in turn and each in the same year was brought face to face with eternity. Gloucester died suddenly, while under arrest in 1447, but if there were foul play the Cardinal himself was not involved. For the past three years he had lived in retirement at Winchester and within a few months of his rival's death, he also met his end. Shakespeare's picture of the dying Cardinal, his soul heavy with the guilt of Gloucester's death, seeing before his horrified eyes his victim's hair uprising "like lime twigs set to catch my winged soul," must give way to one of more sober hue. Henry Beaufort died, resigned at the end, after bidding farewell to the monks of St. Swithun's and listening to the solemn phrases of the burial service, bequeathing part of his large fortune to the poor and the prisoners of Southwark. The final word rests, after all, with Shakespeare:

> Forbear to judge for we are sinners all.
> Close up his eyes and draw the curtain close
> And let us all to meditation.

The Austin Canons at St. Mary Overie's enjoyed their most prosperous years during the first half of the fifteenth century, while Beaufort was in possession of Winchester House and Henry Werkworth, for forty years, held the office of Prior. Just as Collingbourne had given them stability and wise guidance when William of Wykeham was Bishop so, after Weston's death, from 1414-52, Werkworth was Prior and proved himself to be as the canons described him when he died *vir industrie laudabilis*, a man of praiseworthy diligence. He would appear to have been trusted by the Pope, for in 1446 he was employed as his agent in a disputed succession to the Deanery of Wells and showed himself a man of character, if not of tact, by his strong action when the canons of Wells disobeyed the Pope's instructions. Werkworth summarily excommunicated them and sent an official of the diocese of Exeter to affix a notification of the sentence upon the church door. On another occasion the King wrote to the Prior of St. Mary Overie's, recommending a not very desirable character to the vacant living of St. Mildred's Bread Street, but in spite of the strong wording of the letter, which extolled the great cunning, virtues and priestly demeaning of the candidate, the Prior appears to have disregarded it and to have appointed someone else. In 1447 a licence was issued to the all-powerful Duke of Suffolk to exchange for some city property the advowson of the parish church of St. Mary Abchurch which he had been granted by Henry Werkworth, a less admirable instance of his activities. In the year following the Priory was licenced to appropriate the country church of Kedebroke [Kidbrooke], the revenues of which did not permit of the appointment of a parson, "and no parishioner now dwells there." All these small items go to build up the picture of a diligent man of affairs. One looks in vain for evidence of signs of spiritual grace: they would be little likely to appear in Patent Roll and Statute Book. There was no open scandal and, in that it seems to have been a community happy in having little history, the Priory may well have been in better case than many of its contemporaries. There is an indication of vitality in Werkworth's triumphant recasting of the bells in 1424, and there are contemporary records extant which show that the parish church of St. Margaret, within the Priory's immediate care, was in a healthy state in the mid-years of the century. What remains certain was the day-to-day celebration of the Mass. Not only in these comparatively peaceful years but throughout the horror of civil war that lay immediately ahead, the prayers and intercessions of the Austin Canons close to London Bridge continued without ceasing and the two-fold duty of work and worship was steadily performed.

There were six bells at St. Mary Overie's in 1424, when Werkworth recast them after the original tower had been strengthened, and added two more making a ring of eight. Trinity, the great bell, Mary, Augustine, Lawrence, Gabriel, All Saints, John the Evangelist and Christopher the treble, their names ring down the years, as the bells rang across Long Southwark and the Clink when Bishop Beaufort lived, as they sounded in the eighteenth century when the society of College youths rang a record peal, as they still ring to-day across the Borough High Street. It was the custom in medieval times to christen the bells in all solemnity, duly anointing them and praying that whensoever they should sound all danger of whirlwind and thunder, lightning and tempests and all devils of Satan should be swept away. Five hundred years ago the men of Southwark heard them and knew that all was well.

One is grateful that the bells have survived for so much has vanished that made their religion real to the folk of the fifteenth century, though there are in existence some account books for the church of St. Margaret that are full of references to lovely possessions and gay practices in which all Southwark shared. The church stood on the opposite side of the High Street to St. Thomas, a short distance to the south of the Priory. It was in every sense a church in the way. The main road ran beneath its walls and its churchyard spilled over the borders so that a man riding in haste might scatter a funeral party as he passed. Immediately on the northern side the road divided, a path branching off towards the Priory, the main highway curving eastward to the bridge. St. Margaret's was indeed too much in the way both for health and convenience, but the accounts leave no doubt of the fact that it was also very much alive. They were discovered in the mid-nineteenth century by Mr. J. Payne Collier and published with his notes in the British Magazine for 1847-8 and they make fascinating reading. They begin in 1444 and cover about a hundred years, recording not only the church's belongings, of which for some reason an inventory was taken in 1485, but also the daily expenses of keeping the church in order. The first entry on the payments side was for £20 for a cross of "silver and gilt" and a year or two later there was £6 6s. 8d. for a pair of new organs and 13s. 4d. for the hire, in Cheapside, "of a player to play upon the same organs." The church was wealthy in those days, with regular collections on all the great festivals, bequests from parishioners and a steady income of fees from weddings and funerals. One source of revenue was the hoke—or hook—money, gathered once a year when a cord was stretched across the road and fastened on hooks on either side and, on the Monday and Tuesday of the appointed week, the men and women in turn levied toll on all who passed. It was a game at which the women, it would seem, were more successful than the men: in 1457 they collected fourteen shillings, compared with the men's total of only five!

One recurrent item in the expenses was the removal of the dirt and dung that lay about the church or was brought in from the crowded highway. Perhaps the frequent laundering that appears to have been necessary was partly a consequence of this. Tilers and plumbers, of course, were often in demand and an entry of ten shillings for the repair of a window serves as a reminder of the fine glass, which added so much to the beauty of the great fifteenth-century churches, built in the new decorated manner. Local craftsmen, who may well have provided the glass of St. Margaret's, were soon to try their hands with glorious success in the chapel of the new King's College at Cambridge. There was colour and harmony all the time, green ivy and holm for the Christmas decorations, flags and garlands for Corpus Christi day and blue and white curtains for the Easter sepulchre, that stood outside the church where all that passed might be reminded of the eternal mystery. Minstrels were sometimes hired for the great festivals and the organ was played, first by John Fichett and then by John Medwall, whose rapidly dwindling salary showed that times grew harder as England became steadily more unsettled. St. Margaret's day was celebrated on December 31st and, after a great procession, a bonfire was lit for which all and sundry had been scavenging wood, for days past, from the high road and the banks of the Thames. St. Lucy's day on September 19th was also celebrated in distinctive manner and on the occasion of both feasts in 1444 and 1445, plays were presented, either in the church or at its entrance, and repeated fairly regularly, at no small expense, for the next twelve years. There are references to the hire of garments, to the "dancing money of the maidens," and to a payment to the clerks in connection with the plays, and though one is left as so often with only scraps of knowledge one can thus trace to the church in the High Street the first appearance of Southwark as the nursery of drama. Another sign of the church's vitality in the mid-fifteenth century comes from another source. In May 1449 the King issued Letters Patent to four parishioners of St. Margaret's to found a Guild in honour of the Assumption of the Virgin Mary. They were to appoint the churchwardens and were empowered to hold property up to twenty marks a year. Guilds of this nature, voluntary associations for religious and charitable ends, were a prominent feature of medieval life. The members cared for each other in adversity and prayed for the welfare of the souls of departed brethren. Some became specifically linked with a craft or a trading project and their worldly characteristics thus developed; others, like the Guild of the Assumption at Southwark, remained predominantly religious in nature, concerned with the welfare of a church or school or other philanthropic aim. There are no specific records of the Guild's activities but it continued in existence during the remaining years of the church's life, a portent of the new age when the welfare of the community would pass from the care of professed brethren to that of individuals of good will.

Changes were imminent and the processions and the morris-dancing, the mystery plays and the canons' recital of their daily office went on against a background of increasing confusion. Henry Werkworth was still Prior in 1450 when another army of

rebels marched into Southwark from Blackheath. But Jack Cade's
followers were not unlettered peasants as Wat Tyler's had been;
many of them were men of substance and they were more concerned with political rights than with social readjustments. The
internecine struggle of York and Lancaster was foreshadowed
for Cade claimed to be a Mortimer and cousin to the Duke of
York, whose recall from Ireland he demanded. The Captain of
Kent, as his followers called him, assembled on Blackheath with
several thousand men and put forward a charter of grievances with
which few sensible men would disagree. When the Council raised
the local militia against him, he fell back upon Sevenoaks where
he turned and routed the opposing army, King Henry withdrew
to Kenilworth and Cade triumphantly re-established himself at
Blackheath. A vivid account of the camp and the discipline he
maintained survives in a letter written to John Paston in Norfolk
by a kinsman who was in the service of the old Southwark knight,
Sir John Fastolf. The latter was anxious to find out the true state
of affairs for he was uncertain whether to garrison his house or
flee to the City. John Payn was sent to investigate and wrote of
his alarming experiences to Paston some years afterwards. "The
captain demanded me, what was my cause of coming thither . . .
and I said that I came thither to cheer with my wife's brethren, and
others that were my allies, and gossips of mine, that were present
there; and then was there one there and said to the captain that
I was one of Sir John Fastolf's men . . . and then the captain let cry
Treason upon me throughout all the field . . . and so forthwith
I was taken, and led to the captain's tent, and one axe and one
block was brought forth to have smitten off mine head." Payn
was saved because John Paston's brother-in-law was Cade's
sword-bearer and he "letted the captain," and Payn returned to
advise his master strongly to send away the old soldiers he had
gathered about him. Fastolf sought refuge in the Tower but Payn
awaited Cade's men, who on July 2 marched into Southwark and
made their headquarters at the White Hart in the Borough High
Street, divesting the unfortunate Payn of his velvet gown and
coat of mail and otherwise maltreating him.

For three nights Cade remained at the White Hart. When on the
first morning he rode across London Bridge, the drawbridge was
down and there was no attempt to stop him. His men were kept in

order and only the house of one Alderman was sacked and in the evening he withdrew quietly to Southwark. Among those who had given him countenance were the Prior of Lewes and the Abbot of Battle; the other leading ecclesiastic of the Borough, Wainfleet, the Bishop of Winchester, had not dared to cross the river to his home on Bankside and remained in the City anxiously waiting on the event. On the second morning, Cade entered London again and Scales, the governor of the Tower, surrendered to him the Treasurer, Lord Saye, who was the people's scapegoat. After a summary trial in Cheapside, Saye and the Sheriff of Kent were executed on the spot and that night a grim procession returned to the White Hart, with the Treasurer's body dragged at horse's tail to Jack Cade's lodging. During that night there was some pillaging, as much by the ne'er-do-weels of City and Borough as by the rebels themselves. Stirred out of their paralysis by the threat to their property, the citizens took action and with the help of the Tower garrison barricaded the bridge. Cade tried to force an entry and battle was joined. Throughout the night of July 5th a fierce struggle continued, and first the Londoners were driven back to the wooden piles by St. Magnus' corner and then the rebels were repulsed to the "stulpes" or posts at the Southwark end till, "both parties being faint, weary and fatigued," they agreed to desist, neither crossing to the other side. Meanwhile the prisoners, whom on the last evening Cade had released from King's Bench and Marshalsea, added to the distraught tumult of the Southwark streets.

In the morning the two Archbishops and the Bishop of Winchester offered to intercede and Wainfleet crossed the bridge and met Jack Cade in the churchyard of St. Margaret's. He brought two pardons with him, the one for Cade himself, made out in the name of Mortimer, the other for his supporters. Cade accepted the terms and most of his men went thankfully to their homes. Cade lingered in Southwark and most rashly failed to disarm and, fearful of a new rising, the Council revoked his pardon. He rode hurriedly to Rochester and tried in vain to capture a neighbouring stronghold, then fled with a price on his head and died fighting in a Sussex lane. Once again the streets of the Borough were quiet; Fastolf returned to his great house in St. Olave's parish and Wainfleet came back to Bankside.

The new bishop was as different from the imperious churchman who preceded him as Beaufort had been from William of Wykeham. Wainfleet was a student; he had been at Winchester and New College and, when King Henry founded Eton in 1440, he had been one of the first Fellows and later the Provost. It would please him to be remembered as the founder of Magdalen College in his beloved Oxford rather than for his not very outstanding exploits as Chancellor to the tottering Lancastrian throne. He was genuinely fond of King Henry, whose piety was congenial to him, and his heart was torn by the increasing turmoil to which Cade's revolt was but the curtain-raiser. In 1452, he ordained a solemn procession through the streets of Southwark from the Priory, by way of St. Margaret's, through St. Olave's parish to the gates of Bermondsey Abbey. All the clergy of Southwark took part, singing their litanies and swinging the censers as they went, with "apt suffrages for defence and increase of the Christian faith and for the prosperous estate of the King and his dominions." A last abortive expedition to France was the immediate cause of the day of intercession, but no victory came in answer to the Bishop's prayers and within a month or two the King succumbed to his first fit of insanity, and Richard of York's protectorate, Henry's recovery and York's recourse to arms followed each other in quick succession. There was to be no "prosperous estate" for many long years to come.

During the Wars of the Roses, the sympathy of the City of London remained consistently with the Yorkists; very probably in consequence, Southwark was biassed in the Lancastrian's favour as were the great ecclesiastics with whom the Borough had so many ties. Not often, however, did the wars impinge immediately upon the Priory. In 1460, before the battle of Northampton, Warwick the King-maker landed in Kent and advanced on London in triumph, and on that occasion Scales, that same governor of the Tower who had yielded up Lord Saye to Cade ten years before, fled before the city mob and endeavoured, by way of the Thames, to reach sanctuary at Westminster. He was captured and cut down on Bankside and his body left by the great door of the Priory church. It was an ironic turn of fortune, for three hundred years before his forefathers had befriended St. Mary Overie's; had he perhaps turned his boat that way in the hope of finding refuge there? Now the canons took in the body and buried it in the church.

Edward IV, when his crown was won at last, naturally wished to reward the loyal Londoners and the new charter he issued in 1462 gave them fuller rights over Southwark than they had hitherto enjoyed, making no fundamental changes but clearing up various ambiguities in their favour. Among other privileges, the City authorities were given the right to appoint an officer to execute writs and to correct all persons including those "exercising any arts whatsoever." Already it would seem the players, whose performances were forbidden in the City, were accustomed to resort to Southwark, and the more stringent provisions of the 1462 charter drove them in particular to Bankside where within the Clink Liberty the arm of the law could not reach them.

There were further provisions in the charter for the holding of the annual Lady Fair, which took place in the first days of September at the southern end of Long Southwark. Only Bartholomew Fair in the City rivalled it in size and noise and junketings and throughout the centuries, though dynasties came and went, the Fair continued. Only in times of pestilence was it forbidden: and the pestilence was a recurrent evil which disturbed far more ruthlessly than civil war the ordered days of ordinary men. In 1467, there was an outbreak of plague that hit the Borough hard and gave the Bishop good cause for another penitential procession. The pestilence appeared to him as a sign of God's wrath: the treachery and cruelty which had so long tormented England, the sinfulness of man deserved such retribution. Once again the canons of St. Mary Overie and the monks of Bermondsey passed through the stricken streets singing their mournful litanies, as much part of the picture of medieval England as the pageantry after Agincourt or the rebels that marched from Blackheath.

Medieval England: for good or ill its days were numbered. In 1469, as if as a sign of impending change, the stone roof of the nave of the Priory church fell down, weakened perhaps by the removal of some flying buttresses in the repairs necessitated by the fire of Richard II's reign. The Prior of St. Mary's from 1462 to 1486 was Henry Burton, who erected a new wooden roof, lighter than its predecessor and less likely to collapse; all that now remains of it are a few of the bosses, preserved when the roof was allowed to decay in the 19th century. They form a delightful collection of humorous and vigorous designs. There is a rebus on the name of Burton, three burrs or thistles and a tun of beer; there are some grotesque heads, including one of the devil swallowing his own false tongue, the pelican always a favourite symbol of medieval piety, and other mouldings that help to show that good craftsmen still lived and worked in Southwark.

In 1470 there was once again bloodshed on London Bridge when Fauconberg struck a last blow for the imprisoned Henry VI, marching from Kent along the accustomed route and bombarding the City from the Southwark side. But it was a half-hearted affair, and the assailants did not persist. News had come of King Edward's triumph at Tewkesbury; within a few days he was back in London and Henry conveniently dead in the Tower. With heavy hearts, the canons beneath their ruined roof prayed for the coming of tranquillity. And for England, though not for them, the years of reconstruction and progress were at hand. Bishop Wainfleet and Prior Burton lived till 1486, just long enough to see the representative of the Lancastrian cause triumphant at Bosworth and established on the throne. The future of England was in the hands of the Tudors: what difference would it make to St. Mary Overie's?


## Note on Sources

See L. B. Radford, *Henry Beaufort, Bishop, Chancellor, Cardinal* (1908); for St. Margaret's church, in addition to a good summary in Rendle, *op cit.*, p. 110 *seq.*, see the article by J. P. Collier in *British Magazine* for 1847–8. For John Payn's account of Cade's rebellion see *Paston Letters* (Everyman Ed.), I, 29–31. The reference to Henry Werkworth's dealings with the Dean of Wells is in the *Calendar of Papal Letters*, vol. VIII (1427–47), p. 470.

# VIII

# CHANGING TIMES

IN the midsummer of 1518 when Henry VIII had been nine
years on the throne the Austin canons met at Leicester for a
general Chapter of their order. The proceedings began on
June 16th with a sermon and a great procession through the
streets of the town. There were one hundred and seventy delegates from all parts of England, and at the Cross in the Market
Place the Mayor and twenty leading citizens toasted their revered
guests in ten gallons of Gascon wine. The conference was one of
particular importance for, at its final session, the King himself
was present with Catherine, his Spanish bride, Wolsey, the Archbishop of York, and the King's sister and her husband, the Duke
and Duchess of Suffolk. All these eminent people were thereupon
solemnly admitted members of the Augustinian order in a great
gesture of Catholic piety fitting to a Sovereign, proud to describe
himself Defender of the Faith.

Yet between the pleasantries in Leicester's market place and the
ceremonial ending of the Chapter, in the period when the canons
got down to business, there had crept in a feeling of *malaise*, a
"querulous and despairing note" as a modern chronicler calls it.
Only thirty-six of the delegates were heads of houses, which
meant that many of the smaller priories were not represented,
and it looked as if, once again as so often before, it would not
prove possible to implement satisfactorily any resolutions that
were taken. The compromise inherent in the order itself, between
strict seclusion and parochial work, and the diversity in the
Observances in use throughout the country made uniformity in
practice impossible and probably undesirable, but it also made it
particularly difficult to initiate effective reform. And with every
passing year, men of intelligence and sincerity became increasingly
aware of the pressing need to reform. This was undoubtedly so

in regard to scholarship and, as soon as the Chapter at Leicester assembled, a letter was read from Wolsey regretting the lethargy of the order in this respect. Not only had there been a scheme on foot for fifty years to found a college at Oxford, specifically for the use of the canons regular, and the scheme continued to hang fire—but in addition all houses with more than twenty members were supposed to maintain a scholar at the University. Yet as far back as the reign of Richard II Henry Collingbourne had appealed against an order to send one of the Southwark canons to Oxford and it was often necessary to fine a number of houses for failing to fulfil this requisite. This was the matter of Wolsey's rebuke, but little practical good would come of it, and of his assertion that true learning contributed more than any other single factor towards conserving and increasing the Christian religion, if, owing to the absence of delegates from a large number of houses, his words reached only a few.

Next morning when the Chapter reassembled a member rose to speak. It was Bartholomew Linsted, the Prior of St. Mary Overie's. He was in a state of deep distress, wringing his hands and in the end falling on his knees in an attitude of prayer, as with tears in his eyes he pleaded for a stricter observance of St. Augustine's rule. Not in closer study, not in tighter discipline, not in royal patronage, did he hope to find the salvation of his order, but in the complete acceptance, the day-to-day practice of a rule that proclaimed without reservation God's love for man and man's duty to his fellows. Linsted's words and his obvious emotion caused considerable stir and some embarrassment, and the subsequent discussion took up the whole of the forenoon. The wealthy and powerful Prior of Merton, who was President of the Chapter, endeavoured to re-establish a normal atmosphere by a reasoned speech well inter-larded with quotations from Scripture, but throughout the royal ceremonies next day the memory of Linsted's words lingered with the more thoughtful among the delegates. Something was radically wrong with the present state of the Church. What was the cure: education, conversion or revolution?

Twenty quiet years at St. Mary Overie's lay ahead of Linsted, before King Henry answered the question in no uncertain terms. The Prior's diocesan until 1528 was Bishop Fox, who had been

VIEW OF LONDON BRIDGE SHOWING ST. SAVIOUR'S CHURCH AND
MONTAGUE CLOSE (TEMP. SEVENTEENTH CENTURY).

This is a very careful and scholarly reconstruction by H. B. Brewer
in *Old London Illustrated*, ed. H. A. Cox. The picture shows clearly the
position of the Chapel of St. Mary Magdalene, east of the south
transept, and also the great west door and window added to the
mediaeval building by Bishop Fox in the reign of Henry VIII. Immediately flanking this is the gateway to Montague Close, formerly the
conventual buildings, and to the west of it St. Mary Overie's Dock.

**THE LADY CHAPEL TO-DAY.**

The altars beneath the four east windows of the chapel are dedicated to St. Andrew for missionary intercession, to St. Christopher, to St. Mary and to St. Francis and St. Elizabeth; the furnishings of the latter altar were the gift of the Guild of Social Workers.

one of Henry VII's chief advisers before and after Bosworth and had spent his prime in helping to organise the Tudor monarchy. As Wolsey increasingly dominated the scene, Fox withdrew as far as possible from public life and in his old age, as he devoted himself to his diocese, his sense of unworthiness grew: so much he might have done and had failed to do for the churches under his care. Most of his time was spent at Winchester but St. Mary Overie's shared in the benefactions by which to some small degree he strove to make reparation, and a new window of six lights and a magnificent doorway were placed at the west end of the church, while two upper storeys were added to the tower. At Winchester and St. Mary Overie's alike great altar screens of stone were erected, the one in Southwark only less grand than that in the mother church of the diocese. Thirty feet in height, it consisted of three tiers, each with eleven niches filled with appropriate figures, and the whole ornamented with a design of oak leaves and acorns, flowers and twisted thorns. The spandrels of the doorways on each side of the main altar were decorated, at Southwark, with grotesque devices of bird and beast which have been happily preserved. The images in the niches and many of the adornments were hacked out by iconoclasts in the years of religious strife, and in 1703 the whole was covered by a wooden reredos of classical design, but in the early years of the 19th century Bishop Fox's screen was rediscovered and restored, and remains after many vicissitudes one of the church's loveliest possessions.

Fox died in 1528 and for two years Wolsey held the see which he coveted not merely for its wealth but because, except for London, this was the only diocese in which a Bishop could remain in residence and still keep his ear close to the heart-beat of the realm. Wolsey's successor, the shrewd Stephen Gardiner, realised this to the full and made his home in Southwark more consistently than any prelate since Henry Beaufort.

The twenty years that elapsed between the meeting at Leicester and the dissolution of the monasteries are recorded in a London diary kept by Charles Wriothesley, a minor court official. The diary shows among other things how close the Tudors remained to the customs and trappings of the medieval age and yet how astir the days were with new beginnings. Shortly after his return from Leicester, Linsted probably took part in the great procession of monks and clergy, which accompanied the Italian Legate, Campeggio, from St. George's Bar in Southwark to Leadenhall Corner in the City on his solemn entry into London. Such religious processions were now once again interspersed with secular pageants, for the Tudors believed in shewing themselves to the people. Henry went frequently from Greenwich to Westminster, sometimes by road through Southwark where his brother-in-law, the Duke of Suffolk, was building himself a fine palace close to St. George's church. More often the King travelled by river and the canons at St. Mary Overie's had a good view on such occasions, when the royal barge passed under London Bridge with trumpets and drummers going before, "a goodly sight to behold . . ." But Wriothesley's pages are also full of entries of another sort, telling of executions, of heresy trials, of swift changes of policy and personnel as Thomas Cromwell took Wolsey's place, as Gardiner succeeded Cromwell and one poor Queen after another passed across the stage. In 1534, the Act of Supremacy declared the King to be the supreme head of the Church of England and in the succeeding years all payments and appeals to Rome were prohibited. The Act of Six Articles in 1539 laid it down, on the other hand, that the dogma of the Church remained unchanged and that any who denied the tenet of transubstantiation should be burnt as heretics, as surely as those who refused to defy the Pope should be executed as traitors. It was a bewildering time for the law-abiding Christian.

The majority of his subjects were in sympathy with Henry in his attitude to Rome, for they had been restive under Papal domination for at least two centuries. When he proceeded to abolish the monasteries opinion was more evenly divided. The idleness and at times the immorality of some of the brethren demanded extreme action, but the fact remained that in an age of rising prices and economic maladjustment, the monasteries were valuable welfare centres that would be missed. In a town such as Southwark, a ready target for the pestilence and the haunt of many undesirables, where a constant stream of wayfarers passed by, the need for some such place as the Priory was self-evident. In 1532 when a dole was distributed at its gates, the throng of suppliants was so great that seven persons were crushed to death, two women and a boy among them. Yet, in spite of "the great lamentation that the poor people made for them," the monasteries were doomed. It is not easy to see the significance of the great procession which the King ordered the Priory to hold in November 1535, when the canons went "with their crosses and candlesticks and verges before them, all singing the litany." It was perhaps a public expression of repentance and submission. The threat of change came nearer in the spring of 1538 when "the image of the rood at the Abbey of Bermondsey was taken down by the King's commandment." Meanwhile, officials appointed by Thomas Cromwell visited the religious houses up and down England, unearthing whatever of scandal or disrepute they might find. Both at Bermondsey and St. Thomas's they found enough and to spare. In comparison, St. Mary Overie's had a good reputation. The last hint of trouble had been in 1501 before Linsted's appointment, when a commissary of the Prior of Canterbury had visited the canons at a time when the see of Winchester was vacant. The then prior, Dr. Michell, described the spiritual state of the house as good but reported a debt of £190, which he had reduced to £100 in his two years of office. His sub-prior blamed Michell's predecessor for the debt and he also reported all well in regard to the conduct of the brethren, stating in particular that silence was kept at the proper times. When Cromwell's men arrived thirty years later, they estimated the wealth of St. Mary Overie's at £624 6s. 8d., of which £283 4s. 6d. came from Southwark rents. There had been a steady falling off in numbers for some years throughout the country and this had been encouraged by the authorities. On October 14th, 1539, when Bartholomew Linsted voluntarily surrendered the Priory into the King's hands, only twelve canons were left in residence, all of whom received a pension. The sub-officers, Thomas Henden and William Goodwin, were to have £8 annually, the rest received £6 and Linsted (or Fowle as he was often called) £100 and a lodging within the precincts, where Dr. Michell had dwelt after his retirement. Here Linsted lived out his days in peace, acquiescing in the new régime but refusing, unlike his neighbour of Bermondsey, to accept office in the reformed church. It was here at his home in the Close that Stow discovered him and heard from him the story of John Overs and his lovely daughter.

The last prior of St. Mary Overie's was not the stuff of which martyrs are made, and his large pension certainly looks like a reward for the voluntary surrender. But one need not go so far as the vigorous but not very scholarly Aubrey, who stigmatised him as the "cowardly and traitorous Prior." The incident at Leicester shows how unhappy Linsted had been about the state into which his order had declined; neither by temperament nor by convinction was he prepared for resistance. The Abbot of Glastonbury, to his honour, had defied the Crown and paid for it with his life. If Linsted lacked the courage for such an act, he probably lacked also the certainty that such an act would be right and without any sense of disloyalty to his beliefs may have agreed that the monastic system had had its day. There were many besides Linsted, Bishop Gardiner amongst them, who imagined it would be possible to accept the fall of the monasteries and even the Act of Supremacy, and to go no further along the dangerous road of reform.

Among those who hoped at first for a workable compromise was Sir Anthony Browne, the man who benefited most from the sequestration of the Priory. He was a personal friend of the King, who gave him the conventual buildings of St. Mary Overie's as well as the lands of Battle Abbey in Sussex. Sir Anthony's father had been slain at Bosworth, bearing Henry Tudor's standard, and the son inherited the family tradition of loyalty. When Henry VIII was about to die, it was Sir Anthony who "with good courage and conscience" told him that the end was near, and it was he whom the Council sent to Prince Edward to ride into London by his side. It is refreshing to find in Tudor times a family whom all parties regarded with respect and affection, but so it seems to have been with regard to the Brownes. They remained staunchly orthodox, and when a cleavage became inevitable held firmly to the ancient faith. Yet they saw nothing amiss in the enjoyment of abbey lands. Sir Anthony adapted the prior's house in the precincts of St. Mary Overie's to be his town residence, and after his death, his son completed the rebuilding, and, when he was created Lord Montague in 1554, gave to his Southwark home the name of Montague Close.

If Sir Anthony Browne, Bishop Gardiner and Prior Linsted all thought it right to accept the royal edicts, without believing that thereby the fundamentals of their religion were undermined, it was natural that the ordinary residents in Southwark, the leather-sellers and soap-boilers, the inn-keepers and hop-merchants, who went to Mass each Sunday at St. Margaret's and St. Mary Mag-dalene's, should continue to worship as before, exercising the Englishman's right to grumble (very discreetly in Tudor times) but leaving it to the specialists and to a few eccentrics to worry about the theological implications of the recent changes. The more immediate concern of the energetic wardens of St. Margaret's was the traffic congestion about their island site and the inadequacy of the church buildings in view of the increasing population. Already in 1537 the parishioners had been granted by act of parliament corporate powers, similar to those enjoyed by the Guild of the Assumption, for the purchase of land for a new churchyard, on the grounds that the original one, "situate in the common street and in the middle of the King's highway," was apt to transmit "corrupt and pestilent infection to those of the King's most natural and loving subjects that should ride that way." In 1539, the last year of St. Margaret's existence, the Bishop had contributed over £24 to a total sum of £45 collected for improvements in the church, possibly the erection of a rood loft, but, as the wardens considered the problems again, they found themselves faced with a great opportunity. Now the canons were dispersed and Sir Anthony had taken possession of the conventual buildings, what was going to happen to the Priory church itself?

It was a general predicament in the England of the time. When the dissolved monastery was linked with an episcopal see its church naturally, as at Winchester, continued in being as the mother-church of the diocese, but all too often, in other cases, no action was taken and the ancient building fell slowly into dis-repair and ruin, the process often accelerated by the removal of lead and brick to assist the construction of the new manor house nearby. Up and down the countryside they stand to-day, Rievaulx, Fountains, Tintern, Waverley, witness to the tragic mishandling of a problem and an opportunity. Elsewhere, progress, of a sort, wiped out every trace of them. Of Bermondsey Abbey only a few scattered stones remain, while, at Merton, board mills and railway sidings cover the site of the finest Augustinian priory in the kingdom.

What then of St. Mary Overie's? Someone had a bright idea. Was it that "honest man" William Emerson, who was a prominent property-owner in the Borough? Was it Thomas Cure, the saddler, competent man of business and a good if conventional churchman? Or was it some unknown, who first suggested to the wardens of St. Margaret's that their problems would all be solved if they made an agreement with St. Mary Magdalene's and obtained from the Crown the use of the Priory church?

They proceeded in a typical English manner, by drawing up a petition of the parishioners and then consulting their bishop, who was most anxious to help them. Through his good offices the scheme was put into effect and, not waiting for legal sanction, the removal took place. Wriothesley's chronicle records under the date 1540, "This year also after Christmas the Priory of St. Mary Overie's in Southwark was made a parish church, and the little church of Mary Magdalene, joining to the same priory was made all in one church and St. Margaret's in Southwark was admitted to the same parish. And on Candlemas Even, to join the same parishes together, the sacrament of the Altar was solemnly brought in rich copes with torches burning from St. Margaret's church to the said church of St. Mary Overie's; the which church, the inhabitants of the said church borough had bought of the King with the bells of the same to their great charges which now is the largest and fairest church about London; the good Bishop of Winchester, now being called Doctor Stephens, putting to his helping hand to the redeeming of the same."

It was fitting that the symbolic act of union should take place at Candlemas, that season of rededication and the proclamation of the Word. It took some time longer to complete the transaction, which was of a three-fold nature. First there was the purchase of the church's possessions, including the bells, plate, vestments and church records, which entailed a considerable financial sacrifice on the part of the hard-pressed parishioners; between 1540 and 1544 the sum of 400 marks was paid to the Crown in large instalments for which Bishop Gardiner and Richard Longe the Bailiff stood surety. Secondly an Act of Parliament was necessary to amalgamate the two parishes. Thirdly in 1543 a lease was obtained for the annual sum of £47 5s. 4d. of the church building and the rectory of the combined parishes, including the right to levy tithe and to appoint the clergy, rights which had belonged to the sequestered Priory and had thus passed to the Crown. The vestry minuté books of the new parish are crowded with details of the troublesome and expensive proceedings entailed in the periodic renewal of this lease, which remained in the wardens' hands except for two years in the next reign when it was held by the then Bishop of Winchester. Meanwhile after Candlemas in 1540, here the parishioners were in their new home. There were drawbacks to be sure, as they discovered when first they were seated in the lofty nave of the old church and listened to one of those sermons in English that were becoming so popular, only to find that most of them could not hear. Some less intrepid spirits must have longed nostalgically for the vitality of St. Margaret's and the comfortable fellowship of the little church of Mary Magdalene. The more robust among them however had a satisfaction that none of the difficulties could undermine. They had saved a church, richly endowed by bishops of the past and by the gifts of humble citizens. Its control and management now belonged to them under the terms of the lease through the church wardens they elected. What a chance there was here of power and privilege, what opportunities of service, what dangers of spiritual pride.

The Act of Parliament of 32 Henry VIII [1540] clarified the legal position, confirming the action that had been taken. It referred to St. Margaret's as already "prostrated and converted to another use" and stated that its parishioners and those of St. Mary Magdalene's were accustomed to repair to the Priory church "and there jointly as inhabitants of one sole parish hear divine service" and receive the sacraments. Wherefore the Act continued, "at the humble supplication of the said several parishioners," St. Margaret's and St. Mary Magdalene's were from henceforth to be "united, knit and joined together" and the parishioners were yearly to "nominate and elect six or four honourable persons dwelling within the precincts of the said parish to be church wardens who shall do and exercise all and everything as any other wardens may do in any parish or place within this realm of England." Upon these wardens there devolved the rights and powers of the defunct Guild of the Assumption of the Blessed Virgin Mary and of the wardens of St. Margaret's, and they were duly created a "perpetual and able body" in the law with a common seal and the right to sue in the courts.

The Act also laid down that the "said church of the said late monastery from henceforth shall be a parish church and named and called the parish church of St. Saviour of Southwark and so at all times hereafter shall be called and not otherwise," but it was easier to inscribe this in the statute book than to curb the tongues of men, and though St. Saviour's it became in legal parlance, St. Mary Overie's lingered in common use well into the eighteenth century and has now happily been restored in the Cathedral's official title. There may have been some idea, in naming the new parish in 1540, of keeping alive the old dedication of Bermondsey. This might make the change more palatable to people who liked the old ways but who could not be permitted, in the new temper of the times, to retain a dedication to the Virgin.

The Act contained one other phrase which proved to be only too true. It referred to St. Mary Overie's as "a very great church and very costly to be maintained in due repair." The authorities made some effort apparently to hand it over in good order, and the Court of Augmentations bore the expense of regravelling the paths at the total cost of £23 8s. 8d. The accounts give details of the carriage of stone and gravel at the cost of 4d. and 2d. a load and of the actual paving at 2d. a yard. Thereafter the upkeep of the "fairest and largest church about London" depended in the main on the exertions of the six church wardens. As Prior Martin had felt after the fire of 1213, and Burton, his successor, when the roof collapsed in 1469, as they felt in the nineteenth century when thousands of pounds had already been spent and the enthusiasts asked for more, so the new wardens of St. Saviour's contemplated a dilemma which was never entirely solved. How to keep the House of God fit for its holy purpose, how to keep it wind and weather-tight, its fittings seemly, its worship dignified, and how, having done that, to have anything left for the spread of the Gospel and the succour of those in distress, these were the questions that agitated them as they puzzle their descendants still. Their mistakes were colossal; there were sins of omission and commission, yet through the centuries, by a mixture of faith and efficiency and through the untiring sacrifice of time and energy, St. Saviour's church stood firm as St. Mary Overie's had stood before it and as the Cathedral Church of Southwark stands to-day.

It was Bishop Gardiner's helping hand which encouraged the wardens of St. Margaret's and St. Mary Magdalene's to rise to their great opportunity in 1540 in spite of the fact that he was more than occupied in a struggle for power with Thomas Cromwell, the King's first minister. Gardiner's pawn in the political game was Catherine Howard, the Duke of Norfolk's beautiful niece, and the gossip writers noted how often during that winter the Bishop entertained the King at Winchester House and how often Catherine Howard chanced to be present. (So that when the parishioners' petition reached Henry the topography of the churches involved would at least be fresh in his memory!) At this juncture Gardiner's schemes were frustrated and Cromwell successfully negotiated the marriage with Anne of Cleves, at which the King's friend, Sir Anthony Browne, acted as proxy. The failure of the match meant Cromwell's disgrace and execution and during the last years of the reign there was no rival to Gardiner of commensurate ability. His intellectual powers and his capacity for taking pains were alike outstanding. It was typical of him to write five books of theology during the very years that he was supreme in the King's Council and to continue as the royal purveyor while he was Chancellor of England, so that in a military campaign of 1543 everything from the tonnage of shipping to the price of biscuits came within his scrutiny. He even found time to relax and at Winchester House, freshly repaired by his predecessor, added new adornments and made himself a "pleasant study" which gave him much delight. He gathered about him there a group of younger men, of the same intellectual calibre as himself, so much so that the antiquarian, Leland, described Winchester House at that time as the home of eloquence and the muses.

Gardiner's personal correspondence and the friendships he made shewed that he did not lack wit or the capacity for human affection, and to his credit his servants were fond of him. But he could not begin to understand either the courage or the obstinacy of ordinary folk. He was, above all, a legalist, an expert both in canon and civil law, and his whole outlook was conditioned by a deeply ingrained reverence for the ordinances of Parliament and the courts. It was his rigorist approach to the business of life which enabled him to accept the enactments of Henry's Reformation Parliament, even to write a book justifying the royal supremacy, and then, like King Canute bidding the tide to stay, to be horrified and uncomprehending when the spiritual ferment of the times produced heretical opinion.

It was this growth of heresy which disturbed and defeated him at the last. It had been fostered undoubtedly by something that had occurred in Southwark in the years immediately preceding the dissolution. In 1532, the Priory of St. Mary Overie had presented to the living of the City church of Holy Trinity-the-Less a certain John Rogers, who two years later resigned the cure to go as chaplain to the English merchants settled at Antwerp. A few months later his fellow-chaplain, Tyndale, was arrested on the continent and subsequently burnt as a heretic. At the time of his arrest Tyndale was engaged on a translation of the Bible into English and his manuscripts passed into Rogers' hands and by him were edited and prepared for the press. Meanwhile, in 1535, Miles Coverdale, a relapsed monk, published an English translation, some of which Rogers used in completing Tyndale's work. When at length his task was finished, the Bible, printed abroad, was duly licensed and imported into England, Rogers hiding his identity under the pseudonym of Thomas Matthew, and in 1537, also, there appeared in Southwark an edition of Coverdale's translation, printed by James Nicholson, a glazier, at the press of St. Thomas's hospital.

It thus became possible, dangerously excitingly possible, for the men and women of the Borough, even the scalliwags of Bankside, to read for themselves the good news of the Gospel. There were a few enlightened spirits to whom this seemed all to the good. Erasmus had declared: "I wish that even the weakest woman should read the Gospel, should read the epistles of Paul . . . I long that the husbandman should sing portions of them to himself as he follows the plough, that the weaver should hum them to the tune of his shuttle, that the traveller should beguile with their stories the tedium of his journey." Stephen Gardiner, on the other hand, disapproved. Miles Coverdale's linguistic powers were limited. His beauty of language (illustrated by his translation of the psalms preserved in the English Prayer Book), and the value of his work as a pioneer did not blind the authorities to his inaccuracies and lack of precision. Thomas Matthew's bible was more scholarly; indeed, Cranmer went so far as to say that he could not see the Bishops themselves doing better until the day after Domesday. But to Gardiner the dangers inherent in any translation were insuperable. The most sacred words in the Vulgate, *Christus, ecclesia, caritas,* enshrined a particular idea and significance, subtly changed in translation, sometimes disastrously so as when Coverdale made "congregation" synonymous with "ecclesia." The fact that he still regarded English as a tongue in a formative stage added to Gardiner's scruples. It "hath not continued in one form of understanding two hundred years," he declared, "and without God's work and special miracle it shall hardly contain religion long when it cannot last itself." But deeper than questions of scholarship and theological terminology was his instinctive distrust of the new reforming temper. He saw, more clearly than many, some of the disturbing results. "Ye flatter the covetous master with putting away holy days," he challenged a Protestant preacher on a later occasion, "that he may have the more work done him for his year's wages. Ye take away distinction and differences of apparel, days, times and places. . . . Ye give women courage and liberty to talk at their pleasure, so it be of God's word." Bishop Gardiner had no illusions about progress.

Within a few months of that Candlemas procession from old St. Margaret's to the new St. Saviour's the dangers inherent in too much thinking were brought more nearly home. In May 1540 three persons were burnt without St. George's bar in Southwark, "in the highway almost at Newington," for "heresy against the sacrament of the Altar." They were simple folk, a French groom, an Italian painter and a low-born Englishman; how could they understand the mystery of the Mass? They only knew what they believed, what they themselves had wrested from the treasure trove of holy scripture, and they held to their beliefs and men watched them burn and were amazed. There were angry whispers that a priest suspected of heresy had hanged himself at the porter's lodge awaiting examination at Winchester House, and another crazed Englishman named Collins was burnt at Newington. The sense of uneasiness grew.

The new opinions threatened to infiltrate into the royal house-hold itself, when a knot of heretics at Windsor aroused the unfavourable attention of a new prebendary who reported the matter to Gardiner. The group centred round a delightful but irrepressible chorister, Robert Testwood, and included among its number John Merbecke, the organist. Among Merbecke's papers there was discovered a concordance in English and, there-upon, he was sent to the Marshalsea for Gardiner's closer attention. The Bishop liked his music and was anxious if possible to save him. There were numerous examinations and at one occasion at Winchester House he was faced by a number of church dignitaries who could not suppress their interest in the way he had produced the Concordance, completed as far as the letter "L." Merbecke knew no Latin but had performed the colossal task by the use of an English Bible, a Latin Concordance and "a good wit with diligence." He offered to shew the bishops his method by tackling on the spot any word they suggested from the second half of the alphabet. The bishops agreed and the atmosphere was so friendly that Merbecke returned encouraged to the Marshalsea. Even Gardiner's scolding barely veiled his liking for the man. "What the devil made thee meddle with the scriptures? Thy vocation was another way, wherein thou hast a goodly wit if thou didst esteem it."

Three weeks later on Whitsunday, Merbecke was summoned to St. Mary Overie's and found the Bishop of Salisbury and Gardiner's secretary, garbed in the official white robe and chain of office, "sitting alone in the church," looking at an epistle of Calvin's which Merbecke had written out. They took him up to a side altar, perhaps in that portion of the Lady Chapel later used as a consistory court, and interrogated him upon certain heretical statements contained in the epistle. Merbecke's defence lay in the fact that he had written out Calvin's letter before the Act of Six Articles had been passed in England. Even so it is fairly certain that he would not have been saved if Gardiner had not liked his music. In July he was taken back to Windsor, tried with the other suspects and condemned, but the officials in charge post-poned the execution for twenty-four hours until the Bishop had been informed and by swift return came a pardon for him alone. Next day Merbecke said goodbye to his friends and watched them go to the stake. There is no hint of the agony of that parting in the calm beauty of his setting of the service of Holy Communion, which in adapted form is sung to-day in every corner of England and in that very church in whose empty grandeur he was brought so near to the challenge of martyrdom. He lived out his life in peace, "singing merrily and playing on the organ," while the shadows gathered round Stephen Gardiner's head and England passed through two brief reigns of instability and nightmare to new hope and endeavour under Elizabeth I.

## Note on Sources

For the Chapter of 1518, see H. E. Salter, *Chapters of Augustinian Canons*, pp. 131 *seq*. Charles Wriothesley's *A Chronicle of England* is printed in the *Camden Society Publications* for 1875 and 1877. Details of the creation of the Parish in 1540–1 are given in a report of a committee of 1835 on *The Properties and Charities of the Parish of St. Saviour, Southwark*, cf. *Dollman*, p. 8 *seq. et alia*. For a fair and scholarly attempt to assess Bishop Gardiner more charitably than is usual, see J. A. Muller, *Stephen Gardiner and the Tudor Reaction* (1920).

# IX

## TRAGIC DILEMMA

D URING the greater part of Edward VI's reign, Bishop
Gardiner was in the Tower. For a brief time John Poynet
was Bishop of Winchester while Winchester House was
in the temporary possession of the Marquis of Northampton,
who added a new gallery but was not tenant for long enough to
make any mark on Southwark. The appearance of the Borough
was gradually changing. The ancient church of St. Margaret,
once the centre of so much life and beauty, vanished from the
scene soon after 1540. It was purchased by Sir Thomas Pope, who
had recently acquired Bermondsey, and by him it was resold to
William Emerson himself who, with more regard for his pocket
than for hygiene, at once built dwelling-houses on part of the
former troublesome churchyard. Part of the old church was
already in use as a court house and it was either further adapted or
a new town hall was built on the same site. It was divided into
three sections, used respectively as a police court, a court of
Admiralty and a prison. The latter, known as the Compter,
appears repeatedly in the future annals of the Borough, as unsavoury a place as the Clink or the Marshalsea. Yet in spite of the
prisons and the waterside taverns, the fine manor house that Pope
made for himself at Bermondsey, later the home of the Earl of
Sussex, Lord Montague's house in the Close and Northampton's
brief tenancy of Winchester House all indicate that Southwark
was still a fashionable district. Until a year or two before King
Henry's death, a familiar figure in the streets was Charles Brandon,
the Duke of Suffolk, whose home at the top of Long Southwark,
known variously as the Manor or Suffolk Place, was the rendezvous of as many notables of a different sort as Winchester
House itself. Suffolk was a soldier born, who regarded learning
as "a great hindrance and displeasure to a nobleman," a man of

blunt ways and easy good nature. He died in 1545 and the Manor, known now as Southwark Place, passed into the King's hands and for a short time was used as a royal residence. In 1549, young King Edward dined there on the way to Whitehall from Hampton Court and, after walking in the garden, rode on in state down the highway, a lad of eleven years old, weighed down with the burden of kingship.

In the spring of the next year Edward granted to the City a new charter extending its domain in Southwark. It already held for the annual payment of £10 the original nucleus of the Gildable manor, and to this was now added certain ecclesiastical lands which had come into the hands of the Crown, consisting of the Great Liberty, hitherto belonging to the Archbishop of Canterbury, and the former possessions of the dissolved Bermondsey Abbey. The estate of the late Duke of Suffolk, except the house itself, was also included in the deal and henceforth only the Clink Liberty remained an extraneous district, under the ecclesiastical jurisdiction of the Bishop of Winchester. For this grant the City paid the large sum of £647 2s. 1d. In May, the Lord Mayor rode in state through the Borough and in the precincts of St. Saviour's, no doubt in the presence of the gentlemen of the vestry, a stone was set up to mark the extent of the City's jurisdiction. To the sound of trumpets the common crier read the royal proclamation, bidding vagabonds depart.

In spite of this ceremony the relations between City and Borough remained indeterminate, though the number of bakers sentenced for giving light weight and of coiners caught in the act shews that a real attempt was made to establish the Lord Mayor's authority. Southwark was constituted an extra ward of the City as Bridge Ward Without, but for some reason, perhaps a form of passive resistance, the Borough never elected its own representative and the ward became a sinecure for London's senior alderman.

In the Clink Liberty progress had been made. In 1546 Gardiner had at length suppressed one of the crying scandals of the district, for in that year the stews were legally closed and Bankside was proclaimed, again "by sound of trumpet, no more to be privileged and used as a common brothel but the inhabitants of the same to keep good and honest rule." This no doubt was an ideal of conduct easier to enunciate than to maintain but it was at least a step forward and certain material improvements in the way of drainage and embankments also contributed to the development of the area. New property began to arise west of the Bishop's Park, and Maid Lane which led from Paris Garden to Winchester House became a well-used thoroughfare. A large contingent from Bankside attended the Sunday services at St. Saviour's but it was an unwritten rule that Banksiders sat in the north aisle, set apart from their more fashionable sisters of the Borough.

The day-to-day business of lighting the streets, cleaning the roads and dealing with the nuisances created by the bad smells of breweries and soap-boilers, as well as the impossible task of coping with economic distress, devolved upon the wardens and other officials of St. Saviour's and the adjacent parishes of St. Olave's and St. George's. There was one result of the changes of the mid-century that added very appreciably to their burdens. The Reformation, which had swept away the monasteries and priories, had left destitute of tenants the great ecclesiastical houses which had once been the glory of Southwark. For another hundred years Winchester House remained a Bishop's residence but the home of the monks of St. Swithun's, leased for a while to the Bishop of Rochester, soon fell into disrepair and with Waverley House and many others was let out as tenements, frequented by families that too often fell victims to disease or poverty. In part to alleviate their needs Edward VI refounded St. Thomas's Hospital, changing the dedication from St. Thomas the Martyr to St. Thomas the Apostle. In November 1552 Greyfriars, across the river, was re-established as Christ's Hospital for the care of fatherless children and St. Thomas's again opened its doors "for poor and impotent persons, lame and sick." Thomas Cure, one of St. Saviour's vestrymen, may have thought to himself that one class of person was still unprovided for, the old who were not "lame and sick" but just tired out with honest toil and who like Gower and the King's aged servants had once found refuge in the Priory. One day he would endeavour to do something about it.

In St. Saviour's itself various repairs and alterations had already been put in hand and some idea had been obtained of the great expenditure entailed. An entrance had been made into St. Saviour's from Mary Magdalene's by breaking down the wall and erecting four clumsy arches. Since the Lady Chapel was no longer in use

**THE SANCTUARY.**

The altar screen is seen as one looks across Bishop Talbot's effigy; beyond the chancel is seen the Humble tomb. There is an account of the modern figures on the Tudor screen in T. P. Stevens: *Southwark Cathedral*, pp. 30-7.

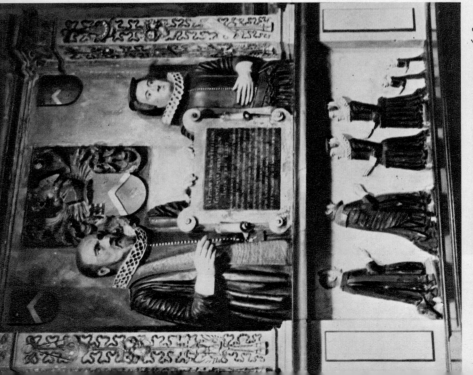

THE CANDELABRUM GIVEN BY DOROTHY APPLEBEE IN 1680.

THE TREHEARNE MONUMENT IN THE NORTH CHOIR AISLE, 1618.

for processions, now the new reign had opened the floodgates of reform and everything was anathema that savoured of popery, it was decided to make some money by letting out for gain that part of it not used by the Bishop as a consistory court. In 1553 it was leased to one Riall, "to stand his carts upon." Another way of raising money would be by the sale of some of the glorious but discredited vestments, and an inventory had already been made with some such purpose in view but before the process was completed, Edward VI was dead and during Mary's brief and tragic reign, the old forms of worship were resumed and Bishop Gardiner was back at Winchester House.

At first the policy of the new government was not severe and King Edward's leading bishops, men such as Ridley and Latimer and Hooper of Gloucester were given every opportunity to leave the country. The majority refused either to recant or to emigrate and persisted in preaching Protestant doctrine till they found themselves in prison. But in the country at large, most people accepted with equanimity the return to the old ways, until a rumour began to stir, and grew too soon to certainty, that the Queen was about to marry Philip of Spain. At once there were signs of dismay in England. The Londoners muttered in angry foreboding and a "frenzy of fear and hate" seized the ordinary, ignorant countryman, "dreading armed invasion, fire, sword and rapine." In January 1554, Bishop Gardiner entertained the Spanish Ambassador at Winchester House and agreed to the terms of the alliance. Within a month there was open rebellion and once again an army swept down unmolested from Blackheath to the foot of London Bridge. A full-scale rising in four different parts of the land had been envisaged, but the government got wind of what was afoot and it was necessary to act precipitately so that only the Kentish rebels with Sir Thomas Wyatt at the head made an effective start. Even so they came within an ace of success, the Londoners, sent down to meet them at Gravesend, deserted to their ranks with the cry: "We are all Englishmen," and in the surety that they would have many friends in the City the rebels advanced to Southwark and encamped there on February 3rd. Yet on that very day Mary had shewn herself true Tudor and, refusing to flee, had spoken to her people, assuring them of her love and favour and promising to submit to the High Court of Parliament in the matter of her marriage. Unlike Tyler and Cade, Wyatt found the drawbridge up and the gates of London shut against him.

For three days he remained in Southwark. The guns of the Tower were trained upon the two churches, St. Olave's and St. Mary Overie's, that rose above the trees on the south bank. The Queen had ordered her officers not to shoot and each side waited, uncertain of the next move. Wyatt was a firm and popular leader; and the victuallers of the Borough did a roaring trade for he paid for all the food he needed for his men. There was no looting, with one grave exception. Gardiner was across the river with the Queen when a body of young gentlemen entered Winchester House and bore down on that very study which had been his great delight. Every book they could lay hands on was torn and cut to pieces, "so that men might have gone up to the knees in the leaves of books . . . thrown under foot." Of casualties, other than books, there was only one in these three days of anxious hesitancy. A waterman was killed by a chance shot from the rebels' guns, and the officer-in-command in the City threatened reprisals. The people of Southwark appealed to their dangerous guest to go on his way, and not to subject their buildings to ruin and themselves to slaughter. London Bridge had proved impregnable and practical necessity as well as a merciful heart compelled Wyatt to turn west to cross the Thames at Kingston. But the wearisome detour took too long; the government was in readiness and the heart had gone out of his assault. After a skirmish around Charing Cross, Wyatt surrendered and died on the scaffold, a young man of promise with a foretaste of Drake and Ralegh in him, who had forgotten how heavily in England the scales are weighted against rebellion. Within a week of their departure, fourteen of the ringleaders were hanged in different parts of Southwark, and St. Olave's and St. Mary Overie's, saved from destruction, sheltered silent and uneasy congregations.

The following summer Philip of Spain landed at Southampton, and the wedding took place at Winchester in July. Among those honoured on the occasion was the second Sir Anthony Browne, who now became Lord Montague. The royal pair proceeded to Richmond and, on August 11th, by water to Southwark. There,

Bishop Gardiner entertained them at one of the last and most magnificent banquets that Winchester House was to see. After the feast the King and Queen retired for the night to Southwark Place and next morning "rode through Southwark, over the bridge and so through London." There were pageants and acrobats and the crowd seemed pleased enough. A royal wedding is, after all, a royal wedding: moreover, not many weeks later, twenty cart loads of Spanish gold drove up to the Treasury, a solid argument for the alliance difficult to gainsay.

During these final years of Gardiner's supremacy, the old church next door to Winchester House undoubtedly came before the public eye more frequently than was its wont. It was in St. Mary Overie's on April 1st, 1554, that Gardiner, assisted by the Bishops of Durham and London, consecrated six new bishops to fill the sees vacated by Protestant divines. Afterwards he feasted his new colleagues with all but royal pomp. In the beginning of October the obsequies of the Duke of Norfolk were celebrated in the church with due solemnity. The bells tolled for two days on end and about the hearse stood four gilded candlesticks and four great tapers, a pool of light in a sombre choir draped in funereal black. On October 29th the distinguished soldier, Lord Audley, who was linked with Southwark through his friendship with the Brandons, was buried in the church and once again the great ones of the land came to St. Mary Overie's.

A Parliament, composed in the main of "the wise, grave and Catholic sort," had not hesitated during 1554 to repeal the measures which had separated the English church from Rome nor to re-enact the laws against heresy originally passed in the reign of Henry IV. Within a few days of the end of session, a number of leading protestants were brought from their various prisons to Winchester House, where Gardiner presided over an informal examination. Its object was not to elicit the prisoners' opinions, which were well known, but to offer them pardon if they would accept the established fact of the reconciliation with Rome and to warn them that if they refused the only legal course was a formal trial on a charge of heresy. Unfortunately Gardiner's impatience and the violent temper, that flared up when he was crossed, was matched by an aggressive obstinacy on the part of the prisoners, which caused the atmosphere of the meeting to be charged from the start with irritation ill-suppressed. Only Thirlby, the kindly Bishop of Ely, spoke gently of the Queen's mercy; the others were too readily involved in argument, taunting the Protestant clergy with the fact that they were married and bickering with them on the nature of the Church. Nobody showed any sign of changing their views, and the prisoners were sent back to their cells to await their trial.

Nobody as yet believed that there would be any need for large-scale persecution. The Queen hoped to put an end to effective resistance by a brief but cogent essay in severity. Not as yet driven to the verge of insanity by her husband's desertion and the bitter disappointment of a false pregnancy, she had no liking for cruelty, and neither had Gardiner. Their views were echoed by a nobleman, who said to one of the prisoners at the Winchester House meeting, "Thou wilt not burn in this gear when it cometh to the purpose, I know well that." One or two recantations at the stake would discredit the whole movement; at the worst, if a few burnings were necessary, it would suffice to warn the masses of ordinary folk. What the Queen and her ministers forgot was the amazing courage of ordinary folk, once given leadership and an example, which was why so much depended on the bearing and the bravery of the seven men who at the end of January were brought back to Southwark for trial in the Lady Chapel of St. Mary Overie's.

Bishop Gardiner's consistory court was set up in the north-east bay of the chapel, and with him sat Bonner of London and some twelve other bishops, with secretaries and legal officials in attendance and a number of knights and noblemen who, though they were present in the role of spectators, commented freely on the proceedings. The new Lord Montague was among them, but there is no record whether or not the wardens of St. Saviour's by virtue of their office were admitted or whether, with less eminent spectators, they crowded in through the openings from the choir. Unauthorised intruders were excluded after the first morning but, throughout the days that the court was in session, the alleys and byways between Winchester House and Long Southwark were thronged with angry, disturbed, excited people.

Of the seven prisoners, Hooper, formerly Bishop of Gloucester, was the most famous, a puritan in the making, "spare of diet, sparer of words and sparest of time," whose severe and grave grace matched the critical moment. Before his examination was ended it was interrupted for another of the prisoners to appear, one John Cardmaker, a Prebendary of Wells, who was said to be ready to submit. The eagerness with which Gardiner and his colleagues welcomed Cardmaker's temporising words indicated the anxiety with which they awaited a like compliance from the rest, who were told at once of their comrade's submission. (Later he said he had only "temporised" and went with equanimity to the stake.) The honour one gives without stint to these "protestant martyrs" should not preclude all sympathy with their baffled accusers who legally could scarcely do other than condemn them, once it was laid down that the heresy laws must be enforced, and who longed passionately for a quiet realm, untroubled by new-fangled thought. But tranquillity was the last quality to be associated with the third of the accused men. The winter afternoon was on the wane when John Rogers was brought before the court, an adversary worthy of all Gardiner's legal skill. He had returned to England in the previous reign and had naturalised his wife and family and set out on a vigorous career as Vicar of St. Sepulchre's and Prebendary of St. Paul's. He succeeded in keeping a secret record of his trial which his wife found after his death in a dark corner of his cell, and in it he described the keen altercation which now took place as the light was fading in St. Mary Overie's. Gardiner, eager to justify himself, declared that the Queen was the prime mover in the matter of the trial. Rogers refused to believe this, and the uneasy laughter which greeted his sharp reply to a bishop, who upheld Gardiner's statement, was a sign of the tension in the air as the shadow of the stake drew appreciably nearer. For Gardiner could delay no longer; rising and taking off his cap he asked Rogers the crucial question; what was his faith in regard to the sacrament, did he believe in the bodily presence of Christ? Rogers hesitated. He was no theologian, to voice as Bradford did next day a philosophical defence of belief in a spiritual presence. "I answered that I had often told him that it was a matter in which I was no meddler." But did this sound like vacillation? He was not going to risk losing his way amid theological concepts and he added with vehemence that, since his opponent's doctrine was false in all other points, it was no doubt false also in this. And, knowing that now his fate was sealed, he proceeded to upbraid the Bishop for keeping him so long in custody without any allowance for his wife and children. Poor impetuous Rogers, he was very worried about his family and pleaded next day "that my poor wife, being a stranger, may come and speak with me as long as I live, for she hath ten children that are hers and mine and somewhat I would counsel her what it were best for her to do." But to give consent would be to admit that Rogers, a priest, was legally married and Gardiner refused—a rigorist in all things till the capacity for human sympathy had frozen in his veins.

The court was adjourned at four o'clock on the first day, and Hooper and Rogers were taken to spend the night in the Compter on the site of old St. Margaret's. Hooper, the senior man, drew back for a word with his fellow-prisoner. "Come, Brother Rogers, must we two take this matter first in hand and begin to fry these faggots?" "Yes, Sir, by God's grace," the other replied. "Doubt not," said Hooper, as the guards hustled them apart, "but God will give you strength." Next morning they were duly found guilty and handed over to the secular arm to be burnt as heretics. That night, after dark, they were led through the churchyard to the highway and over the bridge to the safer custody of Newgate. The authorities, fearing a demonstration, had ordered all lights in the streets to be extinguished, including those on the coster-mongers' stalls, and they hoped that the prisoners would pass unrecognised, but the people thronged the streets with lighted candles in their hands and greeted the doleful cavalcade with words of cheer and encouragement. Hooper was sent down to Gloucester to be burnt, and his passing was not easy; Rogers died on February 4th at Smithfield, the first of those whose courage, beheld by a vast crowd of aghast spectators, made nugatory from the first the Queen's hope of a quick end to the business.

Four others appeared before the consistory court on the second and third days of the hearing. Lawrence Sanders, the learned and respected rector of a City church, was well known already to one section of Southwark's population for he had spent the months awaiting trial in the Marshalsea. John Ferrar, the Bishop of St. David's, was sent down to Wales for a further trial; he had begun life as an Austin Canon in the Priory of St. Mary at Oxford; with what conflicting thoughts he must have stood, that morning, in St. Mary Overie's! For he was a man of imagination, impetuous in temper, with a fantastic strain in him, refreshing after Hooper's puritanism and Roger's pugnacity. He prided himself on his whistling and declared that thus he could keep a seal quiet for an hour, as maybe he had sometimes done in solitary peace among the rocks at St. David's. After he had been sentenced, when one in doubt asked him for reassurance, it was Ferrar who dared—and what a magnificent risk it was—to bid the doubter watch him die, and if he wavered not to believe a word he had told him. He went then to the stake, and the one who doubted watched to the end and believed.

Rowland Taylor and John Bradford, the two others sentenced at Southwark, were again alike only in their courage. Taylor was a big jolly man from a country parish in East Anglia who spoke with the thick Suffolk accent of those parts. They all knew him in Hadleigh, from the old man and his wife in the corner almshouse to the local drunkard who alone could be persuaded when the end came to set fire to the stake. When after fifteen months' exile in a London prison, Taylor learnt that he was to be sent home to Hadleigh to die, his chief emotion was one of thankfulness that he would see his parishioners again and smell the Suffolk air. He went resignedly, nay joyously, to his death, throwing his glove filled with his spare cash into the corner window of the almshouse as he passed.

Bradford, the last of the seven to die, had learnt his Latin at Manchester Grammar School, earned his living in the service of a royal official and only at a mature age turned his thoughts to divinity. He had become Ridley's chaplain, a well-known figure in St. Paul's: "very gentle he was to man and child, tall and slender of figure, with an auburn beard and seldom without a book in his hand." It was six months before they burnt him, so earnestly did they hope he would submit. In July he died at Smithfield in the company of a young apprentice, for as the months passed the humble and unlearned had shewn that in them also faith bred endurance and in the nearness of God's presence they were strong.

Gardiner, ageing fast and suffering from a painful disease, was clear-sighted enough to know that the royal policy had failed. He did not preside again over a trial for heresy and while he lived, no one was sent to the stake in the Winchester diocese. Three men, one a stranger, were burnt in St. George's Fields in 1557, but though Gardiner's successor did not object to persecution, the heretics in these parts were either few or fortunate and during the three nightmare years, in which London was harried by Bonner, turbulent Southwark was quiet.

Gardiner died before the end of 1555. In October the French Ambassador visited him in Winchester House and was distressed to find how ill he was, although he insisted on escorting his guest through the long gallery to the door so that he might shew the crowd of onlookers that he was still alive. When Parliament met in November he forced himself to mount his mule, and, supported by four servants and in excruciating pain, he rode to Westminster to make his opening speech. He died on November 12th at his lodgings in Whitehall, murmuring in his last agony that like St. Peter he had gone out and denied his Lord, but that even now he had not learnt to weep.

His body was brought back to Southwark speedily, in the small hours. He had been suffering from an internal infection, and the same morning before daybreak the body was disembowelled and the entrails burned before the high altar of St. Mary Overie's. Once again for two long days, the great bells tolled and a dirge was sung in every London parish. It had been intended to transport the body to Winchester for immediate burial, but heavy rains that winter had made the roads impassable, and so for ten days it lay in state in St. Mary Overie's, till some wretch stole the pall that lay upon the coffin. Afterwards it was placed in a temporary vault until the spring. On St. Valentine's day 1556, after further obsequies in Southwark, the solemn procession to Winchester took place. That faithful friend Lord Montague, with the Bishop of Ely, rode at the head of two hundred men all clothed in black, and the princely prelate went on his last journey in full state and beneath the trappings with which in life he had hidden so ruthlessly the man he might have been. From the Borough and Bankside they gathered to see him go, and in all the little villages upon the route the small and curious crowds watched in silence, as along the ancient Roman road, over Leatherhead Downs, through Guildford's High Street and Farnham, which he had loved, the last great Bishop of the old dispensation went to his resting place.

## Note on Sources

For the Brandons' connection with Southwark see Rendle, *op. cit.*, pp. 96, 100–2; for Mary's reign see H. M. Prescott, *Spanish Tudor* (p. 283 *seq.*; for Wyatt's rising) and J. A. Muller, *Stephen Gardiner*, who gives an unbiassed account of the trials of Hooper, Rogers, etc. These are described by Foxe, *Acts and Monuments*, VI, 587, *seq.*, based largely on Rogers' account of his own experiences, discovered in his cell after his execution and later printed.

# X

# NEW BEGINNINGS

TOWARDS the end of Queen Elizabeth's reign her Principal Secretary, Robert Cecil, returning from France, landed at Portsmouth and asked for a carriage to meet him at Staines to bring him up to London. "By London," he added, "I mean not the merchants' London but Sir Walter Ralegh's." This early distinction between the City and the West End indicates a change in topographical emphasis which had an immediate effect on Southwark. A hundred years previously, Mr. Secretary would, in all likelihood, have either landed at Dover and ridden up the Old Kent Road, or would have travelled from Portsmouth by the Stane Street, and in either case have crossed London Bridge to the Tower where his sovereign, if in London, would have been in residence. By Queen Elizabeth's reign however, the new palace of Whitehall had established itself as the Queen's London home and, while the Tower continued to fulfil its gloomy role as prison and in part became a show place where visitors were brought to see the captive lions, the great of the land came less often over London Bridge. When the Queen went on progress, or her successor on a hunting expedition, the route now lay along the great west road or north through the home counties, or over the horse ferry at Lambeth to Kingston and beyond. The royal cavalcades, that had brought the crowd in their dangerous hundreds to throng the narrow passage of London Bridge, no longer came and went between the Tower and Southwark, nor was there any longer the repeated sight of the great ecclesiastics going into Westminster from their town houses on the south bank. It is true that for a large part of Elizabeth's reign Bermondsey was the home of the Earls of Sussex, but Southwark Place became the royal mint and, through the chance of the priory buildings passing into the hands of a family that remained true to the Pope, uneasy recusants more often than not were the guests that frequented Montague Close. Even such items on the credit side as the draining and embankment of the land in the Clink Liberty and the building which ensued, the introduction of new industries, the development of the postal and coaching services, all added to the noise and crowds and danger of plague, which caused prelates and nobles to eschew Southwark in favour of more secluded seats.

Thus the character of Southwark altered, and the story of St. Saviour's in the first century of its existence is the story of ordinary men, engaged in the everyday business of earning their living, merchants, victuallers, industrialists, showmen, who also undertook the colossal task of keeping up and caring for a church, the size of which was entirely out of proportion to their needs, far larger indeed than any other parish church in England. That they succeeded, and not ingloriously, was due not only to their faith and enthusiasm but to that deep sense of public responsibility which characterised the generations that defeated the Armada and fifty years later faced each other in the civil wars. They were not in the main of heroic mould and possessed a shrewd capacity for making money and for equating public interest with private gain, but they were men of vigour and, like most of their contemporaries, they were prepared to contribute, at some cost to themselves, to the welfare of the community in which they lived.

In its changed character Southwark prospered. It became, for example, the centre of the starch industry, which was by no means unimportant in an age when every man, woman and child of any social standing wore a ruff that needed regular starching. It remained, as it had been before, the mecca of the transport trade, for whether kings passed that way or not, as times grew more settled travelling increased. It was not surprising that Thomas Cure and John Bingham, who succeeded him in the counsels of St. Saviour's vestry, happened to be saddlers. It was as natural as it would be to-day to find the local garage proprietor prominent in the affairs of the town on the by-pass. As the roads improved, the carriers did a regular and thriving trade and made their headquarters at the various inns of Southwark; a list of a slightly later date, 1637, notes that the carrier from Tunbridge, Sevenoaks and Staplehurst came and went from the Catherine Wheel, while the one from Leatherhead and Dorking used the Greyhound and the carrier from Reigate was to be found at the Falcon, the fine new inn on the boundaries of the Clink Liberty and Paris Garden. In the High Street of the Borough, between St. Saviour's and St. George's, the larger hostelries, the Grapes, the King's Head, the George, the Tabard, the Queen's Head and the White Hart, catered for the wayfarers that were as frequent as of old, concerned now upon their private concerns and the welfare of their own pockets rather than upon a pilgrimage or warfare in France or any distant crusade.

In these years of growth and successful endeavour, which stretched from Queen Elizabeth's succession to the beginning of the troubles in Charles I's reign, another interest competed with that of industry and transport to make Southwark a place brimful of life and energy. When Henry VIII died and Stephen Gardiner ordered a solemn dirge to be sung at St. Mary Overie's, he discovered to his annoyance that the players of Bankside had announced a spectacle to be performed at the same hour to celebrate the accession of the new king. The Bishop requested the authorities to make it clear whether mourning or rejoicing was the order of the day, and his protest is recorded, but whether or not the rival show took place and whether the church or Bankside attracted the greater crowds, history is silent in her usual tantalising way. But the incident serves as a pointer to the future. At the very time when the art of drama ceased to be the concern of vagabonds and enjoyed the patronage of kings and queens, Bankside became for a while the home of the theatre and two such leading figures in its story as Philip Henslowe and Edward Alleyn, the C. B. Cochrane and Lawrence Olivier of their day, were in turn respected wardens of St. Saviour's. The hangers-on of the entertainment world continued to contribute their quota to the unruly element in the Clink Liberty and to the population of the Compter and the Marshalsea, but there also were to be found in increasing numbers the less fortunate denizens of the new tenements and those who for conscience sake, recusants and anabaptists alike, had cut themselves off from the ordered living of respectable society.

It was thus a place of strange and moving contrasts, much poverty, much solid wealth, gaiety, fear, pestilence, bustle, steady industry and the occasional hatching of treason, every human emotion jostling its fellow in the crowded highway as the burghers and their wives jostled each other for a seat at the Globe or competed more soberly but with equal insistence for a convenient pew at St. Saviour's. The dominant characteristic was perhaps vitality and, as Elizabeth's reign progressed and the sense of security grew, hope and vigour unlocked the gates of the future, giving to men the power to carve out fortunes for themselves, to write a master-piece, to discover a new world—or on the income of a small parish to maintain a magnificent church and not leave entirely unaided the poor and needy at their gate.

All this happened by degrees. When St. Saviour's history as a parish church began in 1540, the conversion of the great houses into tenements, the new building along the river, the erection of the first theatres were all events of the future. A print of the Borough drawn by Anthonie van den Wyngaerde in the middle of the century reveals a scene still predominantly rural, Hollar's famous drawing published in 1647 shows clearly how the houses are increasing in number, particularly in the liberty of the Clink, though the Bishop's Park itself remained an enclave of quiet beauty for a few more years. It is against this background of steady growth, but with the recollection that the parish was still a small and pleasant spot, that one turns to the old records of St. Saviour's to glean from them what one can of this chapter in the church's story.

There is in a vestry order-book, bound in old parchment, a copy of the rules drawn up in 1557 to govern the conduct of the church officials. Gardiner's successor, Bishop White, was a former Warden of Winchester College, a scholar and a staunch Romanist, who after Elizabeth's accession was deprived and died in prison. It was under his chairmanship and with his guidance that the rules of procedure were drawn up for St. Saviour's, probably repre-senting practices which had gradually evolved in the course of the preceding years. They contained one clear deviation from the 1540 Act of Parliament, which had laid down that the parishioners were to elect their own church-wardens. The orders of 1557, on the contrary, stated that this all-important task should be per-formed by thirty vestry-men who, yearly on the 2nd of March, were to choose six wardens, four of whom should not have been in office in the previous year. The consent of the assistants, as the vestry-men were termed, was required before new leases could be issued or repairs of more than 40s. put in hand. Nor were the churchwardens to "put out or take in" any priest, clerk or sexton if the assistants did not agree. The other responsible officials, such as the surveyors of the church property and the collectors for the poor, were also elected by the assistants, who thus, contrary to the letter of the law, constituted themselves a closed vestry which continued without challenge for fifty years and, surviving a crisis then, controlled St. Saviour's until the middle of the eighteenth century.

The Bishop's orders did however make it clear that the vestry-man's job was no sinecure. There was a rigorous system of fines for absence from meetings and other misdemeanours, whereby in these comparatively simple days, the poor box was kept in funds. It cost an assistant 4d. and a warden 8d. if he failed to attend without lawful excuse, provided he had twenty-four hours' notice of a meeting; if he "burst out in choler," he was fined 2s. 6d. and as much as 5s. at the discretion of the vestry if he "carried talk out of the house," spreading indiscreet gossip about parochial affairs. There were of course compensations such as feasts, much appreciated by the women folk and famous for the traditional dish of calf's head pie, which were held twice a year on March 2nd and fifteen days after Easter when the accounts were presented. On these choice and audit days it was said that the vestry-men began the festive occasion by drinking, as their first toast, a round to the church's legendary patroness, affectionately termed "Old Moll."

The first extant minute book dates from July of 1557 and no doubt was one of the results of a general clarification of procedure under the Bishop's direction. The first entry is significant: it records that John Sadler, the clerk, and Lawrence, the sexton, have been sent to the Compter "for disobedience in serving of God within the choir." What omission of ceremony or aggressive protestant gesture caused their disgrace is not revealed, and fate was kind to them for the pendulum swung before they were punished further and after Elizabeth's accession they returned to their respective duties. One would wish there were more such entries to indicate something of the spiritual progress of St. Saviour's but like all church committees, before and since, practical affairs loomed all too large. There is only an occasional reference to the "preaching chaplains" in the vestry minutes but a large number to the lease of tenements, indications of the vestry-men's behaviour but not a word of the Gospel of Christ. Some idea emerges of the warden's day-to-day problems in maintaining the fabric and fulfilling such duties of local government as the care of the roads and the suppression of vagrancy; it is more difficult to discover whether or not they succeeded in guiding a bewildered congregation through the turmoil of the mid-century, obeying the letter of the law and accepting Elizabeth's doctrinal compromise and yet growing by degrees in faith and discipleship until a live worshipping community had been created. At least the uncomplaining expenditure of time and money in the service of the church and the sacrificial giving its upkeep entailed were genuine signs of spiritual vitality, and only when the latter failed at a later epoch did a corresponding confusion and neglect appear in the vestry's practical affairs.

In 1558–9 the wardens surrendered their lease and received a new one, which gave them the specific right of electing their own chaplains and imposed upon them the new and onerous duty of establishing a Grammar School. The relevant entry in the minutes under the date, August 31st, 1559, laid down that the school should be set up in "the church house, late in the parish of St. Margaret's" and that "the old chapel behind the chancel" should be "let out toward the benefit of the said school." The immediate concern of the vestry was less with education than with cash. It had been an expensive business, obtaining the lease, and in September they passed another motion that certain Popish ornaments should be sold to defray the charge of the new lease and of repairing the church. Some of the priory's lovely adornments had already been sold in Edward VI's reign, and in 1552 the royal commissioners had come down to compare what remained with the inventory drawn up a few years previously. The parochial officials had replied to their enquiries in an unco-operative way, typical of the independent temper they so often shewed: "and where it is a parcel of our oath to present how and to what use the money coming of the sale of our ornaments and plate is employed and in what place of our church it is bestowed, to that we say it is not in our wits to tell . . . and surely if there be not much more reparations done upon the said church shortly it will

utterly decay." The amount received in Edward VI's reign was
estimated at nearly £166; the wardens, who decided to complete
the process of sale in 1559, made just over £50, £14 of which
came from a miscellaneous collection of oddments, communion
plate, silver-gilt candle-sticks, fine altar-cloths and "a little
narrow thing like a valance with the name of Jesus in gold,
sold for 8*d*." The vestments also were listed in detail, black
velvet and crimson satin, blue damask and flowers of gold, all
these accessories that had contributed so richly to the worship of
St. Mary Overie's were lost for ever.

As to the lease of the Lady Chapel, posterity judged even more
harshly. It was let in the first place to a baker named Wyatt, and
not retrieved for the use of the church until the influence of
Andrewes and Laud emphasised in a new century the beauty of
holiness and the sin of such a desecration. During those sixty
years, the chapel was rented by a succession of bakers; one Peacock, who followed Wyatt, let the place get into such a foul condition that members of the vestry in 1576 called to inspect his
bakehouse and found it full of "hogs, a dung heap and other filth."
His lease was called in, but three years later he obtained a new
one on the understanding that he should keep the building
"sweet and clean and in sufficient repair." The bakers who
succeeded him, Claybrooke and Wilson by name, did not apparently offend, but the 17th century commentator on Stow
described the Lady Chapel in his time as "lathed, daubed and
damned up," and added "in this place they had their ovens, in
that a bolting place, in that their kneading trough, in another (I
have heard) a hog's trough."

The letting of the Lady Chapel and the sale of vestments were
unhappy symbols of the new spirit that was astir, eager to sever all
links with "popery," in spite of Elizabeth's own wish to maintain
a modicum of continuity. She herself had authorised the use of a
certain amount of ceremonial, but advanced protestant opinion
would have none of it, and to some at least of St. Saviour's vestry,
elaborate vestments were suspect as luxuries that distracted the
mind from the true hearing of the scriptures and a Lady Chapel
was superfluous since processions in church were no longer to be
held; therefore since ready cash was non-existent and must be
found, if the school were to be established to the glory of St.

Saviour's and the advancement of learning in Southwark, there was no doubt in the minds of the honest William Emerson, the benevolent Thomas Cure, Robert Curtis and the rest, that the sale and the letting were not only common-sense but commendable. Thank heaven that no precision or coppersmith among them suggested that the bells also savoured of popery, and arranged for them to be melted down!

These signs of protestant fervour were encouraged by the personality of the new bishop. When White was dispossessed in 1560, Robert Horne succeeded, a north countryman of more zeal than charity, whose narrow protestantism as Dean of Durham in Edward VI's reign had been manifested in his treatment of St. Cuthbert's tomb, which he removed from the cloisters with his own hands. He spent Mary's reign in a far from peaceful exile, disputing with his fellow countrymen at Frankfurt and at Strasburg, and when he returned in the new reign to become Bishop of Winchester and visitor to the University of Oxford, his aggressive temper and virulent opinions caused an unfriendly contemporary to write: "he could never abide any ancient monuments, acts or deeds that gave any light of or to Godly Religion." In the chapel of New College the lovely east end was defaced and white-washed, and in Winchester Cathedral he pulled down the cloisters and chapter house, "to turn their leaden roofs into gold." It was perhaps as well that, at St. Saviour's, the Lady Chapel was let to a baker and disfigured only by the daily business of ignorant men, not permanently destroyed by the conscientious vandalism of a fanatic.

The only known structural alteration at Southwark, beyond the defacing of Bishop Fox's screen, was the removal of the rood loft which was noted in a vestry minute of June 1st, 1561, when it was ordered to be "taken down and made decent and godly, as in the other churches in the city." On the previous day, the minutes recorded an instruction that is near to being incredible: "that the church books in Latin be defaced and cut according to the injunctions of the Bishop." So runs the laconic entry and it is perhaps relevant to note the vestry's determination that there should be no doubt upon whom the responsibility lay! If, indeed, they were uneasy at the wanton destruction and not fired by a like spirit to their diocesan, their unspoken reproaches have been uttered without stint by the generations that have succeeded them, for thanks to Bishop Horne's detestation of all that came before the Reformation the medieval records of the church were lost.

It was 1562 before the Grammar School was established for there had been some difficulty in finding a satisfactory site. The suggestion of the old church house came to nothing and a tenement known as the Green Dragon, originally part of the Cobham property, was eventually leased from a certain Matthew Smith after a good deal of bargaining and shilly-shallying. It stood to the south-east of the church on land now covered by the sheds of the Borough Market. A charter was received from the Crown, which in its exordium recorded the names of the twelve members of St. Saviour's vestry who, with "other discreet and the more sad inhabitants of the parish, had erected and set up a school," and in the list there are many names that recur frequently in Southwark's history. The school, which was to give free tuition to children of the parish whether rich or poor, was also to admit fee-paying students up to the number of forty from other districts, but the total was not to exceed one hundred for the sound reason that if it did the masters might be so oppressed with multitude that they were "not able to set forward and further their charge to their honesty and the children's profit." The master, according to the regulations, was to be a paragon of virtue, "sound in the Christian religion, according to the law of the land, and sound in body and mind, in conversation gentle, sober, honest, virtuous and discreet, skilled in the Latin and able to teach grammar, oratory, poetry and Greek"; alas, when the rules were revised fifty years later, it was thought advisable to add another proviso, that he should not frequent ill houses nor do anything else to hinder his diligence! The first founders concluded with some wise advice to parents; "for the master may do much but good and discreet government at home makes all sure, and doth the greatest good."

The entrance fee at St. Saviour's School was 2s. 6d., and 2d. a quarter towards "brooms and rods"; it was also the parents' responsibility to equip the child with books and writing material and candles in winter. On entry the pupil had to be able to read English and a modicum of Latin; and, once a year on the eve of St. Bartholomew's, "men of learning and worship" examined the boys either at the school or in St. Saviour's. The master was assisted by an usher and there were six governors, among the first of whom were Emerson and Cure and William Browker. The endowments were few and it was fortunate for St. Saviour's that the neighbouring parish of St. Olave had also set out to found a school, and one Henry Leeke, a brewer who lived at the southern end of London Bridge, had left money for this purpose. Until such time as the scheme fructified, Leeke's money went to St. Saviour's and the extra £8 was of no little value in setting the school on its feet. In 1571 St. Olave's received a charter and went ahead with their own project, making a provision for a grammar department so as to secure Leeke's legacy. At first however they were concerned in the main with more elementary teaching and St. Saviour's remained the chief grammar school of the district. The founders had great visions of its future, though the young residents of the Clink Liberty, making their way along Bankside at six o'clock in the morning, only knew that at such an hour on a summer day nobody wanted to work; perhaps it was a Grammar School boy whom Shakespeare watched dawdling past the Globe, "creeping like snail unwillingly to school."

The "discreet and sad" members of the vestry had much to occupy them besides the school. The primary business of keeping the church clean and in good order devolved on the sexton and a minute of 1562 shows that Lawrence Robinson was reinstated, "to keep the clock and chimes, to blow the organ, to clean the church, the gutters, walls and windows when need shall require for 44s. a year." This sparse salary could be supplemented by perquisites, the money received for "tolling the bell and digging the graves" and "all the profits of the pigeons resorting to the church steeple," for which privilege he paid, presumably to the vestry, four dozen pigeons a year. Fortunately for themselves, if not for Lawrence's successors, no such source of profit is provided by the starlings, who to-day have usurped the place of the pigeons and chatter incessantly round the Cathedral tower.

In January 1565 the old chaplain, Mr. Kelle, had notice to quit, for Elizabeth's church settlement was now completed and a ruling laid down as to the use of ceremonies. The views of the extreme protestants had been disregarded and one instruction was that the surplice should be worn at the Communion service. This, Chaplain Kelle would not do, and sacrificed his place by his refusal to conform, but the vestry agreed that "Master Kelle should have at his departing of our goodwills for because that he is an old man, the sum of £4, I say £4." The attempt to help Master Kelle in his need was a typical gesture. The chaplain's salary remained totally inadequate—at the moment it was £20 per annum—but whenever their clergy were in financial straits, as frequently happened from illness, size of family or removal expenses, the church wardens either made a donation out of their own pockets or put their hands into the bag, in which, in the absence of banking facilities, the rents and fees were kept that made up the church's income. Just occasionally the more cautious members asked to see the annual account before being generous with the balance they might not have, but a bonus of £10 at Christmas and rent-free houses made by degrees a valuable addition to the meagre stipend. In renewing the lease in 1591 the wardens asked that there should be no rigid proviso as to the payment of the chaplains, "part of whose entertainment proceedeth from our own estates." "We assure your lordships," they continued in their petition, "the parsonage is not able to bear the same and therefore our parishioners are very unwilling to be tied unto the continuance of that which must come (and grow) of their own benevolence."

Master Kelle's colleague was James Holyland, whose wife was also given a small wage of 10s.; perhaps she superintended the cleaning of the huge rather awe-inspiring edifice, so different from the comfortable little country church she had probably known hitherto. In July 1565, Mr. Harman was elected to take old Mr. Kelle's place, at a salary of £20 a year and on a fortnight's notice! It was customary to appoint two chaplains, no doubt because St. Saviour's had come into being as the result of the combination of two parishes. Their salaries and theoretically their status were equal but in 1585 when Masters Hansonne and Ratclyffe were appointed, a distinction was made between the former's role of preacher and Ratclyffe's position as minister, a sign that St. Saviour's was still advanced in opinion and paid considerable attention to the sermon, one of the points at issue in the middle years of the reign. Hansonne however soon got into difficulties and displeased either the government or St. Saviour's vestry. It looks as if a ban were placed upon his preaching, which in these dangerous years of the Martin Marprelate tracts might easily alarm the worried authorities. In September 1587 the vestry agreed to wait till All-Hallowes to see whether Hansonne "shall be admitted to preach again or no, if not then presently to call a vestry to take further order concerning him." On November 18th he was told to look for another post and in the following August Edward Philips was appointed preacher with an increased salary of £30, raised to £40 in the following spring. In return, the new chaplain was to give two lectures a week, the one on Sunday and the other "every Thursday in the forenoon." Mr. Ratclyffe the minister was consoled by a new study, which the vestry agreed to build in a convenient part of his house, but in the allocation of the Sunday sermons the morning duty was usually given to Philips, and in spite of the trouble Ratclyffe took over his sermons in the new study he usually found himself at evensong with many empty pews before him. For Sunday afternoon was the great time for bear-baiting, the Tudor equivalent of to-day's greyhound racing, and it was almost impossible to entice people to church. It was agreed that if necessary the chaplains should switch over their Sunday duties to see if that made any difference! There was no such difficulty on Thursdays for, in the absence of a *Times* or a *Daily Mirror* to guide one's thinking, a week-day sermon was as good a way as any of hearing what was on foot. The wardens' frequent reference to the Thursday lecture in their replies to visitation articles shew how proud of it they were.

As one handles the old records of these years the ghosts of the past walk again. There was a rising in the north in 1569 and a public collection was made to purchase the soldiers' equipment which the parish had to provide. When the crisis was over a surplus in cash was left in the wardens' possession, an intoxicating circumstance which placed them in somewhat of a dilemma. They decided to spend most of it on buying buckets, ladders and hooks as part of the church's equipment in case of fire, and eventually agreed to put the remainder towards the repair of certain houses in Chequer Alley, recently given by Cure to the parish. In order to do this they themselves waived their right to receive back half the money they had paid in 1569, which was to be done in the case of ordinary parishioners. But Brian Pattinson, a newcomer to the vestry, objected, claimed his right to the money and was eventually expelled. A few years later Mr. Pattinson became church warden, his earlier recalcitrance forgiven, though he was still a man of decided views, it seems, and did not hesitate when in office to take £20 out of the bag to pay the choir. St. Saviour's has always been proud of its music and in 1571 the vestry dismissed the clerk, for whom they found another post, and looked for a successor, "who shall be a good bass," deciding also to engage "a tenor, that the choir may be the better served."

So one reads on, and one aspect after another of the church's life is briefly and fitfully illuminated. There are a bundle of old accounts for a year in which a good many repairs were undertaken, and there the slips of paper still remain on which Robert Lewes, the tiler, and Philip Norton, the carpenter, together with the plumber and barrow boy and the odd man, make their mark to acknowledge the receipt of small sums for various days' work. There are the details of those presented by the wardens to the officials of the Archdeacon of Surrey, at the annual visitations, the innkeepers who had transgressed by serving drinks on Sundays in the hours of divine service, the keepers of disorderly houses or the woman who insisted on sitting in the wrong pew. There are the token books, listing all who attended Holy Communion, divided into those of the Borough and the Clink, with their fascinating statistics and details of street and alley, and the parish registers with the crabbed crowded entries of the deaths in a plague year, when there was something heroic in the mere continuance of the record and fear lingers in the very page. But the vestry minute books remain the principal source of information, whether it be of the fines imposed on its members for speaking out of turn or details of the commitments that never ceased, the paths to be kept in order, palings to be repaired, houses to be leased, rents collected, or the well in the precincts to be kept clean and in working order. How like much of it is to the minutes of church committees in every age, the incessant pressure of practical details, the problem of money, the claims of charity; how different, also, as the unexpected entry shows, which records St. Saviour's undertaking to deliver sixty cartloads of hay into the Queen's barns at Greenwich! The second minute book began in

1587 and the clerk who kept it was something of an artist. The title page is a delight, for he decorated it with fanciful sketches of birds and beasts and flowers. A diminutive dragon adorns the capital letter, round another an earth-worm rears itself, a small monkey perches in an upper corner, while the flowers are scattered jewels among the dry-as-dust deliberations of the vestry. These men who paid their dues in cartloads of hay, who filled their margins in idle moments, not with pictures of an aeroplane or varied makes of car, but with the little creatures of the hedgerow and the field, these men were never far removed from the beauty of Elizabethan England that pressed in upon the Borough and starred the river side with the flowers that William Shakespeare knew and loved. Not one of the vestrymen, hard-headed though they were, who did not know a bank whereon the wild thyme blowed.

When the second minute book began, a few years before the defeat of the Armada, the first generation of St. Saviour's vestry were passing from the scene. William Emerson had died in 1575 and was buried in the chapel of St. Mary Magdalene, which was used frequently for this purpose during the coming centuries. Emerson's memorial stone, displaying an emaciated corpse and the proud record that he lived and died an honest man, was removed to the south transept of St. Saviour's when the chapel was destroyed in the 19th century. He had reached the ripe age of ninety-two, a sturdy old gentleman, who amassed a large amount of money and was ready to give of his fortune and his time to the service of the common good. It was a pity he did not last two years longer to welcome the Queen when she visited Southwark in 1577, on the occasion of the wedding of the Earl of Cumberland to the Earl of Bedford's youngest daughter. It probably took place, not in St. Saviour's, for it is not recorded in the registers, but in Bishop Horne's chapel in Winchester House, for there is a con-temporary reference to the bridegroom's sister marrying Lord Wharton at Winchester Place on the same day. But whether or not the Queen visited the church, it must have been a royal occasion, with decorations on all the little houses and the bells from the great tower pealing merrily forth.

Thomas Cure, a much younger man than Emerson, outlived his old friend by some years and died in the year of the Armada while the threat of invasion still lay over England. He had attained a position of some eminence and had served three Sovereigns as "master of the saddle horses," as loyal a subject to Mary as to Elizabeth. He had twice represented Southwark in Parliament, but his chief concern in his latter years had been the welfare of the aged and before he died he had completed the arrangements for the almshouses that perpetuate his name. In 1579 he had bought from his friend Lord Montague the property to the south of Winchester House, owned prior to the Reformation by the Abbot of Waverley. Five years later he obtained letters-patent authorising the erection of his almshouses on this site and endowing it with the rents of the surrounding property in what is now Stoney Street and Park Street. About the same time, in 1580, the wardens built six almshouses on a site immediately adjacent to Waverley House, on that plot of land bought by St. Margaret's for a new churchyard. These parish almshouses and Cure's new foundation were amalgamated and remained a prominent feature of the Southwark scene through the vicissitudes of the coming years until they were removed to West Norwood in 1863.

Thomas Cure's will laid down in considerable detail the rules he had in mind for his old people. He provided for the maintenance of sixteen "honest and godly" poor men or women, who had been resident in the parish for not less than three years, specifying the order in which they should be chosen. Aged labourers who were past work should be given the preference, and then in turn, cripples and the blind, any brought from riches to poverty by sudden calamity, the chronically sick, and if a vacancy yet remained those "over-charged with a burden of children." There was to be a small weekly pension of 1s. 8d. out of which all fines were to be paid, and there were fines in plenty for any pensioner tempted to be other than "honest and godly," whether his misdemeanour was absence from daily prayers, allowing his children to beg, frequenting a tippling-house or refusing a day's work should a job be offered him by a member of the parish! Provided only one pension was received there was no objection to a successful candidate bringing his wife or children to live with him in the college, an enlightened attempt to preserve the "family unit." Elections took place at St. Saviour's after evening service, and the choice lay with the minister and church wardens and twelve of the "ancientest and discreetest of the vestry men." There was a ceremony of admission, at which the new pensioner was vouched for by two referees, who each gave a bond of £20, lest their nominee "should have any children chargeable on the parish," the continual nightmare of Tudor local officials! The pensioner was then examined by the wardens, as to his or her ability to repeat in English the Lord's Prayer, the ten commandments and the articles of the Christian faith, and the keys of the vacant lodging were duly handed over. Two of the places were filled by nomination, the one by the church-wardens who were constituted Governors of the College, and the other by its President, the Lord Chief Justice of the Common Pleas, who was to receive each year on his annual visit a pair of gloves worth 3s. 4d., as a token of appreciation,

When Cure died and was buried in the north choir aisle of St. Saviour's, those who wrote his epitaph made play with his name equating it with the Latin word for "care." *Respublica Curae semper erat Curo*; the state was ever a care to Cure. "He cared for the welfare of the people and the support of the aged." He cared: it is that perhaps which is the distinguishing mark of all the most worthy of those Tudor and Stuart benefactions which were the Christian's attempt, in the new capitalist age, to fulfil his duty to his less fortunate neighbours. The founders of schools, of hospitals, of almshouses, admitting their responsibility for the work that the monasteries had performed in their prime, had also a personal concern in the community in which they lived, a clearly conceived society with the £5 subsidy men at one end and at the other the poor, themselves subdivided into "honest and godly" and "idle, filthy and stubborn." They girded their gifts about with rules and regulations, that must have been extremely galling to the beneficiaries, and they savoured to the full the power of doing good their money gave them, money often earned in questionable ways. But at least they cared, for the souls as well as the bodies of those they helped, in a way that often eludes the generous donor of to-day who signs a cheque and, if he has time, glances through the pages of a Society's annual report.

The Armada sailed within a few weeks of Thomas Cure's death, and the vestry duly provided equipment for the parishioners who marched in Southwark's militia. In June, thirteen spades and blackbills were purchased and there were already corselets, forks and halberds stored in the church. When the Queen rode down to Tilbury to inspect her troops, foremost among those who greeted her was old Lord Montague, with his son and grandson and a company of men, as staunch and loyal as his coreligionist, the Admiral, Lord Howard of Effingham. He was a fine man, this first Lord Montague, who had spoken true words earlier in the reign when he voted against Elizabeth's Act of Uniformity. "What man is there," he had asked on that occasion, "so without courage or stomach or void of all honour that can consent or agree to receive an opinion and new religion by force or compulsion?" The vote went against him but his loyalty to the Queen and to his religion did not falter. His commonsense honesty secured him many friends and he was undisturbed in his religion. He remained on good terms with his Southwark neighbours; in the vestry on one occasion someone offered to pay his tithes if he refused to do so, and the door, by which in the old days the Prior had entered the church from the cloisters, was left conveniently open for his lordship to make a brief appearance at matins and slip quickly out again. But compromise of such a sort was not to be possible much longer. The Armada was defeated but England was still at war with Spain, the champion of the Roman Catholic faith. It was not as heretics but as traitors, that the Queen's ministers hanged the Jesuit missionaries who came with such fine courage to recapture England for their faith. During the remaining years of Elizabeth's reign the prisons of Southwark were crowded with suspect Papists, in particular an ancient hostelry known as the White Lion, now set apart for this purpose. Government agents reported regularly that secret masses were held in the Marshalsea, that priests were in hiding in Montague Close, that seditious speeches had been overheard. In the vestry of St. Saviour's, a member moved that the door in the north wall of the church should be closed up and there was some angry talk about the non-payment of tithes, on which subject a new vestry-man, Richard Humble, was particularly voluble. Lord Montague died in 1592, leaving the Close as a dower house for his widow, whose charm and humility ensured her the continued friendship of the majority of her neighbours. Soon afterwards the wardens ordered that a new door should be made for her convenience, but it is doubtful whether Humble and his associates were pleased and there are signs every now and again that the harmony of earlier years was threatened. For on the other wing of opinion, also, there was a growth of acerbity, a new zeal that brought fresh stresses and strains into the political and religious beliefs of the second generation of Elizabethans. In 1586, a new headmaster was appointed to St. Olave's school, perhaps at the instigation of Lord Burghley who must often have passed through the parish on his way to visit the Earl of Sussex in Bermondsey. It was a troublesome kinsman of Burghley's, Robert Browne, who was appointed upon terms, one of the first of the puritans to declare that the bishops were anti-Christ and that parish churches deserved to be rooted up, believing that the only true church was a congregation of covenanted believers. He even extended his nonconformity to matters of scholarship, for he wrote to Burghley in 1590, "I have justly altered the arts and rules and terms of Art, by evidence of the Word (or God) and have corrected many errors of all our Professors. . . ." At St. Olave's after two years they dismissed him and he went to Stamford, his birthplace and Burghley's, to see what he could do with the school in that place. But his brief appearance is a reminder of the dissidents, whose advanced views as to the relation of church and state seemed just as likely to prove subversive as the recusants' flirtations with Spain.

Troubled years they were as the century drew to a close, and the more unsettled the times the heavier the duties that devolved upon the parish officials, the constables, the scavengers, the collectors for the poor, and the overworked wardens upon whom fell the responsibility of preserving the peace, giving succour or punishment to an alarming number of vagrants and co-operating with the magistrates in the local government. It is as a collector for the poor that Richard Humble's name first appears in 1586. A year or so later he took out a twenty-one year's lease of the Well house, agreeing to set up and keep in repair "a new pump . . . for the inhabitants within the chain-gate to use without controlment," provided that they washed no linen or filthy bowls therein. He proved a somewhat difficult tenant, quick to take offence, humble by name but not by nature, but he had money and personality and in due course was elected to the vestry. Another new member in 1594 was John Bingham, who thereafter gave steady and devoted service to the church, while the name of Thomas Garland recurs so often that when at length the token books reveal that he has moved to another parish, one feels that an old friend is leaving the district and is anxious to know whether he had crossed the river to some new venture in the City or retired to the rural solitudes of Battersea or Camberwell.

John Bingham was churchwarden in 1598 when the vestry, having regained its numbers and its equanimity after two or three summers of recurrent pestilence, took into consideration the state of affairs on Bankside. In between a recommendation that Mr. Philips should begin the Thursday lecture again and an enquiry as to a plan of Mr. Ratclyffe's to build himself a shed (and a note also of Brian Pattinson's death) there are two entries that strike entirely a new note. The first refers to Mr. Langley's new building in Paris Garden, the Swan theatre, and recommends that Mr. Langley, Mr. Henslowe and Jacob Meade should "be moved for money for the poor in regard of their playhouses." The second, two months later, is an agreement to petition the council concerning these same playhouses, "wherein," the anxious vestrymen continue, "the enormities shall be shewed that comes thereby to the parish . . . that in respect thereof they may be dismissed and put down from playing." One cannot be certain whether the incompatability of the orders was due to a desire to make the best of both worlds or to a genuine cleavage in opinion. Yet however unanimous the vestry's dislike of what was going on within a stone's throw of the church, the tide of events was too strong for them. For a while at least the show business had come to stay, the watermen were busier than they had been for years and the south bank had come again within the purview of the fashionable world.

## Note on Sources

The inventory of vestments, etc., made in 1552 as part of a general investigation by the Crown, is printed by J. R. Daniel Tyssen in volume XVIII of the *Surrey Archaeological Society; Inventories of the Goods and Ornaments of the Churches in the County of*

*Surrey in the reign of Edward VI*. It is commented upon and quoted freely in Appendix IV of Worley, *op. cit.*, 105–11.

The *Records of the Corporation of Wardens of St. Saviour's* include the minute books of the vestry, vol. I of which covers the years 1557–81; vol. II, 1582–1628. In addition, there are the Token books for the "Borough-side" and the Clink from 1578 and 1588 respectively, which give the names of householders and the numbers receiving the sacrament at St. Saviours. The records also include the registers of births, marriages and deaths; numerous accounts for church repairs and such miscellaneous documents as the charter of incorporation of the Grammar School; Thomas Cure's will and details of other charities; records of parish officers (*e.g.* constables, surveyors of highways) and particulars of periodic visitations. For the Grammar School see *V. C. H. Surrey*, II, 172–81, and for Browne, *Writings of Robert Harrison and Robert Browne* (ed.: A. Peel and L. H. Carlson), p. 538.

# ON BANKSIDE

WHEN the Church withdrew its patronage from the drama, and miracle and morality plays no longer delighted, on festive occasions, the wayfarer who passed the threshold of St. Margaret's, the future of the theatre was in the hands of the showmen. The professional actor of the 14th and 15th centuries had been drawn from the ranks of masterless men, adventurers home from the wars, vagrants of gypsy breed or outlaws sentenced for some crime or misdemeanour. Throughout the Tudor age, however, the status of the actor steadily improved. Gradually it became the custom for companies of strolling players to place themselves under the protection of some nobleman or court official. They thus rid themselves of the stigma of masterless men, could look the constable in the face and wear their lord's livery with an air. At the same time a spirit of friendly emulation among their patrons led to the improvement in standards and a pride in their men's achievements, which contributed not a little to the development of Elizabethan drama. Yet a new problem presently emerged. For now that it was fast becoming a mark of good taste and distinction to own a troupe of showmen, it was no easy matter to find a place in which to perform. Churches were no longer available and at first the yards of the City hostelries provided the best alternative, and such inns as the Bell and Cross Keys in Gracechurch Street and the Bell in Bishopsgate had their regular performances. It was no doubt in one of the inn yards of Long Southwark that Lord Oxford's men produced the show that clashed with Gardiner's solemn dirge in 1547. In 1576 James Burbage, the father of the famous actor, built a playhouse which he called the Theatre outside the City walls at Shoreditch, copying the shape of the inn yards in which his men were accustomed to play, with the pit for the groundlings at a penny a head and the tiers of galleries for the well-to-do. In this Theatre and at its neighbour the Curtain, in the succeeding years, most of the companies played to the Londoners in between going on tour and red-letter appearances at court.

There was another old playhouse at Newington Butts, which as a rule was the first stopping place of companies on tour. One of the persons with a financial interest in this concern was a certain Philip Henslowe who lived next door to the Clink prison. He was a Sussex man, the younger son of a respectable family for his father had been Keeper of the Game in Ashdown Forest. He came to Southwark in the service of a certain Mr. Woodward and in due course laid the capacious foundation of his fortune by marrying his master's rich widow. Philip Henslowe was fascinated by money in all its aspects, the variety of ways in which it could be increased or dissipated, the control that it gave him over the lives and destinies of other men, the power to help or hinder in the affairs of the community. He was no miser and got on reasonably well with his family and his friends; he was not even particularly hard-headed, but there was about him a good deal of the adventurer, whose medium was coin of the realm and the foibles of other men, and he had the wit to see that, in the immediate future, there was no greater opportunity for the exercise of his talents than in the exhilarating gamble of the show business. Of his early years in Southwark nothing is known. The Montagues had large estates in Sussex and there may well have been some connection with the Close, for his lordship's bailiff was also called Woodward and may thus have been a kinsman of Henslowe's master. Certainly at a later date Henslowe referred to Bailiff Woodward as his friend. Henslowe appears to have been engaged in business transactions of a varied nature. A document of 1584 described him as a dyer and a large purchase of skins in the same year indicates that like so many Southwark men he was connected with one branch or other of the leather trade. But it was the buying and selling rather than the type of commodity which chiefly interested him. As his wealth increased he acquired property up and down the Borough, notably in the rather unsavoury district of the former stews.

It was in 1585 that he identified himself more nearly with the world of entertainment by purchasing a plot of land known as the Little Rose, rather further from the river and some distance to the east of the old bear-garden. The land had belonged to a city fish-monger and been bequeathed by him to the parish of St. Mildred, Bread Street; the site, rather less than half-way from Winchester House to Paris Garden stairs, stood approximately where the modern Park Street (then Maid Lane) runs to-day under South-wark Bridge Road. Here in the course of the next few years, Henslowe in partnership with a London grocer erected a fine new playhouse to which he gave the name of the Rose and at the end of 1591 there appeared at this first of the Bankside theatres a company of players, fresh from a triumphant season in which their pre-eminence had been established by no less than six summons to appear before Her Majesty the Queen.

The company had for some time been performing at the Theatre but had quarrelled with Burbage and were on the look-out for new quarters. They were a composite group, most of them owning as their patron Lord Strange, the Earl of Derby's son. Their star actor, however, always subscribed himself the "Lord Admiral's servant." His name was Edward Alleyn, a man of fine figure, with a "well-tuned audible voice," rather given to histrionics but at his best in the passionate verse of Marlowe's *Tamburlaine the Great* or *The Jew of Malta*. Though a less thought-ful actor than young Burbage and hampered by the scarcity of suitable plays, he was now at the height of his powers and his dramatic ability was unsurpassed. In Thomas Nash's words "not Roscius nor Esope, those admired tragedians that have lived ever since before Christ was born, could ever perform more in action than famous Ned Alleyn."

In February 1592 the season at the Rose began and lasted for eighteen weeks, with performances every day except on Sundays, Good Friday and two other days. Among the twenty-three plays in their repertory, in addition to the two by Marlowe and some by Edward Chapman, there was the first part of *Henry VI* and *Titus and Vespasian*, a play later remodelled by Shakespeare in *Titus Andronicus*. All was going like a song, and Alleyn was just falling in love with Philip Henslowe's stepdaughter when, as summer came, the plague broke upon London and the suburbs. The theatres were closed by order of the Council, in view of the danger of infection, and the companies went on tour, making ends meet as best they could. In the autumn, when the virulence of the pestilence was for a while abated, Alleyn returned to Southwark and in October he and Joan Woodward were married. Henslowe had just been made a groom of the Chamber to the Queen, as a recognition of his services to the theatre, and in spite of the plague it was a pleasant winter in the house by the Clink, where he lived all his Southwark days and where Ned Alleyn and Joan lived with him while their new house on Bankside was building.

There were occasional performances at the Rose but in the spring the Council's prohibition again came into force and Alleyn had once more to take the road. Henslowe remained in Southwark and, through intermediaries, ran a pawnbrokers business which during these years of hardship was a real help to actors in distress and had the double advantage of making money and re-stocking the Rose's wardrobe with various pieces of unclaimed finery.

Joan Alleyn stayed at home with her step-father and Ned's letters to his "Mouse," as he called her, and the replies which she and Henslowe concocted between them leave a refreshing impression of mutual confidence, which is a pleasant change from the bickerings of many Tudor households. Henslowe reported on the ravages of the epidemic; "it hath pleased the Lord to visit me round about and almost all my neighbours are dead of the Plague." Henslowe's own household was not exempt but his two wenches had recovered and were "thanks be to God very well." Alleyn urged them to keep the house clean and a good store of rue and herb of grace, and his father-in-law assured him that in addition they strewed it with hearty prayers unto the Lord, which were more available "than all things else in the world." Henslowe and Mrs. Alleyn also reported that the garden was doing well, the spinach beet had been sown and, as requested, Alleyn's orange-coloured stockings dyed black to wear in the winter.

When winter came and the Rose was re-opened there was a considerable change in personnel. In all probability, during the summer Alleyn and Burbage had acted together at Newington for the last time, and some of the ablest of Lord Strange's men now left the Rose to join Burbage in a new profit-sharing venture he was organising under the Lord Chamberlain's patronage at Shoreditch. Lord Strange, who had succeeded his father as Earl of Derby in September 1593, died in the spring of 1594 and it was under the Lord Admiral's sole patronage that Alleyn reconstituted the company at the Rose. During the last years of the century, on either side of the river, the two companies played in magnificent rivalry. Burbage was the younger man and Alleyn's histrionics were beginning to pall but on the whole they were evenly matched: that the Lord Chamberlain's men gradually pulled ahead was due to the greater attraction of the profit-sharing system and to the fact that one of the shareholders, William Shakespeare, had adapted various plays and was now writing fresh copy which appealed to the groundlings and the galleries alike in a way that Alleyn's rather mediocre repertoire entirely failed to do.

At the Rose, Henslowe's financial backing took the form of binding the actors to himself as hired men, and he often tightened his hold on them by personal loans. Yet on the whole he remained on good terms with them, bailing them out when they were arrested for debt or duelling, advancing money to purchase plays, costumes and other necessities, and treating the company not infrequently to a meal or drink at one of the local inns. He always took for his rent half the profits "gathered" from the galleries and recouped himself for his advances by adding a portion of the other half. The players divided between them the remainder, as well as the pennies from the pit. It was said that the satirist Day had Henslowe in mind when he wrote: "Most of the timbers that his state repairs, he hews out o' the bones of foundered players," but the latter's account book, still preserved at Dulwich College, allows of a different interpretation. In between notes of money advanced for various costumes and the cost of mending "the tawny coat eaten by the rats," there are more personal entries, recording loans to Alleyn and Ben Jonson, £3 12s. 9d. "laid out for the company of our meeting at the Tavern when we did eat our venison," and £5, "to discharge himself from the White Lion," to a troublesome nephew accused of stealing a horse from a hatmaker of Bermondsey! A bit of a rogue he may have been, with a keen sense of his own interests, but Philip Henslowe was not cold blooded enough to be a villain and his best defence is his happy relationship with his son-in-law who found him, in a partnership of more than twenty years, much easier to get on with than his second father-in-law, the distinguished and difficult Dr. Donne.

In 1594 Henslowe and Alleyn made the first move in a new

venture by acquiring the lease of the old Bear-Garden some distance up river from the Rose. There were however, by this time, competitors in the show business on Bankside, the Jacob Meade and Francis Langley who were coupled with Henslowe in the vestry minute which advised a request to them "for money for the poor." Meade was a waterman, mainly interested in bear-baiting and kindred sports; Francis Langley of the Draper's Company had practised as a goldsmith and bought the Manor of Paris Garden as early as 1589. Here he began to build a fine new theatre, named the Swan, during the winter of 1594–5.

It was not an easy time for the acting profession, for in the City in particular a more serious attitude of mind was developing, adding fresh venom to the authorities' dislike of stage-players. In 1596, under the pretext of danger from the plague, all performances were prohibited in London and the suburbs, and when the playhouses without the walls began to function again, the City authorities still maintained the ban in regard to the inn yards. Burbage's men began to turn their eyes towards Bankside and it is probable that this company, with Shakespeare among them, performed at the Swan in the autumn of 1596. Next summer the Earl of Pembroke's men appeared at Langley's theatre in the *Isle of Dogs* but this occasion proved inauspicious, for the play was thought to have political implications and all theatres were shut down in consequence. The part-authors, Thomas Nash and Ben Jonson, and some of the actors languished, for the rest of the summer, in the Marshalsea. Then Henslowe saw his chance to draw even with his rival. He stepped in, bailed out Nash with a loan to be repaid at his convenience, and negotiated with some of the Earl of Pembroke's players to transfer their services to the Rose. Alleyn was on the point of retiring and the company needed strengthening; during the next season, Gabriel Spenser took the lead at Henslowe's theatre, until he was slain in a duel in 1598 by the quarrelsome Ben Jonson.

A scandal such as this gave weight to the argument of those in St. Saviour's vestry, who disliked the theatres not merely because they offended the new puritan spirit but because, as the Lord Mayor had once put it, they were likely meeting places of "vagrant persons, masterless men, thieves, horse dealers, whore-mongers, cozeners, coney-catchers, contrivers of treason and other idle and dangerous persons." Yet though in the summer of the duel, the vestry petitioned the Privy Council to put down the playhouses, next year, the Lord Chamberlain's men again crossed the river, and the consequent addition to the amenities of the south bank was too productive of custom of every kind, to vintners, watermen, shopkeepers, showmen, for any of them to resist for long. Burbage had had a dispute with his ground landlord after the expiration of his lease and eventually decided to remove the Theatre, piece-meal, across to Southwark. It was rowed across and erected section by section in Maid Lane, between the Rose and Winchester House, and was duly given the new name of the Globe.

The ground where the Globe stood has been covered since the eighteenth century by Barclay's great brewery, and to mark the approximate site an inscription has been placed in one of the brewery's walls. In the Cathedral there is a new window com-memorating Shakespeare and below it a memorial depicting behind the effigy of the poet, the Southwark scene he must have known so well. How often he worshipped in the church we do not know, though his brother Edmund, also an actor, was buried at St. Saviour's in 1607, "with a forenoon knell of the great bell." Many of Shakespeare's colleagues lived in Southwark, such as Lawrence Fletcher and Augustine Phillips the clown, who may have married Alleyn's sister-in-law, and there is good reason to think that Shakespeare himself moved from Bishopsgate to the Clink Liberty when he began to act on Bank-side. But his name has not been traced in the token books and there is little one can say with certainty. Thomas Dekker in *The Shoemaker's Holiday* makes one of his characters declare that the guineas jingle in his pocket like the bells of St. Mary Overie's. With these bells, at least, Shakespeare must have been familiar, as with the Clink and the precincts and the Borough High Street. There he must often have wandered in his years at the Globe, his fancy caught by such Southwark names as that of Fastolf, meeting in tavern and thoroughfare those men of varied sorts he captured for posterity, as his actor's eye noted their speech and bearing and his poet's heart read the meaning that lay beneath.

At the turn of the century the Lord Admiral's men ceased to perform at the Rose, for Alleyn had been tempted back to the stage and, considering that Bankside was more suitable for a summer rendezvous, had built a new theatre in Clerkenwell called the Fortune. During the next few years, the Globe dominated the south bank. It was during this period, immediately after James I's accession to the throne, that the fortunes of the theatres were in their hey-day. Not only did the King himself enjoy a good play, but the Queen and the younger members of the royal family each had their chosen company, while they indulged their love of amateur dramatics in the production of numerous masques, to which the combined genius of Ben Jonson and Inigo Jones gave a fortuitous glory.

In 1608 Burbage and his associates followed Alleyn's example and acquired a private theatre in Blackfriars for their winter season. It was increasingly clear that the south bank was more suitable for summer entertainments and that the Londoners would not be enticed across the river in bad weather. Henslowe had already realised this and been anxious for some time to increase his interests in the bear-baiting which had been carried on at various places in the Clink Liberty, at least since 1550. The property, including one of the bear-gardens, which he and Alleyn had acquired in 1595, was not yet developed and in the interim Henslowe had characteristically used it for the manufacture of starch. In 1604 he and Alleyn obtained, after many delays, the joint Mastership of the King's Game, but the plans still hung fire, perhaps because James, an enlightened person in most ways, favoured the sport much less than the theatre. It was not till 1611 that the persistent masters received a grant of £42 10s. 0d. and 12d. a day, for the upkeep of two white bears and a young lion to be housed in Paris Garden. The dogs required for the baiting were forcibly requisitioned each year by the masters' agents, whose reception, particularly in the north of England, was unfriendly in the extreme.

The time was now ripe to develop the old site and in 1613 Henslowe engaged one Gilbert Katherens, a carpenter, to demolish the former ring and to build a new theatre "convenient in all things both for players to play in, and for the game of bears and bulls to be baited in same." He had chosen an opportune moment, for in that same year, during a performance of *Henry VIII*, the Globe caught fire and was completely demolished. Henslowe pushed ahead with the completion of the Hope as he called his new theatre, and in partnership with Jacob Meade opened it, amid general acclaim, with a performance of Ben Jonson's *Bartholomew Fair*. For another forty years it continued, as Henslowe had planned, with alternate stage plays, wrestling matches and bear-baiting, attracting, we are told, "a mixed society, with many noble worthies amongst them."

There were new heroes to tread the board of the Bankside theatres in these latter years. Nat Field, a clergyman's son, played the lead in *Bartholomew Fair*. Shakespeare had retired to Stratford and, when the Globe was rebuilt and reopened, it was John Fletcher and his friend Beaumont who wrote the plays that made the King's men still pre-eminent. As for Henslowe and Alleyn, they grew with every year richer and more respectable. In 1607–8 they had both become members of St. Saviour's vestry and had taken a prominent part in the church's affairs at a critical moment in its history. Henslowe was rated as a £10 subsidyman and Alleyn, who combined a most genial temper with a financial flair exceeding even that of his father-in-law, was rated at £12 and was negotiating for the purpose of an estate in Dulwich. The transaction was completed in 1613 and the old actor said goodbye to his old haunts to play the new role of a country-gentleman. He visited Southwark frequently and with an exchange of compliments St. Saviour's desired him to remain a member of the vestry. His thoughts were turning from making money to spending it, and he was planning a foundation in Dulwich resembling in part Thomas Cure's college and in part a miniature St. Saviour's Grammar School.

Henslowe remained obstinately in his house by the Clink. Why uproot himself? Hither he had come some fifty years before as a servant; now he was churchwarden and a governor of the school and held an honorary post at court as server to the King. He had just done the parish yeomen service, in assisting it to buy the rectory from the Crown and he, who had once been regarded with suspicion by Bingham and his colleagues, now in the last years of his life rejoiced in the friendship and goodwill of all who filled the best pews on Sundays. He was one of Southwark's outstanding personalities, happy in his family relationships so that the occasions when Ned and Joan visited him from Dulwich were still red-letter days, happy in the respect of his fellow townsmen and loving the gossip of Bankside as much as he enjoyed the Thursday lecture at St. Saviour's. He died in 1615, after making a will disinheriting the troublesome nephew in favour of another relative he loved, and his last acts were characteristic. He was suffering from a stroke but he succeeded in recognising and talking to an old friend who called to see him, and he summoned sufficient strength to cancel the I.O.U. of an insolvent actor whose wife petitioned him for relief.

Then he passed on to the next stage of his journey, well content, one imagines, at the deal he had received in life, not the most heroic nor the most saintly of Southwark's dead yet a benefactor to whom posterity has cause to be grateful, for the money and the service which he gave to church and stage alike, for his imagination and vigour and for the lively part he played in the brief and exuberant flowering of Bankside.

## Note on Sources

For the Elizabethan Theatre see *inter alia* E. K. Chambers, *The Elizabethan Stage* (1923); J. Dover Wilson, *Life in Shakespeare's England*, chapter VII, and L. Hotson, *Shakespeare versus Shallow* (1931), pp. 9–19, who establishes Shakespeare's presence at the Swan in 1596; cf. *Survey of London; Bankside*, pp. 66–77, for arguments against the certainty of Shakespeare's residence in Southwark, which Hotson considers as proven. For Henslowe and Alleyn, there is a brief account of the men and materials in E. T. Hall, *Dulwich, History and Romance* (2nd enlarged edition, 1922), and see C. I. Hosking, *The Life and Time of Edward Alleyn* (1952); cf. J. P. Collier, *Memoirs of Ed. Alleyn* (1841); *Alleyn Papers* (Shakespeare Society, 1843); and W. G. Greg, *The Henslowe Diary* (2 vol. 1904; 1908); *Henslowe's Papers* (1907).

Mrs. Golden draws attention to Dekker's quotation in *Old Bankside*, and her chapters on the theatres and the bear-baiting (pp. 110–58) are most attractive.

# XII

# PARISH POLITICS

A GREAT deal was happening in Church and State during the years of the Rose and the Hope and Bankside's emergence as a fashionable resort. In Southwark there were changes in the close, in the vestry, in the borough which must not go unrecorded. In the Close, a new bailiff called Love had succeeded Mr. Woodward. Things had not been easy of late. At least on one occasion the house had been thoroughly searched for gunpowder, the chambers, cellars and vaults, and until peace was made with Spain in 1604, there was always the danger of a scare which filled the prisons again with despairing recusants. The well-to-do smuggled their children abroad to Jesuit schools and there was a waterman on Bankside who did a secret trade carrying young gentlemen down to Tilbury, there to take boat for Calais. The refusal to pay tithes was like a nagging toothache to the vestry and they had less patience with the new Lord Montague than with his father for he was much less one of them. He had married the heiress of the Earl of Dorset, whose estates matched his in Sussex, and he moved among the charmed circle of Catholic nobility of whom the Howards were the doyens. After the eleventh-hour discovery of the Gunpowder Plot in 1605, even Montague found himself in disgrace and with other suspect lords was confined to the Tower while the Close was searched again. The fact that he had once employed Guy Fawkes made his position particularly delicate, but Dorset, his father-in-law, was Lord Treasurer and he was released in the course of 1606 on payment of a fine of £200. Thereafter he prospered and his Sussex interests grew; he seldom came to Southwark and eventually sold the Close to a local family, called Overman, who were not slow in cluttering it up with small property, the potential slums of the future.

To a certain extent Montague's place was taken by Sir Edward Dyer who rented apartments at Winchester House. He seems to have come to Southwark about the turn of the century for in 1600 he presented the wardens of St. Saviour's with a buck for their annual dinner. In his young manhood he had been linked with Philip Sidney and Fulk Greville in a close friendship and was reckoned one of the most gifted of Elizabeth's brilliant court. But when Sidney died the savour went out of life. He never married and though he once went on embassy to Denmark and was knighted in 1596, his desire for seclusion grew. Some years later a rhymester addressed him as "Thou virgin knight that dost thyself obscure from world's unequal eye," and the refuge he found was beneath the shadow of St. Saviour's. There he lived out his days, finding a satisfying hobby in the study of chemistry. This new interest in experimental science was as yet closely linked with the practice of alchemy and one of Dyer's few visitors at Winchester House was Dr. John Dee, the kindly but eccentric old scholar from Mortlake, whose daughter was married to a flaskmaker in Southwark so that he could conveniently visit her and Sir Edward on the same day. Dyer died in 1607 and was buried in the choir and all that remained was the one imperishable piece of verse:

> My mind to me a kingdom is . . .
> I laugh not at another's loss;
> I grudge not at another's gain;
> No worldly waves my mind can toss;
> My state at one doth still remain:
> I fear no foe, I fawn no friend;
> I loathe not life, nor dread my end.
>
> .            .            .
>
> But all the pleasure that I find
> Is to maintain a quiet mind.

Stow in his survey described Winchester House as being in good repair in 1598 and though Dyer's presence shows that part of it was already let out to tenants, it was still used as an episcopal residence. Horne's successors were none of them very distinguished men and they made little mark either on the Kingdom or the Borough. William Wickham II, who died in Southwark only ten weeks after his translation to Winchester from Lincoln and was buried in St. Saviour's in 1595, found an opportunity during his brief tenure of the see to protest at the depredations made by the Crown upon church lands. If they were continued, he declared "there would hardly be a cathedral church found in good repair within England." It was well for St. Saviour's, as for more august buildings, that a new school of thought now appeared among Anglican divines, inspired by Hooker's writings and a desire to preserve in England, before it was lost forever, something of the beauty and spiritual grace of the old Catholic tradition. In 1597 Thomas Bilson, a man of German descent, succeeded to the see of Winchester and in his nineteen years as bishop was able to introduce his fellow-parishioners at St. Saviour's to this new interpretation of the Elizabethan compromise, and to a fresh appreciation of the ancient church that had passed into their care. "He carried prelature in his very aspect," wrote Anthony Wood, the Oxford biographer, while Sir John Harington compared him to "a commander in chief in our spiritual warfare." He regarded King James as the embodiment of that divine right of kings, which he traced back to the old testament conception of kingship and this subservience, as it seemed to many, made him unpopular with a large proportion of the denizens of the Borough. But the references to the Bishop in the vestry minute books are sufficient to shew that his interest and help could always be relied upon, and it was to him that Bingham and Trehearne and their colleagues turned in an unhappy dispute in 1606 and in the negotiations to buy their lease.

This lease of the rectory of the church, including the right to appoint the chaplains and collect the tithe, had already been called in three times and re-issued in 1559, when the obligation to found the school was added, in 1585 and in 1591, when the chaplain's stipends were fixed at £30. It was a constant source of expense and worry, for any legal transaction in Tudor or early Stuart times was fraught with financial hazards and interminable delays. In 1605, certain of the "ancients" of the vestry had an interview with the Lord Treasurer and the suggestion was made that the parish should purchase the lease outright. But at a vestry meeting on May 29th Mr. Garland reported that "a Scottishman hath gotten a lease of the Parsonage for fifty years whereupon it is supposed that he will seek the means he can to wrong us in our terms."

The cuckoo in the nest was a certain John Elphinstone, a member of the Queen's household who had been recently naturalised, and his intrusion on the scene added an urgency to the vestry's deliberations. King James was always prepared to make those around him happy by an indiscriminate giving away of offices and reversions, whether or not anyone else had a previous claim upon them. There was much talk and agitation in the vestry that summer and legal proceedings ensued in the Exchequer, though Elphinstone's claim seems to have petered out before the conclusion of the negotiations to purchase.

Meanwhile the whole course of events was thrown out of gear by an unexpected mutiny in the parish when a body of malcontents came boldly into the open, pointing out that legally the vestry had no status whatsoever. In this contention they were indubitably right, for the act of 1540 had provided for the election of churchwardens by the whole body of parishioners as clearly as the practice of the past fifty years had left the choice to the thirty vestry-men. The latter filled up their own numbers by co-option when required and formed a close oligarchy which worked so long and only so long as it retained the confidence of the people. Bingham and his colleagues felt in 1606 that this was still the case. Conscious of their sacrifices in time and money, they defended their position with vigour and on the whole with commonsense, entrusting their case to Sergeant Archer, their legal adviser, and consulting the Bishop as to what action to take. The malcontents had also consulted the Bishop but found him unwilling to help them and so took their course boldly to Parliament, where they succeeded in obtaining a bill in their favour which passed the lower house.

The bill did not provide for any revolutionary change but merely for the addition of ten extra members to the vestry, all of whom were to be £5 subsidy men. These ten, and all new members in the future, were to be chosen by the whole parish assisted by the two chaplains who were also to have a say in the election of wardens. This latter choice was rather surprisingly left in the hands of the reformed vestry and the chaplains. It would have seemed on the surface a reasonable compromise and the amount of heat the dispute generated was out of all proportion to the change involved. The defence declared that one hundred and forty-two

out of a hundred and ninety-five ratepayers had certified that they
desired no change, that it was absurd to have forty £5 (or over)
subsidy men in the vestry when there were only fifty-four in the
whole parish, and that the attempt to improve the status and
authority of the chaplains was merely an artifice to impress the
parliament men. These arguments the traditionalists advanced
with zeal and some acerbity and they were certainly able to draw
up an impressive list of the wardens' duties, which they claimed
were adequately performed under the present system. "In gathering the tithes and delivering of tokens to 1442 householders, not
less than forty days. . . . In ending controversies among poor
people, many days. . . . In enquiry after defaults and abuses, making
presentments, providing for the poor, putting out to keep and
prentice poor children, avoiding inmates and vagrants above
twenty days. . . . The churchwardens do make at the least 2,000
receipts and payments yearly. . . ." Not any one parish in the land
had so much business, they declared. The rebels might well reply
that all this was irrelevant to the dispute, but there was a certain
cogency in the defence's argument that the chance of the wardens
approaching their arduous task with zeal and wisdom was greatly
increased if they had served an apprenticeship in the vestry and
shared in its fellowship and the sense of a common purpose.

It was a similar stress on the importance and value of fellowship
that enabled them to justify the feasts and junketings on choice
and audit days, and on three special occasions to which the critics
took a particular exception. These were the annual visitation, the
perambulation of the parish bounds and the periodic survey of
church-property. The malcontents naturally felt sore at being
excluded from the merry-making but the defence put up a good
case. In regard to the visitation, if they did not entertain the
diocesan official they would have to ride out, wardens and sidesmen, chaplains and schoolmaster and all, to the place appointed—
and spend the money on the hire of as many as seventeen horses!
At the perambulation, only thirty pence were spent on refreshment for the six churchwardens, ministers, schoolmasters and
many others, and "if this be now less," wrote the ruffled church
official, "they may walk alone in future." The description of the
annual survey gives an equally vivid picture of the times: "the six
churchwardens, four surveyors and six or eight of the gravest

and most sufficient of the vestry, a carpenter, bricklayer and plumber with a clerk to take note of defaults, do spend yearly more than one whole day in viewing the church bells, school, alms-houses and parish tenements; for the churchwardens may not do any repairs till viewed or ordered by us vestry." Certainly, whatever the legal position, there was a sense of responsibility in evidence at St. Saviour's, and the present set-up worked. For this reason alone the Bishop was averse to changing it and whether through his influence or the pressure of other business no more was heard of the bill which was not sent up to the House of Lords and lapsed with the end of the session.

It is impossible at this distance of time to say how far the revolt was based on principle and how far it was merely the result of personal feuds and jealousies. The latter certainly existed in plenty, and there was a garbled statement by one Melluish, who had inherited the Emerson fortune, complaining that in 1591 the out-going warden had absconded with £51, which should have been handed over to his successor, Humphrey Emerson. The stormy career of Richard Humble, in and out of the vestry, is an indication that there were some at least of the well-do-do parishioners who were not in the little clique that ran St. Saviour's and were critical of it in consequence. Humble's name was not mentioned among the dissidents, but there is a reference to a person "expelled from the vestry for his misdemeanours against the state of the parish," which might well refer to him. He had recently been fined for interfering with some workmen, sent by the wardens to remove certain posts which adjoined his property, and upon his refusal to pay he had been turned out of the vestry. Humble's political opinions are uncertain, but he was said to have refused to act as Alderman after the Essex rising, and it may well have been that he possessed popular sympathies which ranked him with the dissidents. For the reliance of the established vestry on Bishop Bilson's support, and their opponents' attempt to invest the chaplains with at least a measure of authority, would seem to indicate certain principles at stake and, though at this stage the murmurs died away and things went on as before, those who could read a sign of the times in the politics of the parish pump might with some justification foresee in the malcontents of 1606 the rebels of the next generation when the harmony of every parish church of England would be rent by conflicting conceptions, not only of worship and belief but of the basis of authority in church and state.

Once the bill against the vestry-men had faded out it was possible to give full attention to the purchase of the rectory: indeed some were ready to suggest that the revolt had been engineered to hamper this transaction. Humble was still intransigent and pastured some sheep in the churchyard without the wardens' permission; but by this time Philip Henslowe had become a member of the vestry and he was used to managing men and could cope with Richard Humble. After "some heat of words," Humble was brought to admit that his sheep were there by grace not by right and the vestry then gave their consent! Thereafter he behaved himself and duly paid his tithe, though he could not refrain from adding the proviso that he would not pay it again if it were demanded a second time "by the Scottish gent."

During the next few years the protracted negotiations with the Crown continued. After 1607 Alleyn and Henslowe took an increasing and effective part in church affairs (Alleyn became a vestry-man in March 1608, and Henslowe in the preceding year). In the spring of 1609, the question of whether or not to go ahead with the purchase was carefully debated and the wardens were authorised to "do their best endeavour to complete the transaction," which it was felt would be for the general good of posterity. The price demanded was £800 and next month after further debate, it was agreed to make an offer in view of the advantage of a church-rate, which the wardens would then be able to impose, over the uncertain tithes upon which their income now depended. It was stipulated that the choice of the ministers should remain in their hands and the school be continued. There were still various delays and it was not until April 12th, 1611, that the King granted to four trustees, John Bingham, Philip Henslowe, John Trehearne and John Payne "in fee, the rectory and church, the burying ground and all glebe lands tithes etc.," for the sum of £800. Even then, three years elapsed before the transaction was at last completed when on August 15th, 1614, the deeds were handed over in the vestry to the nineteen "bargainers" (Bingham and Marshall prominent among them) who had raised the required sum of money. Some years later, the parish was called upon to pay an extra £100, on the ground that the rectory had been under-valued, and on this and another occasion the then wardens stated that the purchase had cost their predecessors as much as £1,500. Certainly, in 1614, the vestry were so conscious of shortage of cash that, on Perambulation day, the company were urged to "drink sparingly."

The feeling that the church was now their own, that the whim of a monarch or their own inability to pay for a renewal of the lease was no longer liable to divest them of all authority gave a tremendous impetus to the work of the vestry. They had cause to be proud, for the money they had raised must be multiplied many times to give any idea of its corresponding value to-day. It was a great achievement both of the nineteen men who rose to the emergency and of the parish who steadily repaid at least a portion of the loan. Their renewed enthusiasm coloured their tackling of the immediate tasks confronting them though the building had not been allowed to fall into disrepair during the prolonged negotiations. In 1605 a good deal of work had been done on the windows. In 1613 while Gilbert Katherens was busy at the Hope his fellow-carpenter John Clark, in the leather apron that was the badge of their trade, was engaged in wholesale repairs at St. Saviour's while, for the love they bore the church, Mr. Mayhew and Mr. Marshall had erected galleries over font and chancel and Mr. Maynard later tiled a portion of the floor. In October 1614 it was agreed to repaint the pulpit "in decent manner" and arrangements were made for a skilled man to view the clock and the chimes, "so that they may go again," and for an armourer to clean and to maintain for a small yearly pension, the armour in the vestry. In 1618, a screen was erected to replace the vanished rood loft, a sign of the new spirit abroad in Anglican circles, and in the same year an inner porch, semi-classical in design, was added at the west end. The building of closed and rented pews also date from these years, an unhappy sign of the growing tendency to equate godliness with prosperity, while the provision of boarding to keep out draughts, and a further alteration in the pulpit to enable the congregation to hear the sermons, serve as a reminder that neither bishop nor bargainers could provide an easy solution of the problem of how to make the huge priory church a suitable home for a parochial congregation.

In addition to their concern to preserve the fabric of the building, the vestry-men were particularly conscious of their commitments in regard to the chaplains and the school. A considerable amount of time and trouble was spent on the choice of the clergy, and there would appear to have been some difficulty in finding chaplains able and willing to reside in the parish. Men already in possession of their cures were prepared to come down intermittently to preach or give the Thursday lecture, but from the beginning the vestry was clear that the parish required a minister, one who would make the gospel known not only to the well-filled pews on Sundays but in the Borough and the Clink from day to day. Marberry, appointed to succeed Edward Philips in 1602, was one of those who refused to commit himself to more than lecturing and he was replaced in 1604 by Snape who professed himself only too ready to perform all ministerial duties and declared that his desire was to dwell in Southwark. But he apparently did not please the Bishop and his appointment was not continued after Christmas, 1605. His place was taken by Dr. Symonds who remained till the end of 1614, not entirely peaceably for, in 1610, he had some grievances and differences with Francis, the other chaplain (about fees not about dogma), and a Mr. Tickner was appointed whom the Bishop declared to be a fit man to take over Francis' ministerial duties. Early in 1614, James Archer succeeded Tickner, and preparatory to his election the vestry drew up regulations that shewed they were already somewhat uneasy about the dangers inherent in their system of choosing their chaplains. In a full vestry (twenty-four were present) in February 1614 it was laid down that the candidates should not indulge in any "instigation, entreaty or persuasion," and that every vestry-man should be "free to give his voice, bean, hand or lot for such preacher or minister as at the time of election in this vestry he shall without fear, affection or malice, by God and his own conscience be moved to judge most fully qualified with learning, utterance and conversation to execute the place for the general good of the people." The candidate for his part was to give no money to the wardens or vestry-men to secure their vote, to be content with the stipend of £30 and a house, and to agree to perform those "ministerial duties here in this parish accustomed, according to the canons of this realm, so long as

God shall send him health." In addition he was to exact no more
than his due in burial and marriage fees, a matter over which there
were continual disputes, and finally, if required to do so, he must
"most willingly and quickly without resistance, disturbance, suit
in law or any composition resign the said place again."

The choice of James Archer proved a happy one and he
remained at St. Saviour's for upward of five and twenty years.
At first he was troubled by poor health and on one occasion he
had the bad luck to be burgled, but the vestry acted generously as
it usually did in such crises, and the affection in which his colleagues held him is indicated in a vestry minute recording that
Boston, the parish clerk, had agreed to read the service when Mr.
Archer was preaching, on the clear understanding that he was
only doing it "for Mr. Archer's sake." In 1614, in the same year
as the latter's appointment, Dr. Symonds removed to a country
cure and Archer's colleague thereafter was Thomas Sutton, who
remained at St. Saviour's till his death in 1623, reading for a
doctor's degree in divinity in spite of extra anxiety and expense
caused by his wife's delicate state of health. Once again the vestry-
men's hands went to their pockets.

Dr. Sutton seems to have been affected by the new puritan
spirit, for not long after his appointment he preached against
the players to Nat Field's great annoynce. Field wrote to him a
long letter of expostulation, vowing that Dr. Sutton had looked
straight at him as he uttered the condemnation and reminding him
that a clergyman's duty was to win souls not to discourage them,
adding the pertinent comments that the trade of acting was not
condemned in the scriptures and since the King patronised the
stage it was disloyal to preach against it. Perhaps Sutton handed
the letter over to the authorities, which would account for it being
preserved in the State Papers, but, if so, they wisely took no
action.

With Sutton and Archer adequately, and it would seem har-
moniously, in possession of the chaplaincies, full attention could
be given to the school, a matter about which Bingham in particular
had very strong views. It must be admitted that up to date its
progress had been disappointing, and its rules and regulations
were now thoroughly overhauled, again with the advice and help

of Bishop Bilson who had once been headmaster of Winchester College. There seems to have been a measure of real imagination among the governors of 1614, for now, for the first time in a school's statutes, physical and other recreations were actively encouraged, "shooting in long bows, chess play, running, wrestling, leaping." It was also laid down perhaps at Alleyn's instigation that, in the frequent exercises in repetition, not merely memory but deportment was to be trained, "to frame the presence, good grace, countenance, standing, pronunciation and everything that may commend their carriage all their lives." Perhaps it was Henslowe who stood out for allowing the lads a holiday each September during the days of Southwark Fair; another more scholarly outing was the annual visit of the top form to Merchant Taylors and Westminster Schools, "that there they may see the manner and fashion of the scholars orations and exercises, which may serve for good directions to them either to do the like or better approve their own." But the crux of the matter lay, as they all realised, in the choice of a headmaster. His salary had been increased to £30 and it was now stipulated that he must be a Master of Arts and (so much more difficult!) "of a wise, sociable and loving disposition . . . not hasty or furious . . ."; above all he was to be "of good experience to discern the nature of every several child . . . to learn with the love of his book." Thus, shortly before this time that Dr. Busby reigned at Westminster, spake the new educationalists of St. Saviour's.

There remained the recurrent problem of money. The school had as yet received few bequests, though Gilbert Rockett in 1587 had endowed it with the Three Tuns on Bankside and Hugh Browker, the son of one of the first governors, left it the Red Lion. Now, Gregory Franklyn, a staunch and respected member of the vestry, bequeathed the Queen's Head to the school and Bingham in 1617 allotted to it the profits of three tenements in Kent Street, the lane that let out into the country where the gypsies and the broom gatherers dwelt. Bingham's gift was to be set aside to endow two scholarships for the University. During the next hundred years and more the school went steadily if unspectacularly on its way, producing no intellectual giants but a succession of sound Bingham scholars and a number of reasonably educated boys who went into their father's business and became the intelligent and not very malleable citizens of the Southwark of the seventeenth and eighteenth centuries.

Now, with the purchase of the rectory completed and the affairs of the church set in order, a generation was passing which had governed St. Saviour's destinies since the Armada sailed and listened at the Rose and the Globe to the plays of Marlowe and Shakespeare. The bargain with the King was barely concluded when Philip Henslowe died in 1615. Next year Richard Humble's busy life ended and his son Peter erected to his memory in the church a fine monument, overshadowing the more modest tombs of many of his rivals and contemporaries. Adorned with his effigy and that of his two wives and six children, it is inscribed with the lovely lines, attributed to Thomas Quarles:

> Like to the damask rose you see
> Or like the blossom on the tree,
> Or like the dainty flower of May,
> Or like the morning of the day,
> Or like the sun, or like the shade,
> Or like the gourd which Jonas had;
> Even so is man whose thread is spun
> Drawn out and cut and so is done.
> The rose withers, the blossom blasteth
> The flower fades, the morning hasteth,
> The sun sets, the shadow flies
> The gourd consumes, the man he dies . . .

It is a fatalistic note for the busy, successful Richard Humble. Was it his son Peter's choice or are we wrong about the man? So much after all is imagination. One knows even less of John Trehearne, who was the next to go in 1618, and who with his wife and children are depicted on a nearby monument, with a fanciful but less poetic inscription than Humble's. It describes John Trehearne as "gentleman portar to King James the First" and begins:

> Had Kings a power to lend their subjects breath,
> Trehearne thou shouldst not be cast down by death.

All we know of him besides his loyal service at court and in the vestry is some trouble over the non-payment of tithes in his hot-headed younger days, and the fact recorded on a vanished gravestone that he and his wife Margaret lived fifty years together. She herself outlived him by twenty-seven years, while the face of England changed and the tragedy of the civil wars shattered the serenity of ordered days.

Of the other bargainers John Bingham remained active to the end, even though in 1620 he was seventy years old while another of the group still active was Robert Harvard, one of the Borough's many butchers. But new names began to appear. William Ward, the goldsmith, who had married one of Humble's daughters, became a member of the vestry in 1624, and in the previous year Mrs. Bromfield sent in "to the use of the poor 13s. 4d. for her license to eat flesh in the time of Lent." There are an increasing number of references to young William Austin, whose mother Lady Clerke was a close personal friend of the Alleyns. Alleyn often dined with her and Austin, when he visited Southwark; he remained till his death in close touch with the vestry, who watched with interest his plans for his college at Dulwich in the management of which the wardens of St. Saviour's were to have a share.

Alleyn had given to his foundation the delightful name of the College of God's Gift, and he intended it to house six poor brethren, six poor sisters and twelve poor scholars chosen from the three parishes, St. Botolph's, where he was born, St. Giles Cripplegate, where the Fortune theatre stood; and St. Saviour's, Southwark. The direction of the college was to be in the hands of four fellows, a warden and a master, the latter of whom, Alleyn laid down, should always bear the same name as himself! It was eventually opened in 1619, at a ceremony which was attended by no less a person than Lord Chancellor Bacon, and in these final years at Dulwich Alleyn might well pride himself on his achievements and his friendships with the great of the land and on all that he had accomplished since the days that he signed himself the Lord Admiral's servant. In the summer of 1623 there was an unexpected reference to him in a letter of John Chamberlain, the news-writer, reporting that preparations were on foot to welcome the Spanish princess whom Prince Charles was expected to marry. He wrote that the Duke of Richmond and six other gentlemen had gone down to Southampton "to arrange pageants and repair of the highways for the reception of the Infanta. Inigo Jones and Alleyn the old Player went with them, and could have done just as well without so many Privy Council." But the important occasion faded out, and the prince returned without his bride.

The pleasant days at Dulwich were saddened a few months later by Joan Alleyn's death, and though soon afterwards Alleyn married the daughter of Dr. Donne, the Dean of St. Paul's, it did not prove a particularly happy match. His love for his young wife was sincere but too possessive and he did not get on well with his new father-in-law with whom one cannot imagine him having much in common. The practical affairs, in which he had always been so capable, clogged his spirit and he was constantly remaking his will and revising the statutes of his college. Within a year or two of its opening he had decreed that a certain number of fee-paying students and day-boys from neighbouring villages should be admitted and this provision assured the continuance of his school, different as its development was from his original conception. After many vicissitudes in the intervening centuries, Dulwich College in the event exceeded its founder's wildest dreams and the old stage-player, as would have pleased him well, is honoured in the achievements of many generations of young men. In 1626, he died and perhaps was not sorry to go, for times were changing and he left behind him in the College of God's Gift an assurance that his name would be remembered, though none were left who could recall his stirring diction or the fine presence that had delighted the visitors to the Rose and gained him a hearing in St. Saviour's Vestry.

## Note on Sources

The records of the Corporation of Wardens include under *Church Wardens Miscellaneous* the papers relating to the bill against the thirty vestry-men, which not only give details of the dispute of 1606 but throw much light on parochial administration. The second minute book covers the years up to 1627. For Dyer, see John Buxton: *Sir Philip Sidney and the English Renaissance* (1954).

David Mathew in *The Jacobean Age* (1938), pp. 230–45, gives a most valuable sketch of the Catholic minority in James I's reign to which the Montagues belonged. The standard history of *Dulwich College* is in 2 volumes, by W. Young (1889).

# XIII

# THE TRANQUIL YEARS

THEY were quiet years that followed the purchase of the rectory before the cataclysm of the civil wars. The parish of St. Saviour's prospered though as yet no large-scale industry had developed to change its character. The main occupation of the merchants of the Borough continued to centre round the transport and victualling trades; along the river where open ground was available there were various kinds of dyeing and soap works, in addition to one or two breweries. The building restrictions in London and the consequent overcrowding in the reign of James I had led to a considerable influx of population over the bridge and though, at the beginning of the period, the City merchants themselves hesitated to cross the water and preferred to buy the large houses as they fell vacant and to rent them to artisans and lesser tradesmen, the number of well-to-do citizens began to increase. The occupants of the Close and the neighbouring alleys were often less reputable. The right of sanctuary which appertained to the Close, as part of the Priory precincts, was not abolished till the eighteenth century, and it was at this stage a favourite haunt of debtors and sectaries and full of "mean cottages and habitations for the poorer sort of people that crowded themselves together." In a satire entitled *The Mystery of Lending and Borrowing*, written by Thomas Powell in 1625, the hero bids his waterman carry him to the south bank when his resources in the city fail him, for there he knows of "an excellent hold indeed commonly called Montague Close." Another unruly element was supplied by the crews from the coal ships which came in increasing numbers from Newcastle and frequently unloaded at some point between Rotherhithe and Lambeth. To such the attractions of Bankside were irresistible!

Bankside was still a centre of the show business. Francis Langley had sold out in 1601, when Hugh Browker, a lawyer and member of a well-known Southwark family, bought the manor of Paris Garden. It remained in the Browkers' hands till the Interregnum, the old Swan theatre falling into disrepair but the manor house itself gaining an evil, if fashionable, reputation after Susan Holland, the procuress, obtained possession in the thirties. The Hope was mainly used as a bear-garden or for other spectacles and the Rose had ceased to function, but the new Globe theatre flourished and though Henslowe and Alleyn, Burbage and Shakespeare belonged to a past generation, Francis Beaumont, a judge's son, and Fletcher, the son of a bishop, showed that the art of drama was the recognised concern of the educated classes. Two men of unconventional mould, they lived together near the Globe, collaborating in their famous plays. *The Knight of the Burning Pestle* is a good example of their exuberant fancy, in which John Fletcher particularly excelled, while Beaumont's main task was "to correct the overflowings of Mr. Fletcher's wit." *The Faithful Shepherdess*, which was Fletcher's own work, had a lyrical beauty in many of its passages and a pastoral charm, too subtle, it seemed, for the groundlings of the Globe, who gave it a poor reception upon its first performance. Beaumont married in 1614 and died two years later, but Fletcher remained on Bankside for a further nine years and the place of his lost friend was taken to a certain degree by Philip Massinger, a free-lance writer of plays, and poems, who after a sheltered life in the Earl of Pembroke's household, was thrown, upon his father's death, into the precarious business of earning his living by his pen. Once at least he was imprisoned for debt and it was a £5 loan from Henslowe that set him on his feet again. But such reverses and the hard facts of life in Southwark could not embitter his temper nor spoil a nature which is mirrored in writings unfashionably free from satire or abuse. Another of like temperament, if his epitaph speaks true, was the actor Richard Benefield, whose memorial in St. Saviour's tells of the "frankincense of his piety, the nard of his probity, the amber of his faithfulness and the oil of his charity."

St. Saviour's parish was thus still a mixed society: merchants, artisans, watermen, penurious actors and actors that had grown to be men of property, the truculent birds of passage from the barges that sailed up St. Mary's dock, and a growing number of religious and political malcontents. Nor must one forget in envisaging the Sunday morning congregation the boys from the Grammar School and the old people from Cure's College and the almshouses. During Charles I's reign, Robert Bromfield, who shared with Thomas Overman the ownership of the Close, made a laudable attempt to clean up his property and replaced the mean cottages by houses "fit for men of better ability." Winchester House also had been repaired and beautified in 1617 and these improvements added not a little to the pleasantness of the church's immediate surroundings, for Bishop Bilson's successor at Winchester, Edward Montague, was a member of a noble family and a man of wealth and good taste, more interested in the fashionable hobby of building than in theological niceties. He found Winchester House in a ruinous condition and, when he had refurbished it, entertained there on one occasion of some splendour, various lords and gentlemen with whom he had recently travelled to Scotland in King James' company. Among his guests was the erudite Bishop of Ely, Lancelot Andrewes, a man of God whose friendly interest in his fellowmen made him at home alike at the court and in the city streets. In 1619 he succeeded Montague at Winchester and found the newly beautified house in Southwark a convenient home when his duties as a privy councillor necessitated his presence at Whitehall.

Lancelot Andrewes was a patristic scholar of great eminence, the speaker of innumerable languages, and something of a saint. He was a Londoner by birth and for many years a don at Cambridge, whence he returned to the City as rector of St. Giles Cripplegate in the year of the Armada. At the turn of the century he had been Dean of Westminster, enjoying to the full the contact with young minds at Westminster school, and thereafter, he became Bishop of Chichester and Ely in turn, the King's Almoner and a preacher of renown. As Benefield's memorial reminds us, it was an age of fine words. King James wrote tracts far more ably than he ever learnt to govern and, in the years when the last heretic was burnt in England and nonconformity came to stay, a concourse of learned men produced the translation of the Scriptures known to posterity as the authorised version of the Bible. Lancelot Andrewes had been

THE NAVE OF THE CATHEDRAL CHURCH LOOKING WEST.

This shows the modern rebuilding of the nave as it was in the thirteenth century. The work was completed in 1897.

LONDON AND SOUTHWARK, *c.* 1600, BY C. V. VISSCHER
(PUB., AMSTERDAM, 1616).

The illustration reproduced above is part of a longer panorama stretching from Paris Garden to beyond St. Olave's. Visscher was born in 1587, and apprenticed to an engraver Hondius, who had himself spent ten years in England as a refugee, living in St. Thomas's parish in 1583. From internal evidence, the drawing seems to have been made about 1600: see Irene Scouloudi, *Panoramic Views of London*, 1600-1666 (1953).

LANCELOT ANDREWES, BISHOP OF WINCHESTER,
1619-26.

WILLIAM AUSTIN OF LINCOLN'S INN (d. 1634),
from the frontispiece to his Collected Works (pub. 1635).

chairman of the committee responsible for the earlier part of the Old Testament and the promotion to Winchester was to some extent a recognition of his share in the great achievement. A certain timidity of temperament, and his inability to criticise the King, lessened his influence for good in the counsels of Church and state, but in his deep personal piety and in the searching power of his sermons he challenged the worldliness and corruption of James' court. In the dissension which grew with the years between those whose watchword was authority and those who, in one or other of its guises, desired elusive liberty, Andrewes knew clearly where he stood. To him tranquillity and order in rule, in worship and belief were God's will for his Holy Church and this was the end he strove to foster, alike in his writings and episcopal duties and in the witness of his own disciplined life, grounded firmly on the daily practice of prayer.

Andrewes had endeavoured to interpret to his countrymen and to Europe the conception of the Church of England as Catholic but reformed, going behind medieval excrescences to the faith and practices of the early Christian fathers, yet strongly national in its stress on the divine nature of kingship and the duty of obedience such a belief entailed. It was Bilson's teaching reiterated and enhanced and one to which many at St. Saviour's took exception, for there was another way of looking at things more congenial to a congregation of merchants, familiar in their daily business with buying and selling, a growing opinion that religion was a personal matter between God and one's own conscience and that sovereignty was a matter of contract between king and people. Throughout England as the years progressed this cleavage of opinion became more clearly evident, and in the counsels of St. Saviour's vestry there were already signs of its existence. After Dr. Sutton's death in 1623, there were four candidates for the vacant post of chaplain and the choice fell upon a certain Mr. Harris, of Magdalen College, Oxford. It proved an unfortunate decision, for Harris could not make up his mind to come and live in Southwark and after two years' vaccillation arrived only to move on almost at once to the cure of a City church. His successor Mickelthwaite was apparently of Andrewes' way of thought, and it is significant that he did not please the vestry and left very shortly to take up a post in the Temple. Later,

Bishop Laud referred to him as one who had suffered, "both at St. Mary Overie's and in the Temple," for being "forward for the good discipline of the church." Moreover, the section of the vestry not in tune with the High Church point of view apparently prevailed at Southwark in the choice of Mickelthwaite's successor for Nicholas Morton who came in 1631 and did settle in the parish and do well there, hailed from that hot-bed of puritan thought, Emmanuel College, Cambridge.

There must, however, have been others who were guided and inspired by Andrewes' leadership as certain items make evident from the vestry's minutes of 1623. William Austin of Lincoln's Inn, who lived in the pleasant triangle of ground between Gravel Lane and Paris Garden, reported that his mother, Lady Clerke, was "well-minded" to provide a new communion table and hangings, and the vestry agreed to add at their own charge a new frame of rails where the people were to kneel. She also gave an altar table of oak, still to be seen in the Lady Chapel. Austin presented a "fair silver chalice and a dish for the bread to the value of almost £40," and these benefactions and others that followed all helped to enhance the beauty and dignity of this most sacred of services, to which the sacramental teaching of Andrewes and Laud had given a new emphasis. Moreover, in August 1623, the vestry decided not to renew the baker Wilson's lease of the Lady Chapel. They adhered to the resolution next spring, when Bingham himself made enquiries about the building which adjoined his own property; the vestry reiterated that it should not "be employed any more to any other use but only for the church" and at once set about the work of salvage. The lofts and partitions were removed and the place thoroughly cleansed and the whole retro-choir, to-day such a precious possession, was thus redeemed and resanctified, probably as a result of the influence of Andrewes who did so much to secure beauty of worship in every place with which he had to do.

There was another very important side to Andrewes' nature. To European scholars he might be best known as an able propagandist, to Whitehall as the King's trusted councillor and the preacher of amazing sermons that held and stimulated, challenged and consoled. But the men and women of Southwark knew him first and foremost as a good neighbour. He spared neither time

nor trouble in investigating hardship and in giving effective
assistance to any who sought his aid. Whenever possible he liked
his almsgiving to be anonymous and in those latter years there
must have been many in the Borough and the Clink who were
helped by his bounty and knew not whence it came. Still less did
they know how earnestly he prayed for them. Every day and
every night he prayed, praising God for His Creation, listing with
meticulous accuracy those things for which in his own life, he had
particular cause to be grateful, abasing himself in humble repentance and interceding day in and day out for all sorts and conditions
of men. His book of devotions bore witness on his death to the
reality of his love for his fellows, for each of whom he seemed to
care with a personal concern as he prayed for the prisoners, the
bereaved, the sober, honest workmen, the wayfarer and women
labouring with child.

Outside the Bishop's windows at Winchester House there was
enough distress to burden the hearts of less saintly men than he.
Across the road at St. Thomas's Hospital, there was a ward known
as night's abode for vagrants and sick wayfarers and a department,
all too small, for midwifery. But the few were indeed fortunate
who found shelter at St. Thomas's. There is no sadder reading
among the records of St. Saviour's than Christopher Fawcett's
report in regard to vagabonds, which he made in 1622. The
Elizabethan poor law had saddled each parish with the duty of
caring for its own down and outs and the over-burdened local
officials endeavoured in consequence to keep out any vagrant who
might become a burden to the rates. New families moving into
the district were required to give sureties before they were allowed
to remain while less respectable wayfarers, especially women
whose bastard children must needs be maintained by the parish,
were mercilessly hounded and sent back whence they came.
Fawcett considered himself a good and diligent servant and
received £5 from the vestry for his pains and an additional
*douceur* to mark their approval of measures which they considered
to be essential if the amenities of the district were to be improved.
Yet how can one reconcile the worship of a suffering Christ with
Fawcett's complacent reports: "I, hearing that Mary Moore
and a child with her [were] lying very sick at St. Margaret's Hill,

being come out of St. George's Parish, made it known to the
church wardens and got her and her child carried away back
again to St. George's and so was rid of her," or, "Having heard
that Elizabeth Rogers, great with child and in pain of child-birth,
coming from the other side of London and sat at the new churchyard gate the 12th of March, went presently to her and with much
ado got her over the bridge and so heard no more of her." Sometimes there was a doubt as to which parish was responsible, which
only made matters worse. "Margaret Younger, great with child,
was brought from the parish of St. George by the constable there
and sitting at Mr. Payne's door at ten of the clock at night, he
went presently and took a constable and had her carried back to
St. George's and there left her and set two watchmen all night to
see that they brought her not again."

A few had imagination and did not entirely let things be, and
the provision of schools and almshouses, gifts of land like Mark
Houses' legacy at Sydenham, and benefactions in coal and bread
and clothing represented the honest attempts of good men to
respond to the challenge of "thou shalt love thy neighbour as
thyself." At Christmas and other great festivals there were still as
in the days of the Priory distributions at the church door: Thomas
Emerson's shilling to two honest poor men; Buckland's gift of
ten brown coats: the Marshalls' more ambitious charity, that
clothed six boys each Christmas morning with grey coats and
breeches and new shoes and provided for six old women kerchief
and apron as well as a scarlet gown: such legacies as these took
the place of the medieval practice of founding masses for one's
soul. A sense of responsibility was also evidenced in the constant
use of the poor box and in special collections in the church: a
poor maimed man, having lost his legs in the late Queen's service,
the widow of a Stepney brewer who had gone to Germany with
the Princess Palatine, Matthew Angel of Wapping whose son had
been taken by pirates, all these had occasion to be thankful that
almsgiving had still a place in the practice of Christian piety. Yet
as the years passed the very size of the problem defeated the best
intentions of persons of goodwill. Nor did the readiness to assist
the "sober and deserving" extend to the "swearing, drunken, idle,
impudent, filthy poor," as one benefactor later termed them. The
continuance of many such in St. Saviour's parish remained for

the wardens a perennial source of anxiety and a problem to which none knew the answers.

One result of the increase in population and the overcrowded tenements was the more frequent appearance of the plague. In 1625 there was a particularly virulent outbreak in London and the suburbs. The entry of burials at St. Saviour's continues in the smeared, untidy crowded pages of the register until August and then stops abruptly. No sweet herbs could save a household now. Robert Harvard died and most of his family, only his widow was left with one son, John, who went with her, presumably, when she left Southwark after a second marriage. Later Mrs. Harvard acknowledged the help that parson Morton gave her at this time and one would like to think it was through his influence that John went to Emmanuel. He emerged so convinced a puritan that in due course he emigrated to Massachusetts, where those of his way of thinking were endeavouring to build a righteous common-wealth. He only lived for a year in the new world, during which time he saw the tentative beginning of a university at Newtown, nostalgically rechristened Cambridge. He left half his money and his books to the new foundation, thereafter named Harvard in his honour, and in the cathedral church of Southwark, three hundred years later, the old chapel of St. John was repaired and refurnished by American citizens. Thus they paid tribute to the memory of John Harvard who was baptised here in 1607 and may well have been confirmed by Lancelot Andrewes as a member of the Holy Catholic Church.

Another casualty of the plague year was John Fletcher the dramatist. Years afterwards, when Aubrey wandered round Southwark picking up bits of gossip for his *Lives*, he found at St. Saviour's an old parish clerk, who had once been a tailor. He told Aubrey that Fletcher might well have escaped, for he had made arrangements to go into the country, but first ordered a suit of clothes and while he waited for the tailor to complete the work, the pestilence struck and he died. Fletcher was buried in St. Saviour's church and Massinger asked that when his turn came he might share the same grave. But death, which had claimed Beaumont so young and Fletcher so suddenly, passed Massinger by. He lived on in his home near the theatre until 1639, thinking often of his dead friends in the paradise of which he wrote:

> There's a perpetual spring, perpetual youth,
> No joint benumbing cold or scorching heat
> Famine nor age have any being there . . . .

John Bingham also died in the September of the plague year, but of honest old age rather than of the pestilence. His bust, moved to the south transept from the chapel of Mary Magdalene, proclaims the man for what he was; shrewd, kindly, vigorous, a little unimaginative, "a good benefactor to this parish, expecting the resurrection of the Just." It is a modest monument compared with those of Humble and Austin but it is worth searching out; like Trehearne's effigy it is the work of a fine craftsman, probably the Gerard Jansen who a few years earlier had made a bust of Shakespeare for the poet's friends in Stratford, and the sculptor's genius, preserving for posterity Bingham's honest features, pierces the darkness of the past more surely than any words can do.

Bishop Andrewes was the next to go, an old tired man of over seventy, fearful for the future of the Church he loved. He had been ill for some months at Winchester House and died there in November 1626. Chaplain Archer conducted the funeral service in St. Saviour's, in a church hung with black baize. A number of Andrewes' large and united family were present, as well as other distinguished visitors, and the two chaplains divided the princely collection of £11 17s. 7d. The Bishop was attended on his last journey, as he had desired in his will, by seventy-one old persons representing the years of his age, all clad in new warm mourning gowns and chosen from St. Saviour's and the other City parishes where he had lived. He had provided in addition legacies for aged persons, widows and orphans and for prisoners, the latter to be chosen preferably from the Southwark gaols. His funeral sermon was preached by Bishop Buckeridge and his body laid in a small chapel, east of the retro-choir, in an elaborate tomb on which another friend and disciple, Matthew Wren, had inscribed a eulogy.

Fifty years later a fire damaged the chapel and injured the tomb. The canopy and inscription were lost, but Gerard Jansen's effigy remained to perpetuate Andrewes' shrewd and scholarly features, and after resting for a while within the Lady Chapel, the tomb now stands in the aisle on the southern side of the choir. There is a copy of Andrewes' book of Devotions beside it, which bears truer witness to the man he was than the elaborate eulogies of Buckeridge and Wren; a wise pilgrim will pause to read it and, in the intercessions, will see mirrored the busy life of the streets and alleyways that surged about the Bishop's house in the years he dwelt in Southwark.

The third book of vestry minutes ends with the year 1627, including in the final pages the report of Andrewes' funeral, of Nicholas Morton's appointment and Mrs. Bingham's gift to St. Saviour's of £50, to supply coal for the poor at Christmas in memory of her husband. She also gave the church two great silver flagons for the service at the Communion table, and these she hoped would remain for ever to bear witness to "her pious and religious respects unto this parish, being the place where she was born and hath always lived." She feared, perhaps, that the necessity of finding a second husband to house and keep her would take her across the river, but the fates were kind. There was another lonely soul in the congregation in William Austin, who had lost his first wife in child-birth a few years earlier and in 1626 was bereft of his beloved mother, whose good works and gracious bearing had made her so dear a friend to so many. Austin, whose learning and elegance was not, one imagines, partnered by a like practical ability, was left with five young children and no woman in the house. Very sensibly, he and Mrs. Bingham married, and the admiring care with which, after Austin's death in 1634, the second Mrs. Austin edited his works speaks well for the way she fulfilled her duty to him.

The temptation to digress about the Austins is irresistible. They were a cultured and hospitable family, and the home beyond Gravel Lane must have been a happy place particularly when Lady Clerke presided over it. She was the widow of a baron of the Exchequer, a woman of breeding as well as of piety and perhaps it was she of whom William Austin thought when he adapted the verse from Ecclesiasticus: "And as the clear light is upon the holy candlesticks, so is the beauty of her face in a ripe age." William, the son of her first marriage, was a member of Lincoln's Inn, one of those grave young men who seem mature at twenty. He was twenty-seven when he joined the vestry in 1617, and his seniors there listened to him with a deference which he liked to think was due to his learning not to the fortune he had inherited. For he had a scale of values different from most of his neighbours:

> I joy in these, which few can discommend
> And most desire, next to a constant friend,
> And these are they that draw me most along,
> A well-writ book, a picture and a song.

His metaphors were those of a contented man, of flowers and gardens and ships in sail as he so often watched them in the traffic of the Thames. He loved and admired the work of men's hands. "No beautiful thing is made by chance," he wrote, "but by some ingenious and operative art." He may have counted Andrewes among his friends, for there is not only in the style of his religious meditations, with their analytical exposition of their theme, but in his whole attitude to life, much of the same love of symmetry and seemliness. "The extent of Christian wisdom is to be wise unto sobriety," Austin argued: "For as of wine so of learning a man may have so much as may make another say he is mad. . . ." "Heaven is built like our churches, high roofed within but with a straight low gate, they . . . that enter there must stoop 'ere they can see God." Only the children and music could stir him from his usual moderation and there is the true spirit of joy in his carol of the angels' singing.

> So loud they chant that down on earth
> Innocent children hear their mirth.
>
> .         .         .
>
> Heaven, Earth, Babes, Shepherds, Angels sing
> Oh never was such carolling . . . .
>
> .         .         .
>
> Up then (my soul) thy part desire
> And sing (though but a bass) in this sweet choir.

He had ten children, five of whom survived, belying his own

love of moderation in this respect! After his wife's death in child-bed, he never entirely escaped from melancholy, and brooded much on death, trying to rationalise his experiences and to argue himself into acceptance.

> Shall there be nothing left me, but a Grave?
> Shall I (at last) no other Dwelling have?

So the gloomy verse runs on, and the hedonist in him wrestled with the Christian and is at last subdued. For at the end he found, as other simpler folk have done, his best reassurance in the promise of the scriptures:

> When through the world's dark storm to heaven we tend,
> One quiet pilot sitting at the end . . . .

and he endeavoured to conquer his horror of the grave by the symbol of recurrent life that he found in the fields and gardens that he loved.

It was this idea of God's husbandry, the thought expressed by St. Paul, "sewn in corruption . . . raised in incorruption," that he attempted to depict in the elaborate monument which he erected over his wife's tomb in St. Saviour's, where he and his mother and others of his family were also buried. Its over-elaborate adornments and its intricate allegory offend the simpler taste of to-day and it leaves one cold while the pathetic beauty of the verse on Humble's tomb still catches one by the heart, but it is none the less an enlightened man's profession of faith, his answer to the skeletons and the harpies that disfigure the effigies of Emerson and Bingham and other of his contemporaries.

Austin's poems, so dutifully published by Anne Austin, his second wife, as a tribute to "some part of the great worth of her ever-honoured husband," are in that metaphysical strain which, transmuted by the genius of a Herbert or a Donne, could reflect eternal truths with gem-like brilliance but which seldom in Austin's case transcends the artificial and verbose. The most attractive of his Meditations is that of St. Thomas' day, the immediate precursor of Christmas. "Till we come to Thomas his confession and faithfully believe and particularly apply it to ourselves Christ is not born in us." When we have learnt to desire Him as well as to doubt, then as we assemble "with His Saints, upon His day, within the doors of His house, He will then be in the midst." Austin's sober piety was characteristic of the generation of Anglican lay-men who grew up into the church as Hooker and Andrewes had moulded it and who ten years later faced death and penury for it and their sovereign's sake. It was because of the solid backing, the abiding affection of men of this type that, in spite of Laud's mistakes and the King's vacillating obstinacy, in spite of the worldliness of many of the Cavaliers, the cause for which they stood survived defeat and came again into its own.

Austin died in 1634, by which date other names were prominent in Southwark. The leading family were the Bromfields, not new-comers by any means (there had been a Bromfield member of the vestry in the reign of Edward VI) but now at the height of their fortunes Edward Bromfield had bought Southwark Place in St. George's parish where he may have worshipped. But he was married to John Payne's daughter, his brother held property in the close and his son John married Joyce Austin, so that he was linked in many ways with St. Saviour's, where in due course he was buried. He was a member of the Common Council of the City of London, Lord Mayor in 1636-7 and later Alderman of Dowgate. He was knighted by King Charles in 1637 and appointed in that year to serve on the corporation of soap makers to whom a monopoly of the trade was given. His Southwark interests were no doubt responsible for this, which proved no easy assignment for the housewives showed themselves unexpectedly obstinate and refused to be dragooned into using one sort of soap.

In addition to the Bromfields, the Overmans and the Austins, there were also the Marshalls and the Richardson family who owned Axe Yard (now Newcomen Street) which ran out of the Borough High Street on the eastern side and formed the boundary between St. Saviour's and St. George's parish. John Marshall senior was a baker and tallow chandler but it is significant that his son, also John, described himself "gentleman" as did Thomas Overman of the Close. The emergence of these rich mercantile families, many of whom had small estates in Kent and Essex and who brought up their children to play the part of country squires, shows that as the amenities of Southwark grew, City families no longer hesitated to settle there. Most of the new-comers lived some distance from St. Saviour's and were interested in the idea of a new church, for which the second John Marshall left money when he died in 1631, empowering his trustees to raise £700 from his estate for this purpose and leaving his house, complete with its "cistern and bedsteads" to be let to the chaplain at St. Saviour's for twenty-one years. The rent was to go towards the cost of a house for the minister of the new church, but Marshall's project was for many long years delayed, and not only the unsettled times which so soon fell upon the country but St. Saviour's reluctance to see their parish divided prevented anyone from taking action.

The loss of the minutes for the years between 1627 and 1660 makes it impossible to trace in detail the history of St. Saviour's or the personnel of the vestry. Archer and Morton continued their ministry and in 1633 there was also a curate, no doubt to assist Archer, who had been much troubled with illness and must have been getting on in years. To a small extent the gap in the vestry minutes is filled by the wardens' answers at the annual visitations which were held by the Archdeacon of Surrey or his representatives, and here again the frequency with which they reply "all well" indicates tranquillity, however insecurely based, even in these very years when John Eliot, the Commons' leader, was a prisoner in the Marshalsea. The visitations dealt with the material state of the church, the conduct of its services and the behaviour of the parishioners, not only on Sundays but in the workaday world. At St. Saviour's the wardens' care for the fabric showed sometimes more zeal than artistic sense and the galleries must have defaced the church's medieval beauty as the horror of the boxed pew offended against the ideal of Christian brotherhood. The burden of day-to-day repairs fortunately prevented any major alterations, for in 1631 the wardens reported to the Archdeacon that some £650 had been spent on the church since the purchase in 1614, and although a survey in the previous June had revealed signs of decay in a corner of St. John's chapel and the tiling in the vestry needed attention, they asked for time to put it right since the work would be very

179

chargeable and "not suddenly to be undertaken." In answer to an enquiry about their records they replied with pride that all was well, "only our register book," they added, "is not of parchment but of good royal paper and so hath always been."

Upon Andrewes' death, his friend and colleague, Bishop Neile of Durham, had been translated to Winchester where he remained for four years before he became Archbishop of York. The High Church tradition of the diocese was thus maintained both in Neile's day and in that of his successor Walter Curle, whose benefactions to the poor and the large sums he spent upon the repair of churches distinguished him as a good diocesan whatever his political colour might be. Yet so inextricably were ritual and worship linked with the ecclesiastical politics of the time, that Curle's desire for beauty and seemliness, his provision of copes and surplices, his use of pictures and images led to trouble in his diocese as elsewhere, the more so as he was as firm as Laud himself and so rigorous in exacting compliance, "that he obliged all churchwardens to take an oath that they would denounce to him, or to his officers, such clergy as were wanting in the observance of his orders."

There was no particular sign of lack of co-operation at St. Saviour's; on the other hand it would appear that, at one stage "Laudian" innovations were introduced in the service of Holy Communion. One of the matters which caused the bishops anxiety was the practice of lecturing by which means the puritan clergy had much increased their popularity and influence. In 1631, the visitation articles laid down that "where any lecture is set up in a market town the same be read by a company of grave and orthodox divines . . . and that they preach in gowns not cloaks." Moreover, divine service, according to the Book of Common Prayer, was always to be read beforehand. St. Saviour's was able to reply that their lecture was always given by one of their own chaplains, that their present preacher Nicholas Morton was "conformable to the discipline of the church of England" and that he maintained the rule of reading the service first, duly clad in his surplice. One of Morton's first innovations had been to set up a sermon and catechism for youths and unlearned people, upon such holidays as did not fall on a Sunday, and the wardens now reported that the afternoon service on Sunday also took the form of a catechism, by way of question and answer, a practice much approved by Laud. The Archbishop's vicar-general once made a survey of his province, dealing with such varied problems as unsightly galleries at Kingston and an old man of one hundred and two at Stafford who scribbled, on the walls of the chancel, his opinion of every preacher whom he heard; when the official finally reached the Southwark deanery and met the representatives of the thirteen parishes, probably at St. Saviour's, he was either so exhausted or so satisfied with their bearing that he reported nothing beyond the absence of one of the clergy.

The case was far less satisfactory when it came to that moral surveillance, which was no monopoly of the puritans but which the Laudian church also ruthlessly imposed. Brawling and tale-bearing were dealt with as cogently as more serious vices and at each presentation there was the usual sorry company of persons living in adultery. Some, "to the great dishonour of God," persisted in their ways but others, avowing penitence, made public confession in a white sheet at church on Sunday, affording thereby, one fears, a vicarious thrill to the matrons of the Borough. The most frequent crime however was that of tippling in forbidden hours. Once service had begun and St. Saviour's congregation was launched on the singing of the psalms the wardens and constables made their rounds to see what was afoot in the Close and Clink Alley. "Thomas Prior in the Close for having two men drinking in his house, the 10th day of June being Sunday in the time of divine service," thus runs an entry in November 1632, paralleled again and again. "Mr. Edwards, vintner, in the Close for having six persons drinking," while in Bankside, in addition to peccant vintners, Margery Walton was presented for "entertaining lewd company and keeping a house of bawdery as the common fame goeth," and Richard Wright, waterman, "for abusing the churchwardens and sidesmen with vile speeches." The watermen objected strongly to this interference with their hours of leisure and often resisted arrest or encouraged the vintner to keep his door barred against the parish officials, but such behaviour only sufficed to increase the gravity of their misdemeanour. One who suffered more innocently was the old woman who sold apples on a Sunday, while another who was surprised to find herself in the company of drunkards and loose women was a lady who insisted in sitting in the wrong pew. The churchwardens and sidesmen had taken great trouble over allocating seats in the church and had found it particularly difficult to satisfy the women, who normally sat together, apart from the men, according to their quality. Each had been given a place and their names written down in a book "in orderly fashion," yet in 1634 Mrs. Chambers of the Boroughside, haberdasher's wife, was presented for refusing the seat the churchwarden had allotted her, even going quite fruitlessly to the expense of procuring a key for the pew of her choice! Mrs. Ware of Bankside in 1639 was another good lady anxious to go up higher, and she seems to have made trouble for the wardens by appealing for redress to the bishop to whom the harassed officials wrote: "we assure your lordship that the pew, wherein one Mrs. Ware sits and pleads to be placed, is and always hath been a pew for women of a far better rank and quality than she, and for such whose husbands pay far greater duties than hers and hath always been reserved for some of the chiefest women dwelling on the Boroughside of the said parish, and never any of the Bankside were placed there."

As the thirties drew to a close, a strange amalgam of tranquillity and foreboding, new forces came into play, new opponents harder to deal with than the truculent watermen. On one occasion a parishioner was presented, "for sitting with his hat on in the time of divine service." Was he fumbling, like the Quakers some years later, after the idea of man's equality in the sight of God, that eternal truth of which the refusal to uncover in another's presence came to be a symbol and which was so openly flouted in the Borough's attitude to Bankside? Or did he wish merely to show disrespect to the episcopal church, as man-made and therefore no true church at all? There was a large majority of men of standing, who objected to the King's arbitrary ways and to Laud's innovations and who rejoiced when Charles' difficulties in Scotland forced him to call a parliament and made possible redress. But behind these, as yet barely vocal, were the wilder spirits of the type that congregated so often in Southwark, who desired revolutionary changes in economics and religion alike. How impossible it is to discover how most of them felt who came to worship each week in the old church, and what was in the muddled mind of

George Miller of the Upper Ground who was presented in 1639 for "disturbing the minister, going up into the pulpit whilst the psalm was singing." One thing only was certain: the tranquil years were over and as the troubles of the mid-century gathered about them, the men of St. Saviour's, as of every other parish in the land, found themselves divided against each other, ranged in a puzzled and unhappy hostility against those they had called their friends.

## Note on Sources

The absence of the vestry minutes between 1627 and 1670 leaves a gap only partially filled by the churchwardens' papers dealing with property, visitations, etc., and the returns of the constables and overseers of the poor. Canon Thompson's *The History and Antiquities of the Collegiate church of St. Saviour, Southwark,* contains detailed accounts of those commemorated in the church, *e.g. Andrewes,* pp. 61–80; *Humble,* p. 105–9; *Trehearne,* pp. 118–22; *Harvard,* pp. 122–30; *Beaumont, Fletcher* and *Massinger,* pp. 273–88. See also Aubrey's *Brief Lives* (ed. Oliver Lawson Dick, 1949): for *Andrewes,* p. 6; *Beaumont* and *Fletcher,* p. 21. Andrewes' *Preces Privatae* are printed with his other writings in the eleven volumes of the Library of Anglo-Catholic theology, cf. *The Private Devotions of Lancelot Andrewes,* ed. E. Venables from J. H. Newman's translation (1883). William Austin's works were published under the titles *Devotionis Augustinianae Flamma* (1635) and *Haec Homo* (1637).

# XIV

# INTERREGNUM

THE records of St. Saviour's for 1616, the year that Alderman Humble died and Chaplain Sutton obtained his doctor's degree, contain no reference to the event of most significance which took place in the neighbourhood of the old church in that period of apparent calm. In a house in Southwark a group of men met on a day of prayer and fasting and bound themselves in a solemn covenant, "to walk together in all God's ways and ordinances." They stood with their hands joined as they pledged themselves in fellowship and then chose as their minister Henry Jacob, who had returned from exile in Holland convinced that a dedicated congregation of this kind was the only true basis for a church. In the ensuing years they met in secret, losing Jacob when he went to New England six years later, tracked down by the authorities in 1632 at the house of a brewer's clerk in Blackfriars, re-assembling after a brief imprisonment but weakened by secession as doctrinal differences arose, until at last another Southwark man, Henry Jessey, gave them wise guidance and a measure of stability. They were the first congregational church to survive in England, but after the years of their inception they met mainly across the river and ceased to be an immediate challenge to St. Saviour's.

In Southwark, however, various other conventicles were coming into existence, generally of a more extreme nature, with anabaptist tendencies which made them particularly suspect to those who feared that too great a stress on free grace and the equality of man would lead to the subversion of all ordered society. In 1621, in Deadman's Place, under the very shadow of St. Saviour's, a group of sectaries met, whose minister John Canne was distinguished for his "mightiness" in the Scriptures and his anabaptist beliefs. This group appears to have migrated to Ireland in the thirties, perhaps to escape Bishop Curle's attention, but in

1640 they were again in Deadman's Place and were apprehended by the Marshal and removed in a body to the Clink. Times had changed, however; the Long Parliament was in session and the sectaries after an examination in the House of Lords were reprimanded but allowed to go in peace. Next Sunday two or three interested peers crossed to Bankside and made their way to the Meeting-house, where they observed the sectaries' method of worship and of administering communion and expressed themselves satisfied, giving liberally to the customary collection for the poor.

Other anabaptist assemblies were listed in 1641 and were particularly prevalent in St. Olave's parish with its large proportion of foreigners and craftsmen. One is mentioned in Chequer Alley and early in the year, when the wardens of St. Saviour's made their accustomed rounds, they found some sixty persons met together "to teach and edify one another in Christ." They came submissively enough before Sir John Lenthall, the Marshal, but grew truculent when they were questioned and when they were asked why they did not go quietly to St. Saviour's answered that it was no true church, that bishops they would never obey and the King "only in civil things."

Sectaries of this type formed the left wing of the nonconformists. But there were many solid, middle-class folk, who eschewed revolutionary notions and could not conceive of worshipping elsewhere than at their parish church and who yet felt that certain reforms and emendations would be welcome. Much was amiss in church and state. How far should the powers of the bishops be limited? What jurisdiction had the ecclesiastical courts over the habits and consciences of ordinary men? What was this system of "thorough" that Laud and Strafford had tried to impose? These were the questions that all were asking, and answering in very different ways. There was however a large measure of unanimity, when Parliament met, in the immediate decision to revoke the more extreme of the Star Chamber sentences. Those who had been imprisoned were released amid scenes of great jubilation, and Dr. Bastwick, who had been a captive in Dover Castle since he had stood in the pillory with Burton and Prynne, was brought in triumph to Southwark and escorted thence to his home in London by the excited citizens. It was another of those strange processions that have so often canalised the flow of English history into that narrow space of roadway between St. Olave's and St. Saviour's churches.

What did the vestry men think about it all? In the main they were moderate men, lawyers and merchants, whose instincts of loyalty were balanced by independence of mind and a deeply ingrained sense of their own rights. For example, Sir Edward Bromfield, the rich alderman, was undoubtedly loyal but equally tenacious of his money. In 1640, during the Scottish troubles, the lords of the council summoned a number of wealthy citizens before them and reminded them of certain loans which they had promised. Bromfield denied the offer of £3,700, which he was said to have made, refused an alternative suggestion of £2,000, and stood to an offer of £1,000 to be lent, and only lent, on good security. In the spring of the same year when the mob at Lambeth got out of hand and murdered one of Laud's most hated subordinates, the trained bands were called out in Southwark until the emergency was over. Bromfield supplied his quota of horsemen, but Overman of the Close did not. The latter was, however, excused a heavy assessment on his small Essex estate in recognition of good service recently given to the King. When the Long Parliament first met in November 1640, at the time of Bastwick's release, there was probably at St. Saviour's as elsewhere a large measure of sympathy for what it set out to do. But those among the congregation who were loyal and convinced churchmen soon received their first shock when the Commons, after redressing immediate grievances and impeaching the King's ministers, turned their attention to religion. The specious unity of the early debates vanished forever as the extremists launched an attack, not merely on individual bishops, but on episcopacy as a whole and the entire Anglican way of worship as it had developed under the influence of Andrewes and Laud. In January 1641 it was ordered that all images, altars, crucifixes should be destroyed and the communion table moved out of the chancel. At St. Saviour's, they still knelt in seemly fashion round the new "frame of rails," that the wardens had built to match Lady Clerke's coverings in the tranquil years. One Sunday in May, when feelings had been raised to fever heat by numerous petitions and protestations, seven or eight men pressed into the church and, before the eyes of the scandalised congregation, made a violent attack on the communion rails, breaking and destroying them "in an insolent and tumultuous manner." The men were taken into custody and were examined before a committee of the House of Lords who ordered the wardens to set up new rails and the culprits to pay for them. Within a month however the prisoners were discharged and, as they were all poor men, they were not made to pay. The examination had revealed that some years previously, there had been innovations at St. Saviour's contrary to ancient practice, so the order of the peers laid down that the new rails should be placed "in the same manner as they have been for the space of fifty years past but not as they were for five years last past."

There were similar disturbances at St. Olave's and St. George's, and this irruption of violence stirred and angered those who had learnt to love the ordered beauty of the Anglican liturgy. Among a host of petitions and counter-petitions that emanated from Southwark in these unsettled times, two which protested against the abolition of episcopacy illustrate the growing bitterness of feeling. The first was restrained in tone though it pointed out forcibly the danger of implacable hatred and discord when every man shall be free, "guided by no other rule than the crooked line of his own discretion." The second complained of the "scandalous disorders" that already existed, "some calling the doctrine and discipline of our church cursed, others refusing to read the Book of Common Prayer . . . others behaving themselves most irreverently at those prayers . . . standing without the church till they be done. . . . And our ministers," the petitioners continue, "are, for making conscience to obey the statutes, mocked and abused by base terms in the church and in the streets, nay some have been threatened so that they dare not wear their ministerial garments. . . . And our ancient vestry-men, who were wont to keep their parishes in good order, are contemned and abused by a rude company of young, poor and unworthy fellows." Thirteen knights, fifteen esquires, eighteen divines and three hundred and eighty-two gentlemen, free-holders of Surrey, and others of good account signed this petition and asked for redress in the vain hope that "combustions" might be prevented and they might again meet quietly and comfortably in the churches "to serve God," as they put it, "unanimously and uniformly as God's word doth lead us and the statutes of the kingdom doth enjoin us."

It was not to be. When Parliament re-assembled in the autumn of 1641, the debates on the Grand Remonstrance showed how many had rallied to the King's side when their church had been attacked. But their narrow defeat, after an all-night sitting, ended all hopes of compromise. In January, 1642, the King left London and next month gave his consent to the bill abolishing episcopacy. It was now only a question of months before resort was had to arms and the various propositions and counter-statements of the next six months were rather propaganda than diplomatic exchanges. The royal standard was raised at Nottingham in August, and after the first pitched battle at Edgehill had shown how tragically and evenly the country was divided, Charles advanced within striking-distance of London. As the trained bands marched out to face him at Turnham Green, Southwark became once again the southern defence work of the City. Ramparts were built at the southern approaches to the Borough and at the foot of the bridge fortifications were erected. If they had not already slipped away to join the King, the men of St. Saviour's could do little now but wait upon the event.

In November 1642 Parliament attempted to raise a loan of £30,000 from various London parishes. A note of the amounts received and the names of the contributors still exists in the Record Office and shows that a small contribution came from St. Saviour's. It contributed only £98 odd in contrast to £953 from St. Stephen, Walbrook, £1,300 from St. Stephen, Coleman Street, and the amazing amount of £11,000 from St. Lawrence, Old Jewry. The average contribution was between £200 and £300 and even had their zeal been outstanding, St. Saviour's, with her few wealthy parishioners, could not have expected to be high on the list. But it went deeper than that. The collection was made in church one Wednesday, being a fast-day, and there were few well-known names among the thirty-five contributors, Joseph Collyer and John Humphreys headed the list with £10 and £6 13s. 4d. respectively; the others gave small sums between 5s. and £5. John Hayman, Jonathan Barford, Samuel Warcopp, these were names that would recur in the years ahead; a certain Thomas Harvard gave £1 but Browker, Austin, Marshall, the Bromfields and their friends, these kept silent and aloof. How much they suffered in person and estate in the course of the next eighteen years it would be hard to compute. When the cause of the royalists was defeated some went into exile but many accepted the inevitable, compounding for their estates when necessary by the payment of large fines. Some references of the second William Austin's, in the poems he wrote after the Restoration, serve as a reminder of the financial straits and continuous exactions to which the "malignants" (the royalists) were subjected. He spoke of the "expensive, ridiculous, cursed and bloody changes of a tedious civil war," and referred with feeling to the "great and noble poor," whose lands had been sequestered, to "dowries escheated . . . of such whose husbands stood not for the cause" and to sons whose rights were confiscated because their sires "would not add fuel to the public fires." Yet in spite of such hardships, for the majority, whether victorious or defeated, life went on with its pattern showing a different emphasis but not entirely changed, as ordinary life so persistently does go on in times of crisis or calamity.

The greatest change was within the walls of the churches. As soon as the puritans obtained control in London, Anglican clergy were ejected from their livings in various parts of the City and its suburbs. At St. George's, the incumbent was replaced by Henry Jessey, who continued to minister to his own congregation across the river in the afternoon while preaching in his parish church in the morning, and by his charity and kindliness gained the respect and affection of many who eschewed his politics. In 1643 Benjamin Spencer, the gifted chaplain of the small hospital parish of St. Thomas, was not only ejected but imprisoned on the charge of bowing at the name of Jesus and other "Popish practices." At St. Saviour's, alone of the four Southwark churches, no ejection took place. In 1638, Archer and Morton still ministered; Archer was old and infirm and it is safe to infer that he died before the war was over; Morton was perhaps tactful or sympathetic enough to avoid interference for, though in 1643 the Parliament was driven by the lack of quick success to ally with the Scots binding themselves to establish the Presbyterian system, it was some years before the assembly of divines at Westminster hammered out the details of rule and worship. In the interim, in each individual church the conduct of the services depended very much on the incumbents' own character, and a tactful man could continue undisturbed on lines not very dissimilar to those to which his congregation had hitherto been accustomed.

The war years brought their train of varied hardships. The winter of 1643 was of exceptional severity and the royalist fleet blockaded the mouth of the Thames and kept the coal ships in harbour at Newcastle. The lack of fuel went near to breaking the morale of the home front. In the alleyways of the Clink Liberty and Montague Close the press gangs hovered and the London and the Surrey militias competed for the bodies of Southwark citizens, for once unable to wrest to their advantage the conflicting jurisdictions. Instead of the cheerful bustle of wayfarers along the Borough High Street, there was a sad procession of sick and wounded soldiers making their way to the harassed wards of Thomas's and every now and again the excited movements of troops. But generally the days were drab and anxious, with eager scanning of the newsheets that arrived periodically from Chichester, Windsor, Winchester and as far north as Manchester and York, as the fortunes of the war ebbed to and fro.

It is good to discover that the Grammar School went on steadily. Hezekiah Woodward, the headmaster in 1644, made a list of his books which included five dictionaries and lexicons of various sorts. There was also a regular succession of Bingham scholars, who often came back on the staff as ushers. But the numbers were not great and clever boys from other parishes tended to go over the bridge to St. Paul's or Merchant Taylors so that the hope of rivalling these great contemporaries had already proved illusory. Yet the school remained a possession of which the folk at St. Saviour's were justifiably proud and it was now on the verge of a period of well-being, for in 1648 Nicholas Onger succeeded Woodward and was "very well approved for his way of teaching and diligence therein."

Winchester House was less fortunate in its fate. Early in 1643 it was put into use as a prison and an "orthodox and godly minister" was appointed to have a care of the spiritual needs of a flock that must have been none too easy to handle. At one stage it included Kenelm Digby, the cultured and eccentric bibliophile and scholar. Digby's chief solace, while under restraint, was the study of experimental science with particular reference to the manufacture of artificial stones. At the end of the war another resident in Winchester House, though not under durance, was John Lilburne with his impecunious family. Free-born John, so it was said, would quarrel with himself if there were no one else to fight, and he enunciated more fervently with every year his distrust of every government, Royalist, Parliamentary and in due course Cromwellian, which invaded individual liberty or transgressed, on the grounds of emergency, the sanctities of the Common Law. The watermen who still gossiped on Bankside, bemoaning their lack of custom now the gentry no longer came on pleasure-bent across the river and reacting against the stringent enforcement of a puritan code of conduct, which made them long for the good old days of the wardens' Sunday rounds, imbibed increasingly the shibboleths of Lilburne's tracts and of the rank and file of Cromwell's army. The moderate politics of the Parliamentary leaders, combined as it was with Presbyterian zeal, began to offend them no less than the malignants' loyalty to kings and bishops so that at length even Parliament assumed the stature of tyrants to those who boldly declared that power lay with the people.

In 1645 the army was thoroughly overhauled and remodelled and under the command of Fairfax and Cromwell won a decisive victory at Naseby. In May 1646 the King surrendered to the Scots and the war was virtually over. Nobody quite knew what happened next and there was tension no less than triumph evident in the victors' ranks. At this juncture, an incident which illustrated the new antagonisms occurred at St. Saviour's. Thomas Overman's young wife, whom he had married in 1641, fell into a decline and died, affected perhaps by the rigours of the war years. Her mother and husband mourned together the loss of one whom all had loved for her sweet temper and brave acceptance of the approach of death. It was natural that Overman should turn to his old friend Benjamin Spencer, who was living at Bromley, and should invite him to come over to preach the funeral sermon. The Presbyterian system was now established and Overman was apparently a respected and prominent citizen who had accepted the recent changes, and before inviting Spencer he had asked permission of "the reverend synod" and of "all those that were interested in the church." Spencer agreed to come and the funeral took place. But as the cortège made its way from the Close to the churchyard it was confronted by a crowd of hooligans who barred its progress and duly produced a warrant forbidding the sermon. Argument proved vain; it was the order of the magistrate against the permission of the church authorities, and it is significant that the former prevailed. The friends who had gathered to do honour to the young dead turned away in silence: one of their number, a "commander," "looked with a brave countenance upon the guilty faces of the funeral disturbers," but they answered him "with mocking faces . . . by pulling one eyebrow up and the other down or else turning their back." Fortunately there was no brawl; Overman in his grief had no heart to protest and even when the sermon was printed and he wrote a foreword and sent it to his friends, he contented himself with the prayer: "But God forgive them (I do) this unseasonable malice to my dearest spousesse." Spencer declared, "the rumour of soldiers raised to support me and malignants gathered together to hear me was but a ridiculous pretence . . .", but there is seldom smoke without fire, and the temporary coming together, in a friend's hour of sorrow, of men of royalist sympathies and officers of the parliamentary army foreshadowed that very combination of moderates which fourteen years later would bring about the Restoration.

The radical faction which unfeelingly disturbed the funeral at St. Saviour's was numerous and resolute in the Borough as a whole. In the summer of 1647 the army and the Presbyterians, who dominated Parliament and the City, came near to open conflict. Southwark seized the occasion to petition the council for a control of its own militia and as a matter of course ranged itself against the City. When the army decided to advance, a contingent marched on the Borough, under the command of Rainsborough, a sailor who had turned soldier to fight for the millenium. He arrived at two o'clock in the morning to find himself welcome as a comrade in arms by those who manned the ramparts while friendly sympathisers thronged about his men and shook them by the hand. Later when he had joined forces with Fairfax, there was an ordered but triumphant march from Westminster through London, "with no disrespective word to anyone," and thence over London Bridge to Croydon, Cromwell riding at the head of the cavalry and Fairfax, who had recently been ill, driving in a coach with his wife and Mrs. Cromwell.

Having thus shewn their mastery in no uncertain way the army withdrew. Many regiments were quartered in the neighbourhood of Putney, and there in the old church that guarded the passage of the Thames they argued out as best they could the meaning of democracy, applauded Rainsborough's plea that the "poorest He" had a life to live as well as the "richest He" and heard with some dubiety Ireton's reply that only men of property who had a pledge in the country should have a share in its control. But on one great issue, Ireton and Rainsborough agreed, that beyond the political and economic liberties over which they disputed there was a deeper liberty, "to know, to utter and to argue freely according to conscience," and in the years ahead after many reverses, that one great treasure was rescued from the ruin of a thousand illusions.

The leading figures at St. Saviour's in 1647 belonged to the minority party in Southwark, that of the Presbyterians who combined a devotion to the ideals of civil liberty with a rigorous attitude in religion, enforcing obedience in matters of faith and worship as firmly as any episcopalian. In December 1647, for example, the two ministers at St. Saviour's, Stephen Watkins and John Crodacott, signed a statement issued by the puritan clergy under the cumbrous but revealing title, "A testimony to the truth of Jesus Christ and to our solemn League and Covenant and also against the errors, heresies and blasphemies of these times and the toleration of them." The Westminster Assembly had had an uphill task in fulfilling their obligations to the Scots. They had drawn up a directory of worship which had been issued early in 1645 after which date the use of the Prayer Book was forbidden. A confession of faith, including a longer and shorter catechism, was also issued, and in June 1646, the Commons had ordered the city of London to try out the over-elaborate system of church government which the Assembly had promulgated. But the desire for freedom which the army agents so fearlessly expressed at Putney was no monopoly of one party; Chillingworth, Jeremy Taylor, Robert Owen, men of vision in every section of the sundered church felt the same need and hope, and though most moderate men in 1647 were alarmed at the excesses of the myriad sects, few envisaged with equanimity a rigorous control by "new presbyters" who were no better than "old priests writ large". The

Presbyterian experiment, only tried out effectively in London and Lancashire, failed through the inertia and uneasiness of the rank and file, and in the testimony Watkins and Crodacott signed, the clergy already lamented: "England's general backwardness to embrace, yea forwardness to oppose, the Presbyterial form of church government."

None the less until 1660, this was the form of worship and of ecclesiastical organisation accepted at St. Saviour's. Every church chose a certain number of elders, not so different from the wardens of other days, and these combined with the representatives of neighbouring churches to form the classis. The classes in turn were grouped into provincial assemblies, with a national synod over all. The City and Southwark were divided into twelve classes, of which the tenth included St. Saviour's, the other Southwark churches and the parishes of Rotherhithe, Bermondsey and Newington. The ministers and elders of each classis were supposed to meet fortnightly to deal with such matters as the appointment of clergy or the exclusion of ignorant and scandalous persons from Holy Communion. Such questions of spiritual discipline were always a potential cause of heated feelings, and one can imagine that the very independent parishioners of Saviour's, George's and Olave's had little mind to submit them to the decision of strangers. Throughout the Interregnum, however, the tenth classis continued to function, better organised than many and sending representatives regularly to the provincial assembly. At that body's final meeting in 1660, when only sixteen out of a possible one hundred and eight persons attended, one minister and two elders came from the tenth classis.

In spite of the rigidity and intolerant temper, which doomed the experiment to failure, there was much that was admirable in a system that gave responsibility to leading laymen and a great deal of devoted and honest service was given by those who strove in these vibrant years to rise to the occasion. It is not without interest to note the names of those appointed by the tenth classis at its inception, to judge the fitness of candidates for vacant cures. These "triers" in 1646 were Thomas Gataker of Rotherhithe, Jeremy Whittaker of Bermondsey and Mr. Samuel Bolton of Mary Overie's: even to a puritan the old name slipped easily off the pen! Daniel Santon (or Sawton) of Mary Overie with three others from Olave's and one from George's (the Popish "saint" was omitted from the title!) were added as assistants in the same year, and in 1648 Mr. Collins joined them, the new clerk describing him more accurately as of "Saviour's."

Except for the veto on the Prayer Book, there was little attempt to interfere with doctrinal teaching. In 1648 however the provincial assembly ordered that children and such persons as were not yet communicants should be catechised on Sunday afternoons before the sermon, use being made of the shorter catechism. Thus it came about that Mary Overie's ancient walls, which had echoed for centuries to the psalms the canons sung and to the balanced beauty of Cranmer's liturgy, now for a while housed other earnest seekers who answered the catechists' query, "What is the chief end of man?" with the challenging affirmation, "To glorify God and enjoy Him for ever."

Of the two ministers, a little is known. Watkins had graduated from Trinity College, Cambridge, in 1637 and was rector of Staplehurst in the weald of Kent in the year that Naseby was fought. Thence he came to St. Saviour's, by way of East Grinstead where he was vicar in February 1646. Crodacott, early in '46, was at Lanteglos in Cornwall; he was the younger man and had only graduated from Magdalen College, Oxford, in the previous year; apparently he was the preacher of the two, for, while at Southwark, he also preached at St. Stephen's in the City, "in the afternoon on the Lord's Day and on Thursdays many years." For upward of thirteen years throughout the Interregnum these two continued their ministry, and when this is compared with the frequent and acrimonious changes in many London churches it would seem that once again those who appointed St. Saviour's chaplains had been either fortunate or wise. Of Crodacott one knows little beyond his powers as a preacher. Watkins was a married man with a son John, who was later apprenticed, and four daughters, Hester, Hannah, Susannah and Dorothy, some of whom must have grown out of infancy beneath the shadow of St. Saviour's. He was evidently a man of strong convictions and some administrative ability; he signed the Vindication of 1649, thereby associating himself with those who approved the King's execution, and in 1651 he was appointed a member of a standing committee of the provincial assembly that took charge of those congregations which did not belong to any effective classis.

But in the pastoral duties of a priest, how little after all do politics count. There is a brass tablet in the church to little Susannah Barford, who died in 1652. "The nonesuch of the world" they called the child of ten, who had never learnt to laugh:

> This world to her was but a tragic play,
> She came and saw it, dislik't and pass'd away.

It mattered more than his politics whether Stephen Watkins could bring solace to her broken-hearted parents. Her father had been among those who gave so hopefully to the loan in 1642, but happiness had eluded him. If Watkins and Crodacott ministered well and truly during those thirteen years, bringing to all alike the comfort of the Cross and shewing in their own persons the fruits of Christian living, they would earn the love and respect of their congregation, as Jessey and Wadsworth did at St. George's and Newington and as Nicholas Morton and old James Archer had done in the days gone by. If not, neither classis nor assembly could assist them.

After the sorry interlude of the second civil war the country as a whole accepted an uneasy peace. The arbitrament of arms could not give them their prime necessity, a settled government, and the execution of the King which had seemed at the moment to end all royalist hopes made their eventual triumph inevitable. All the army's zeal for freedom, Cromwell's desire for an ordered rule, the Saints' visions of Utopia foundered on the fact of this initial injustice. Yet for a while hope and vigour persisted, in particular in the years when Cromwell's acceptance of the office of Protector put one in charge who could win the respect of Europe and who increasingly at home aimed to heal rather than destroy.

In Southwark the signs of vigour were not lacking, though all were not to the good. Few would quarrel with the council of state's decision to put down the bear-baiting, but many were sickened by the barbarous way in which the soldiers carried out the order, shooting the bears and wringing the necks of the fighting cocks. It was an ugly end to Philip Henslowe's Hope, which was now pulled down. Yet the destruction of the theatres on Bankside—for the Globe had gone as early as 1644—was at least an integral part of the effort to raise the standards of decency and purity of living. There were other far-reaching changes, less consciously fostered, which set the tone for the Borough's future development and are difficult to forgive. With the establishment of the Commonwealth, the crown and church lands passed into the hands of the state, from the great palaces of the Mint and Winchester House to the King's barge-house, falling into decay, the royal barge standing within in melancholy idleness. Most of what was pleasant in the Clink Liberty derived from the possessions of the King and the Bishop. Though Andrewes' successors ceased to live at Winchester House, the park had remained in the years before the war a lovely enclosure amid the encroaching streets, while west of it stretched the royal Pyke Gardens with their asparagus beds and Pimlico Path where the lads and lasses of St. Saviour's paraded in their new spring finery.

In the Interregnum all this ended. A large portion of the confiscated lands including Winchester House and the park was bought by Thomas Walker of Camberwell for a total sum of over £8,000. Walker, originally a petticoat-maker in Cannon St., made the purchase as a business speculation. He had no intention of living in the neighbourhood, learning to love and adorn his new estates as General Lambert did at Wimbledon. He at once set about developing the site, leasing out the house in tenements and cutting Stoney Street across the park to link up Clink Street with Deadman's Place. Slowly and ruthlessly as the area was built up the beauty of the park vanished for ever. Within a year or two of Walker's purchase the Browker of the day sold Paris Garden to a London grocer, called William Angell. His aim, like Walker's, was that of development and he began by selling the disreputable manor house to a woollen draper, whose widow occupied it on his death and used the spacious ground for stretching and bleaching cloth. Better that, than the immoralities of Holland's leaguer; better Walker's new roads, than the gambling and brawling of the bear-pits. There was much clearing up to be done and there was a century immediately ahead when Southwark would be a pleasant place in which to live: there were as yet no qualms of conscience, no inkling of the more distant future, but none the less it was during these Interregnum years that for good or ill the activities

of Thomas Walker and William Angell laid the foundations of the
unsightly Southwark of to-day.

When the bear-pits were destroyed, two of those instructed to
take action were Thomas Pride, as High Sheriff of Surrey, and
Samuel Hyland the magistrate, both well-known names during
the Interregnum. When Cromwell forcibly dissolved the Rump in
1652, before he became Protector, he summoned a parliament
nominated by the churches to set the country to rights, unable to
believe that good men did not necessarily agree and were not
always wise. Samuel Hyland, the Southwark J.P., was one of the
two members nominated by Surrey, and in the debates of what
came to be known as Barebones parliament, he ranged himself
with the intransigents who urged the abolition of tithes and other
impracticable reforms. Hyland was clearly one of the fanatics and
his influence in Southwark was considerable. He was the member
for Southwark in both of Cromwell's parliaments. In 1654, in the
hope of a settled government, Cromwell tried to secure the
Presbyterians' support and there was consequently a close contest
in the Borough, although Hyland was still elected. The defeated
candidates, Colonel John Hardwick and Peter Lannoy petitioned
against the result. They declared that the bailiff was the father of
Hyland's colleague, Robert Warcopp, and that he called for a poll
although the shout in the petitioners' favour was far greater than
that for their opponents. He then polled his own party first and
many were later prevented from voting, "the day being far spent
and a great rain falling which enforced persons of quality to withdraw to neighbours' houses." Warcopp was accused of atheism,
tippling, gaming and bribery and Hyland of "condoning the fines
of Sabbath breakers, favouring levellers . . . and granting warrants
to carriers to travel on days of humiliation". Moreover he did not
speak the truth and had seduced the electors by a "glozing speech
of self-praise." Hyland and his fellow-candidate were not unseated
but the petition shows again a fairly equal division of parties, with
the leading men of St. Saviour's among the defeated in uneasy
alliance with the government.

One duty Hyland performed that brought him in touch, in a
more pleasant capacity, with a number of people. Cromwell
decreed that marriages were civil contracts and that the ceremony
should therefore be performed not by the minister but by the

magistrate. Samuel Hyland's name occurs frequently in this connection in St. Saviour's records, though it is worth noting that as
early as 1655 one couple was married by the minister, a number
increased to three in the following year and six in 1657. From then
until 1660 the clergy officiated as frequently as Hyland, for when
it came to the point even the Protector's daughter wished her
union to be blessed by a minister of the Church.

Colonel Pride, the Sheriff, Hyland's colleague in maintaining
order, was a man of low birth who according to some had begun
his career as a brewer's drayman in this very town, and though he
might be respected in the army, as a man of determined character
and conviction who dared to match his actions to the challenge
of the hour, to the "men of quality" growing old in an unfriendly
world this petty autocrat from the Borough's byways must have
been as salt in their wounds, an insult barely to be endured. Yet
rather surprisingly some managed to prosper and Sir Edward
Bromfield apparently was still doing well in soap. In 1653 there
was a petition of soap-boilers and freeborn people of England
against the vexed question of the soap monopoly. They specifically mentioned Bromfield's company, and declared that they had
suffered from the patentees "riotously and barbarously breaking
into our houses and warehouses and seizing and destroying our
soap materials." This no doubt referred to events before the war
but they had, they said, received no redress from Parliament and in
various law-suits lasting over thirteen years, Bromfield and his
friends had obtained twelve special verdicts through the "mightiness of their purses." In 1658 Bromfield died and was buried in
St. Saviour's, the first of three Lord Mayors who were buried
in the church during the seventeenth century.

Two things perhaps may be said with a measure of certainty,
though one knows much less than one would like of the ordinary
lives of folk during these years of political and religious upheaval.
On the surface, for the large majority, life went on as before; and
the country was sufficiently prosperous for those who had come
out on top, and some who compounded, to build, to found
families, to publish books of singing games or write the first
English opera. But to one change, some could never be reconciled. Only at a risk, in one's own home, could the Prayer Book
be read in secret and only very occasionally could the sacraments

be administered according to the Anglican rite. Those who remained politically docile were seldom molested; but they were never secure. And meanwhile in private houses up and down the country, men who had once been bishops taught the children of those who had died at Marston Moor and Naseby, the doctrine and the liturgy of the church for which they had suffered.

When Cromwell died and after eighteen months of insecurity Charles II came into his own again, there was a profound joy that had nothing to do with soap or tenements in the heart of many who watched this gayest of all processions wend its way from Dover to Whitehall. To Austin and the younger Bromfields, Richard How, John Marshall, with rather more uncertainty to Overman and the Newcomens, in 1660 the good old days had returned. The confusion, the ugliness, the devastating problems of the centuries ahead were hid from them. They were content that, at last, they could worship once more in the old way in the old church, that the bells should call them once again to matins and evensong, that the vestry should meet as of old and toast "Old Moll" and the wardens should owe no duty to classis and assembly. They proudly erected the King's Arms once again and underneath they wrote: "Fear God, honour the King. Meddle not with those that are given to change"; then, remembering the compositions and the inconsistencies of the past twenty years, they continued in contrite mood: "Although you are forgiven by an earthly king know ye that hereafter you must come to judgment. Repent from the evil of your ways and sin no more unless worse befall you." And so they ended, setting out optimistically on the new chapter that was beginning in church and state: "God bless King Charles II and send him long to reign."

## Note on Sources

See the *Lords Journals* for 1641, for the disturbances at the Southwark churches. There are occasional references in the *Calendar of Domestic State Papers*, and a host of contemporary tracts and leaflets, which illustrate the prevailing factiousness of the period and the painful gestation of many new ideas. Benjamin Spencer's sermon with Thomas Overman's foreword were printed in 1646 under the title *Memoriale Sacrum* [Brit. Mus. reference *C.54 aa 1 (3)*]. For the rise of dissent, see W. K. Jordan, *History of Toleration in England 1603–40* (1930); and for the Church of the Interregnum, W. A. Shaw, *History of the English Church, 1640–1660* (1900); W. Wilson, *History and Antiquities of Dissenting Churches . . . in London* (1808–14); and for Watkins and Crodacott, A. G. Matthews: *Calamy Revised*, pp. 143 and 513. For Walker's purchase of Winchester House see the *Survey of London: Bankside*, pp. 48–9, and *re* Paris Garden, *ibid.*, pp. 98–9.

# XV

## THE LATER STUARTS

"NO more change," cried William Austin the younger, writing adulatory verse to the King and the Duke of Albemarle; "no more change," echoed John Bromfield, knighted in 1661 and wishing his father had lived to see the day; "no more change," Sir Richard How agreed, M.P. for Southwark and an Alderman of the City of London.

But there could be no putting back the clock. Changes there were in plenty, in things spiritual and material. During the Interregnum the face of Southwark had changed and theories and ideas had flourished in turbulent adolescence that could not now be banished by wishful thinking. For one thing dissent had come to stay, carrying yet a stage further the unhappy breach in the church's unity that the Reformation had begun. Bankside, no longer the centre of the show world, was now the haunt of the sectaries and, when times became easier, the site of the first nonconformist chapels. Though the bear-pit was reopened near to the old spot and various spectacles alternated with the battles of bear and dog, tastes gradually changed and the final reference to the sport dates from 1682. The home of the legitimate drama passed to Covent Garden and Drury Lane, and in due time Vauxhall and Ranelagh were to take the place of Paris Garden. Folk still came to Southwark when they wanted amusement, often of a questionable kind, as Pepys visited the Bear tavern or more innocently Southwark Fair, and until the privileges of sanctuary were abolished undesirables still haunted the Close and the Clink Liberty, but now they were more likely to be political malcontents than penurious players, sufficient of the old faction surviving to give Southwark a bad name with government agents who reported once that "an honest constable was hardly to be had."

After the Restoration Winchester House was not reoccupied as an episcopal residence. No longer was St. Saviour's to have the strength and comfort of their father in God as a good neighbour just across the way, and not till the creation of the Southwark diocese fifty years ago was the close relationship between the old church and its bishop to be happily restored. In 1662, John Morley succeeded the aged Brian Duppa in the see of Winchester and finding that the damage done by Walker was too great to be remedied he obtained an act of parliament granting him permission to lease out the Southwark property for building purposes, at the same time that he bought land in Chelsea for a new town house. He did not entirely forget Southwark, this river-side urban community, so different in character and potentialities from every other part of his diocese. He allotted the rents of certain of the new tenements in the Park to provide almshouses and gave £100 to buy coal annually for the benefit of poor housekeepers "in our parish of St. Saviour Southwark in the depth and hardness of the winter season." But one wishes he had lived at Winchester House and gone in and out of the neighbouring church as his predecessors used to do. The story loses something of its *panache* when both the prelates and the players have departed.

Bishop Morley had been one of the most attractive of the Caroline divines, a member of that group of fine spirits who met at Falkland's home on the edge of the Cotswolds in the days before the wars. Though a moderate in politics, he was stubbornly loyal when the crisis came, and after 1648 had proved himself a trusted friend and pastor to the frustrated band of exiles in Bruges and Brussels and Paris. To Hyde, another of Falkland's friends who returned in 1660 as Lord Clarendon and Chancellor of England, Morley always remained "the best man alive." To the end of his long life he was vigorous in mind and body, rising early, living temperately, generous with the wealth his changed fortunes brought him, so that Charles II averred that even Winchester would not make him rich, and exercising the Christian privilege of hospitality so that Isaac Walton and Thomas Ken counted him their friend and benefactor.

Enlightened though he was, Bishop Morley's attitude to dissent was courteous but adamant. He would not accept the ideal of comprehension which the best of the Presbyterians, men of Baxter's mould, so earnestly envisaged after 1660. The first ecclesiastical pronouncement of the Crown was in tune with such a hope for, if there were no sequestered clergy still alive to claim readmission to their former cures, it allowed the Commonwealth ministers to retain their livings unless their extreme theological or political views made them dangerous. Watkins' signature of the Vindication placed him in the latter category and early in 1661 he left Southwark and with his growing family moved to Lee, where he earned his living as a school master till his death about 1674. Crodacott stayed a little longer though he was in difficulties even before Watkins left. As the first Christmas approached since the Restoration, the Lord Mayor issued an order that it should be kept as a holiday in the good old way but Crodacott, it was said, concealed the order, "and consequently several people had opened their shops and tumults had been caused in the streets." Both Crodacott and Watkins, on this count or another, were summoned to appear for seditious conclusions against the doctrines and discipline of the Church of England, but the case was referred to the Surrey Justices and the matter appears to have lapsed. Crodacott remained at St. Saviour's until St. Bartholomew's day in 1662. On that date those clergy who could not accept the Prayer Book as revised in the previous year were ejected from their pulpits. Episcopacy had been restored and the full sacramental faith triumphantly proclaimed, but it took twenty years of renewed bitterness and suffering to make men realise that toleration was the only alternative to comprehension, and three centuries and more before toleration was enriched by understanding.

Crodacott went to live in Montague Close, which was described next year as a house "with many ways to go out above and below." Some of his adherents in the congregation may still have come to him for spiritual guidance; others may have joined the large body of Presbyterians who now met for worship secretly in Globe Alley. In 1669 when the penal laws were temporarily relaxed, the Archbishop attempted to ascertain what conventicles were in existence and those reported in St. Saviour's parish included one in Montague Close, composed of about one hundred Presbyterians "for the most part tradesmen," directed by "several non-conformist ministers", as well as a mixed company of Presbyterians and Independents in Globe Alley in "two large meeting houses built on purpose." The latter were about six hundred in number with ministers of repute in John Chester and Thomas Wadsworth. There were two distinct congregations here, Wadsworth's in Deadman's Place and Chester's in Globe Alley, both of which received licenses in 1672. The little community in Montague Close had by then either dispersed or joined one or other of the larger congregations.

In 1669 there were still various Anabaptists and Fifth monarchy men meeting in private houses; one group which was described as "far gone in enthusiasm" met in the house of one Bloxsom a tailor at St. Mary's Dock. It obtained a licence in 1672, when Barnabas Bloxsom's address was given as Winchester Yard, and continued for about a hundred years, still rather frowned upon by the other Baptist churches as composed of people who could not settle elsewhere. The Globe Alley chapel also continued, respected and respectable, till it broke up with the influx of Arian opinion in the mid-18th century. The present Pilgrim Church of Gt. Dover St. claims, with justifiable pride, its direct descent from the congregation in Deadman's Place, nor should one fail to pay tribute to the steadfastness of the Roman Catholics, who suffered so many vicissitudes during the latter half of the seventeenth century but through them all continued loyal to their ancient faith. It is not easy to write with equanimity of these dissensions. In medieval days the church was (among much else) the symbol of community. Henceforward when the old bells of St. Mary Overie's rang the people to prayer, a section—an increasingly large section—remained without.

At St. Saviour's, the former régime was restored after Crodacott's departure though the minute books are not available again till 1670, when Dr. Martin and William Hoare were chaplains. When in 1665 the last catastrophic outbreak of plague swept through London and Southwark we do not know how St. Saviour's fared, though there is nothing to support Defoe's accusation that the Anglican clergy deserted their flocks. The Rector of St. George's died in harness, and the registers of St. Saviour's at least bear witness that burials were continued in a seemly fashion and that the children were baptised, who came so inopportunely into the world during that hot and agonising summer.

The Borough escaped the fire of 1666 but the influx of homeless persons from London added to its problems of town-planning. There was all the more reason to push ahead with the building of the new church for which John Marshall had left money over thirty years before. It was true that St. Saviour's was large and well provided with seating accommodation in the way of pews and galleries, but there were many that complained that it was not a comfortable church, and it was so built that all the parishioners could not "come near enough to hear with profit and therefore many, especially in winter, went to other churches." That was the position in 1644, when a section petitioned for the new church to be built; twenty years later there was still more reason to go ahead for, as Strype put it when he edited Stowe's Survey, "the inhabitants on this west part of Southwark bordering on the Thames were multiplied considerably, consisting of wood-mongers, timber-merchants, ship-wrights, bargemen and such whose living depended on the river. And being a good distance from St. Mary Overie's Church, it was a seasonable and pious act to provide a nearer place for this people to meet together for divine worship." In 1663 only one of Marshall's executors was alive, so a new trust was created, headed by Edward Bromfield, Sir John's heir, and Richard How and including to one's surprise Samuel Hyland, who had evidently managed to ride the storm. William Angell offered them a site on his Paris Garden estate if they would build the new church there and, on the assumption that one does not look a gift horse in the mouth, the trustees accepted his offer disregarding the marshy nature of the ground.

The wardens and vestry-men of St. Saviour's were reluctant in the matter, in part because it meant to them a considerable loss of tithe and because the disruption of a parish is always a painful process. The new church would rob them not only of the ship-wrights and bargemen that lived beyond the Falcon but also of the Austins and Marshalls and Alderman How. Their opposition delayed matters for some time, but at long last in 1671 Christ Church was built with John Marshall's legacy and consecrated in December by the Bishop of Rochester. For fifty years it prospered, but in 1738 it was found to be already "in a very decaying condition," on account of the inadequate drainage. At that date it had to be entirely rebuilt. To-day it stands a shell, gutted by incendiaries in 1941, but within the chancel the services of the church continue and plans for its rebuilding are in hand.

In 1671 an Act of Parliament authorised the creation of Christ Church parish and went carefully into the financial position of both churches. It was agreed that St. Saviour's "was very great and spacious and so very chargeable to be maintained in due reparations," and in order to give the wardens sufficient money to bear this expense and to pay the salaries of chaplains and schoolmaster they were authorised to levy on the Tuesday or Wednesday of Easter week an annual rate, not exceeding £350. As the salaries now amounted to £230 and there were certain administrative expenses, the wardens were thus left with a bare £100 for repairs. This proved quite insufficient and during the next two centuries a constant process went on whereby the maximum amount of the rate which might be levied was periodically increased without ever catching up with the growing expenditure. The draughty, beautiful, impracticable parish church became with every generation more of a "white elephant" and to meet their liabilities the wardens had either to impose a higher rate than they were legally entitled to do or expend upon the fabric of the church rents and money given them for charitable purposes.

Their immediate difficulties were not lessened by a disastrous fire which devastated the Borough just ten years after the conflagration in London. It began in the cellar of an oil shop in the High Street. In the early hours of the morning some passers-by, who had been gathering herbs and were on their way to market, noticed a light within the sleeping house but took no action. Soon afterwards, "letter carriers, going according to their custom early to the post office," saw the fire in the cellar, but before they had succeeded in breaking down the door the flames had reached the oil and the rest was chaos. Soon the whole High Street was on fire and as the flames devoured in turn the Talbot and the George, the White Hart and the whole of the meal market, men's eyes began to turn with anxious gaze to the old church and the hospital. Whatever else went, if humanly possible St. Mary Overie's and St. Thomas's must be saved.

The City magistrates had hurried over the bridge and tried to allay the panic by enlisting the help of the onlookers in fighting the flames. The trickle from the fire engines was ludicrously inadequate, so recourse was had to gunpowder and the Lord Mayor gave order for the demolition of the old court house and the Compter, acting so precipitately that "several unwary people that could not be got out of the way" were killed in the explosion. The action saved the narrow streets that lay behind the Compter and for a while lessened the threat to the church. But on the eastern side of the street the fire steadily advanced, until it came within a few yards of the porch of St. Thomas's. Though it seemed incredible to the weary fire-fighters, it was still only midday when, at this critical moment, the wind veered slightly and the flames were halted. The hospital was saved! But the crisis was not yet over. Throughout the rest of the long day desultory fires broke out in the lower part of the High Street, the Grammar School in Green Dragon Court was burnt, the roof of the bishop's chapel caught alight at the church's easternmost end and the flames crept on and threatened St. Saviour's on the northern side. There was a last hurried demolition which damaged some of the houses in Montague Close and shattered many of the windows in the church. It was nightfall before the last flames subsided and the magistrates could return to the City and to bed. But few slept that night in Southwark as they looked out on the rubble of the old court house and the smouldering ruins of some five hundred homes. The church still stood, surviving this crisis, as so many before and after, its strong tower rising in the midst of desolation. The men to whose care it was committed and who had fought so hard to save it, looked at it with fresh eyes, with a more lively sense of its beauty and their responsibility, as they set about repairing the windows and the wall which the blast had weakened and the bishop's chapel where Lancelot Andrewes lay.

The years immediately succeeding the fire were brimful of rebuilding problems. In renewing the various leases, the wardens took care that no encroachments were made on church "lights, gutters and water courses" and strongly recommended the use of brick. In the Borough, a court of record was set up by the Lord Mayor to consider conflicting claims without the delays of the ordinary processes of law. Among its members were more than one of St. Saviour's congregation. Sir Richard How of Christ Church and John Applebee were prominent and it may perhaps be taken as a tribute to their experience in the vestries that the court of record worked so smoothly that there were no appeals from any of its decisions. Rebuilding went on apace and in the High Street new taverns rose under the former signs, and the old George of to-day, that treasured link with the past, was the new George Inn that was built after the fire. The Grammar School was rebuilt "in a comely and substantial style," on the southern side of the churchyard as before, on what was still a fair and spacious stretch of ground.

Though the minutes are extant after 1670 to record their names and though they did such yeoman service for church and borough, there are no outstanding figures among the men of St. Saviour's during the Restoration years. There is a "neat memorial tablet" in the south choir aisle to James Shaw, a man of property and owner of Moulstrand dock, who was warden of the Great Account in 1670 and died early next year. His widow gave the church a velvet pall and mourning gowns in his memory and lived on herself till 1693, spanning in the course of her eighty-four years the whole tragic gamut of the Stuarts in England. There was only one daughter, who married William Overman of the Close and retained the name of Alice Shaw Overman. The "neat memorial tablet" tells us less than nothing of what sort of people they were. More revealing is another of the church's monuments to one who died soon after Mr. Shaw—the quack doctor, Lionel Lockyer. He claimed that his pills were distilled from the rays of the sun and would keep people in good health in fogs and "the contagious air." Was he on the track of the modern vitamin tablet? His man of business lived in Southwark and asked leave to set up the memorial, extolling alike his employer's virtues and his pills, but posterity perhaps unfairly has been content to write him down a charlatan.

No stone marks the spot where Elizabeth Newcomen lies, who died a year or two later in 1675 and left her money for clothing boys and girls and teaching them "to read and write and cast accounts." At one time of her life, according to tradition, she had lived in Bowling Green Alley and "vended milk," and there perhaps it was that she first made friends with the children of the Borough, whose need and whose ignorance touched her motherly heart. She married a rich mercer but she never had any children of her own and when her husband died and left her possessed of property in Axe and Bottle Yard and in the High Street, she had more than enough for her needs and to lavish on Thomas Lant, her only nephew. He was her dead brother's son and a ward of Sir Edward Bromfield's; when his aunt died he was fifteen years old and it must have grieved her not to see him settled in life. At least she could provide for him in her will.

Dear Mrs. Newcomen, left a widow with little to do except to consider the disposal of the fortune she could not spend, one imagines her making her will shortly before she died and taking great pains and pleasure over the process. One sees her faithfully tended by her serving woman, Elizabeth Briskett, who settled her comfortably in her wicker chair and arranged her pillow for her so often and so lovingly that the old lady left her not only an annuity and £100 in ready cash, her rings and her bedding, her silver and her clothes, but the wicker chair and the pillow in remembrance. The remainder of her fortune she left to the wardens of St. Saviour's, to be held in trust for the use of Thomas Lant and his eldest child if he should have one. When they too died and needed her money no more the rents of those houses, that would not grow less in value, should go to provide suits of linen and wool for a number of boys and girls, of whom two-thirds should come from the Borough where she lived and a third from the Clink for charity's sake. When they had been taught "to read and write and cast accounts," the boys should be apprenticed "at five pounds apiece at the age of fourteen years," and there would also be £5 for the usher of the Grammar School, "for his better encouragement to teach such boys as shall go thither from my intended school."

One day, Briskett would die, too, and then that money also would be available. Mrs. Newcomen decided very properly that it should be used to help poor women, twenty of whom should be given each year a petticoat and a waistcoat and twenty shillings for headgear, for she had not forgotten how all women like new hats. And then as she thought back over the years she remembered Stephen Watkins and his young family in the distant days that now it was the fashion to condemn, which had not seemed so different in the joys and trials of daily living, and taking up her pen again to complete her will she left to Susan Watkins, "daughter of Stephen Watkins of Lee, schoolmaster deceased," her two strings of pearls and her pendant pearl.

Mrs. Newcomen was a business woman and everything was clearly worked out. A small sum was set aside to pay the rent collector and each year on her birthday—for the old lady loved parties as well as children and new hats—the wardens were to spend £5 on a dinner, "the women to be present one year and the boys and girls with their teachers the other year." Elizabeth Briskett must have died soon after her mistress for twenty poor women received the promised gowns in 1680, and a poor dumb boy (Richard Harris) was also clothed, but it would of necessity be some years before the school could be started. The wardens ordered a decent stone to be laid upon Mrs. Newcomen's grave, as "a good benefactor to the poor of the parish," but it has long since vanished and a later memorial window was destroyed in the second world war. In the church to-day a nineteenth-century tablet commemorates the name of one whose true memorial is the school in Newcomen Street, at the corner of that same Bowling Green Alley where once she lived.

Dorothy Applebee, the other woman of this period whose name ranks high in the annals of St. Saviour's, was the wife of a brewer of Deadman's Place, the owner of the Queen's Head and a prominent figure, as has been seen, in the vestry and the Borough. His wife possessed not only wealth but charity and good taste, and in 1680 when her husband died she presented to the church in his memory the glorious candelabrum that still hangs beneath the massive tower at the entrance to the chancel. On festive occasions when all its candles are lit, it delights the eye and fills the heart with gratitude for this brewer's wife of three centuries ago who knew beauty when she saw it and dedicated it to God.

Dorothy Applebee also left money to provide coal for the poor of Cure's college, and a rent charge of £20 for an English school for thirty boys under the direction of the governors of the Grammar School. In April 1682, Mr. David Jenkins was appointed as master of the intended school on Mrs. Appleby's recommendation. Perhaps she had talked with her husband of Mrs. Newcomen's bequest and glimpsed something of the grievous need of so many of the children of the parish, to whom the Greek dictionaries of the Grammar School library could not bring salvation but who at least should have the chance to read and write their native tongue. The seeds, that Dorothy Applebee and Elizabeth New-comen planted in this manner so many years ago, under God's blessing mingled with others and grew in due time into that system of modern and technical education of which this country has cause to be so proud.

To these years also belong the benefactions of the three Henrys, Jackson, Young and Pratt who each gave money to found two almshouses in 1684, 1694 and 1704 respectively. (There is a pathetic note in the minutes of 1703 of 20s. for subsistence, given to Rebecca Jackson, daughter-in-law to Henry Jackson, "one of our benefactors," "she being very poor and crazed.") Endowments such as these, and many others of an earlier and a later date, reflect the attempts of Christian men and women to fulfil the proviso of the 38th article of their religion. "The riches and goods of Christians are not common as touching the right, title and possession of the same, as certain Anabaptists do falsely boast. Notwithstanding every man ought of such things as he possesseth liberally to give alms to the poor, according to his ability." Yet despite these many charities there were two disquieting features beginning to appear. If Christian giving, not a revolutionary change in the order of society as the levellers had urged, was to be the church's answer to the problem of the poor it must be linked with personal service and a genuine concern for the less fortunate neighbour. During the latter part of the 17th century there were signs of a lessening of that sense of personal responsibility, so marked in the previous generation. There was an increasing reluctance to take office and the habit of paying a fine instead of giving service grew rapidly. It eased the immediate pressure on the poor box, but in the event only added to the confusion as the parochial system gradually broke down. For those who continued to accept office found too often that the work was beyond their powers and their resources quite inadequate. Thomas Worrall's complaint, as warden of the general poor in 1675, was typical of many: to brave out his year, he declared, he needed a considerable sum of money "for relief of the random poor." After the fire the vestry was forced to impose a fifth quarter's assessment in the effort to make ends meet, nor were their difficulties only financial. Their attempts to say to the tide of industry, "thus far and no further," were bound to fail but they struggled on, preserving a free passage and clean water for the almshouses in spite of the propinquity of the soap yards, trying to prevent the new building in the Park from spoiling the look of the new churchyard and waging a losing battle against the encroachments of the butchers, who persisted in displaying and selling their meat within the chain gate that marked the entrance to the precincts from the High Street. On one occasion in 1688 the parish was indicted "at the several quarter sessions . . . for not setting up posts and rails along against the ditches in Maid Lane and by Beggars Hill," while in between their other preoccupations the wardens worried about the property at Godstone or the lease of the farm at Shere or abuses that had crept into the College at Dulwich.

Eventually the State at local or national level would take over the duties the constables and scavengers and harassed wardens could no longer adequately perform, and although much corruption would vanish in the process there would vanish also that sense of fellowship which had seemed possible of achievement when Philip Henslowe went from the vestry meeting to feast with the players at the Cardinal's Cap. For some decades yet, the vestry of St. Saviour's struggled on, and in spite of much confusion in the accounts, a number of favourable leases and the tendency to rob Peter to pay Paul, as in the suggestion that they should borrow from Mrs. Newcomen's rents if Mrs. Shaw's money was not forthcoming, none the less much honest work was put in, many unfortunates were helped, and the fabric of the church was preserved.

When the damage done by the fire had been repaired, the wardens were able to tackle less essential jobs; the vestry ceiling was whitewashed and a porch built outside the south door, "next the Bull Head to keep the body of the church from cold." A good deal of work was also done on the tower. In January 1703, it was resolved that the whole building should be repaired and beautified and agreements were duly signed with carpenter, foreman bricklayer, painter, glazier, smith and a hundred labourers and the church was shut for the work to proceed apace. The beautifying was not always to the good. The new painted altar-screen which was firmly affixed over Bishop Fox's masterpiece appeared to contemporaries as mighty fine and they approved, also, of the "good, decent and handsome pulpit" that was now set up. Alas, for the transitory nature of fashion in church furnishings! In the nineteenth century F. T. Dollman, the authority on the architecture of St. Saviour's, wrote in scathing words: "In 1703 extensive alterations, possibly considered to be for the best, took place. A Corinthian Altar-screen, with blazing fire-pots and volant cherubim, . . . whole length full-dressed portraits of Moses and Aaron, a pulpit with a huge sounding-board ready to drop and thus literally shut up the preacher *in toto*, pewing galleries and other incongruous erections all these *cum multis aliis*, were introduced with impunity, and it may be presumed, met with general approval." At least the authorities have a good word to say for the memorial to Richard Blisse, who died in 1703, aged sixty-seven, and who had been one whose counsels had weight in the vestry of these years: "a beautifully executed bust," as Taylor describes it, commemorates him in the north transept. Another large item on the credit side appears two years later when a new organ was installed by voluntary subscription. The minute book contains a note of the agreement with Bartholomew Isaac who was appointed organist at a salary of £24 a year. He was to attend in his own person and play twice every Sunday, as well as on certain royal anniversaries and on March 2nd, when the choice of parish officials was marked by a service as well as a feast. There might also be other special occasions, but they were not to exceed ten in every year. Four years later his son succeeded him on the same terms. William Neal was paid £4 a year for blowing the bellows and so, through the combined efforts of Neal and the Isaacs, the proud tradition of music at St. Saviour's was continued.

The purchase of the organ and the wholesale repairs of 1703 were visible signs of a spiritual quickening, paralleled throughout the country in the reign of Queen Anne. It is not easy to estimate how genuine the religious life of the parish had been during the intervening years, though it is not likely that the excesses of the Restoration court were mirrored in England as a whole. Many God-fearing folk must have been abashed at the low standard of morality that had crept into social and political life, and the existence within the Church itself of various small societies and groups, endeavouring by prayer and works of social betterment to witness to their faith and deepen their own discipleship, precludes too easy an assumption of decline. In Southwark, this chapter of the church's life was lived against a background of mercantile well-being, which made possible the preservation and refurbishing of the old church and gave the fortunes they used so well to those generous benefactors whose names are still commemorated. It is not without significance that during this period two more Lord Mayors worshipped and were buried at St. Saviour's, George Waterman, in 1671, whose funeral by torchlight was a noteworthy occasion, and Sir John Shorter, the enlightened friend of nonconformists.

It was the persecution of dissenters which more than any other single cause vitiated the witness of the established church, whatever the piety of individual members. Nonconformity, on the other hand, was purified and stimulated by the necessity for decision and sacrifice which this generation of dissenters was called upon to face. Few would deny that the two greatest men who preached in the vicinity of St. Saviour's between 1660 and 1702 were not chaplains at the mother-church but the nonconformists, Richard Baxter and John Bunyan. Baxter came twice to Southwark, first as a prisoner in the King's Bench where he lived in "tolerable comfort" for eighteen months, and in 1676 to preach at the meeting-house in Deadman's Place. With what bitter regrets must he, who loved to write himself "mere Christian," have heard the church bells ringing and passed St. Saviour's by. Soon afterwards John Bunyan preached at a Baptist church in Southwark, a ruddy, well-built man, getting on in years, who had found in his captivity, power to write with vigour and truth of man's spiritual adventure. He stayed with his friend, Sir John Shorter, and rejoiced at the crowds who came to hear him, as sane and forthright in a prosperous old age as once he had been as a tinker, striding across the open Midland fields. At St. Saviour's in 1900 the children of the parish and other well-wishers placed a memorial window to his honour, which in 1941 was destroyed by enemy action. In 1953 it was restored and rededicated, at a service attended by the Cathedral clergy and leading ministers of the Free Churches, a sign of the renewed fellowship for which one gives thanks to God.

Not only the persecution of dissent but too close an intermingling of religion and politics hampered the church's progress. Whig or Tory, High Churchmen or Latitudinarian, these factions were evident in every congregation not least in St. Saviour's as the century drew to a close. Those who returned from exile in 1660, and the young men bred at home during the Interregnum, were imbued with a fanatical hatred of disloyalty not unnatural in those whose fathers had died and been defeated in the battles of the civil war. So there grew up the theory of non-resistance, of loyalty as a twin virtue with godliness, a return, with a yet greater stress on the sin of rebellion, to Lancelot Andrewes' principles alike as to kingship and as to modes of worship. At the same time, the new scientific temper of the age, the cool devout reasoning of the Cambridge platonists and the influence of Locke's philosophy influenced another type of churchman in the direction of tolerance in religion and liberalism in politics. To these Latitudinarians, the majority of the merchant class belonged, and there must have been many of them at St. Saviour's; but there was also in the vestry a strong High Church element and the clash of opinion was evident, especially when it came to the choice of the chaplain. Although they would scarcely at this stage be treated in so summary manner as Philip Jones, the vestry clerk, who was dismissed for "divers miscarriages, irreverent speeches, affronts and enormities" and because he was "not skilful in setting the psalms, to the offence of the congregation," the chaplains were still regarded as their employees by the vestry who insisted on exacting from successful candidates a bond to be forfeited if they failed to reside in the parish. When William Hoare died in 1687, there was trouble. One faction wished to push ahead with the choice of his successor on the very day they heard of his death and, having gained their point by a small majority, they elected Samuel Barton, for whom thirteen beans were cast against nine for his opponent. Their aim appeared to be to face the Bishop with a *fait accompli* when his lordship sent, as he duly did, a letter of recommendation for a third candidate. A fortnight later the vestry replied to a further letter from the Bishop, assuring him that his recommendation had been read out on various occasions and answering his objection to the imposition of the bond of residence by the assertion that it was according to ancient usage and custom. They ended on a firm note that notwithstanding the misrepresentations that have been made to the Bishop, upon whose power in ecclesiastical affairs they had no wish to entrench, they did "unanimously consent and adhere" to their choice of Samuel Barton. The Bishop appears to have agreed to license Barton who remained for twenty-two years as chaplain. His colleague, after Dr. Martin's death in 1691, was the latter's son who held the cure for eleven years and was a man of considerable standing, a prebendary of Westminster and chaplain to the third troop of Guards.

Bishop Mew, Morley's successor, was an efficient bishop and an honest man but he had been a soldier for many years before he became priest and, according to the Whig historian Burnet, he "knew very little of divinity or of any other learning." His portrait at Farnham still shews him as a soldierly figure, with a black patch over his eye to hide one of his innumerable scars. Perhaps his happiest hour as bishop occurred in 1685, when he once again had the joy of fighting for his king, for he was with the troops at Sedgemoor who defeated the wretched Monmouth. With him was Trelawney, Bishop of Bristol, who followed him in the see of Winchester. Both these men were Tories and High Churchmen and both found themselves in an impossible position in 1688 when James II's arbitrary methods and unpopular religion led to the Revolution. Trelawney was one of the seven bishops whose resistance to the King's demands matched the mood of England, yet when his sovereign reproached him with disloyalty he fell on his knees in great heat and confusion, protesting that none of his family could be guilty of rebellion. Eventually both Mew and Trelawney accepted the Revolution, but for them, as for all of their school of thought who did not go to the length of refusing allegiance to the new régime, it was an uneasy and illogical compliance.

In every congregation during the next twenty years there was a nucleus of smouldering Tory opinion. It became more vocal after Queen Anne's accession but the Whigs' successful war policy and Marlborough's "famous victories" kept that party in the ascendant. By 1709 however, as every victory grew more costly, the desire for peace became more pronounced and it was accompanied in the churches by a genuine growth in spiritual fervour which gave new depth to the old shibboleths of "non-resistance" and "high-church piety."

At this stage they elected a new chaplain at St. Saviour's, a man in his thirties, of academic distinction, who came, as more than one of his predecessors had done, from Magdalen College, Oxford. Henry Sacheverell was the grandson of a dissenting minister, ejected in 1662, and as so often happens had reacted violently against his upbringing. While at Oxford he had already aligned himself with the extreme Tories, inveighing against the practice of occasional conformity, the compromise whereby dissenters evaded the provisions of the Test Act by taking communion once a year at their parish church. So bitter was his feeling against nonconformists that according to rumour he nearly shook the life out of a favourite college-servant when he discovered he attended a meeting-house. One cannot believe onetenth of the aspersions cast upon him; suffice it to say he was a man of strong conviction, hot temper and excessive vanity. On the night of his election to St. Saviour's, one contemporary tract asserts, he visited the Mitre Tavern in Fenchurch Street and boasted of his success, "reflecting very barbarously on his competitor Mr. G." and declaring that "he had heard him preach for the place and thought him a very dull soul."

It is usual to state that Sacheverell was chaplain at St. Saviour's from 1705–9 but this is borne out neither by the vestry minutes nor contemporary statements. Richard Martin junior had died in 1702 and was apparently succeeded by Thomas Horne, who was in office when Dr. Barton accepted the living of Christ Church in 1709. At that juncture Horne applied to be forenoon chaplain, which was regarded as the position of seniority, and it was agreed that the new chaplain should preach in the afternoon. There can be no doubt that this new chaplain was Sacheverell, who came down from Oxford that year and preached a most provocative sermon at the Assizes at Derby in August 1709. The *Pious Life* written in 1710 states categorically that he was appointed chaplain at St. Saviour's between this sermon and a second one preached at St. Paul's in November. That he remained chaplain of St. Saviour's at least till 1713 is apparent from various references in contemporary tracts.

In the catalogue of the British Museum library there are more than twelve pages listing the material, mostly contemporary, that deals with the Sacheverell controversy. For the two sermons at

Derby and St. Paul's had remarkable results and made of 1710 a year of "extreme violence and confusion such as cannot be matched . . . a year through which nothing but an almighty Providence could have brought moderate plain-dealing Protestants alive and unmaimed." Thus speaks the Whig pamphleteer; to his opponent, who saw this sudden outburst of Tory fervour as a sign of grace, Sacheverell was the hero of an *annus mirabilis*.

In his two sermons Sacheverell had attacked the false brethren in church and state, his eloquent turgid sentences sweeping on regardless of expediency, charity or grammar. He reviled the "wily Volpones" who were in power (and the nickname of Volpone belonged to the Treasurer Godolphin), and spoke with bitter satire of the license given to rich dissenters as if only "fools and beggars" could be damned. There was some truth in this and no doubt of the preacher's sincerity; a clergyman, who sat next to him at St. Paul's during the prayers that preceded the sermon, watched his neighbour's fair and effeminate features spread over with "fiery red" as he whipped himself into a passion before mounting the pulpit. When he had finished, the Common Council in some agitation advised against printing the sermon, but with or without the Lord Mayor's connivance, Sacheverell sent it to the Press. It contained certain reflections on the Revolution which gave some ground to the charge of sedition, but any government in its senses would have disregarded it. In a momentary aberration, Godolphin, usually the most discreet of men, prosecuted. It was a fatal thing to do. Every Tory in the country was—metaphorically speaking—up in arms. The trial took place, after various delays, in Westminster Hall; Sacheverell was lodged in the Temple and whenever he appeared, devoted supporters thronged about him determined to treat him as a martyr. The Queen, when she passed, was cheered and challenged: "was her Majesty for Dr. Sacheverell?" and poor Anne, tired of the Duchess of Marlborough's tantrums, increasingly under Mrs. Masham's thumb, began to see a chance of a change of ministers and thought the Doctor over-vehement yet a fine figure of a man.

In the end he was adjudged guilty by sixty-nine votes to fifty-two; the sermon was ordered to be burnt and he was debarred from preaching for a period of three years. A motion that he should be prohibited from accepting preferment during that time was lost by one vote! It was tantamount to victory. The bells rang and the bonfires blazed and when the victim accepted a rich living in Wales (though he had so vast a parish upon his hands already, as his critics pointed out) his journey thither was a great triumphal procession. Almost immediately the government fell and the Tories came into power, though when the millennium still tarried, feelings quietened down.

During the first weeks after Sacheverell's trial, St. Saviour's became a place of pilgrimage. The chaplain could not preach in view of the prohibition, but folk came to look at him and to hear Thomas Horne, or a curate, preach High Church sermons to their heart's content. One visitor, identified as Bishop Kennett, described his impressions of the scene. He pleaded with the preachers to desist from political sermons, particularly at this juncture when "curiosity and other very opposite motives draw such crowds of people thither." It was an opportunity for the staff at St. Saviour's, to "allay the proneness of the common people to riots and tumults"; let them instead of politics, speak of the Queen's goodness, of the victories abroad and all that had been accomplished in the space of seven years to strengthen the constitution and "to promote true Church of England piety by our charity schools." To arraign the government as the preachers continued to do was, Bishop Kennett declared, suitable for sermons preached in the statesmen's presence, "not before the Governors of Boats and Barges in their furbelowed galleries at St. Saviour's."

None the less, the writer ended his tract with a tribute to Sacheverell's conduct of the service. "He is audible without noise or any harsh grating accent to impress the close of a sentence upon the ears of a congregation, and as every gesture and turn of both his voice and body is suitable to what he is reading through the whole course of the prayers, creeds, chapters and hymns, so he is entirely solemn and reverend in the composure of his person, without affectation, nay, in his very passage to and from the desk." One begins to realise something of the secret of his power.

Sacheverell would appear to have held the Welsh living in plurality and when the three years' ban was over, it was at St. Saviour's, Southwark, that he preached again for the first time on

March 29th, 1713. He chose for his text, "Father forgive them for they know not what they do"; though he added charac-teristically, that they were also to pray, in regard to their enemies, that God would "abate their pride, assuage their malice and con-found their devices." On the whole he spoke in muted tones to which no one could take exception, and there was a true eighteenth-century flavour to his prayer that all would foresake "the wild freaks of enthusiasm, to embrace a religion without superstition, plain, pure and apostolical." Queen Anne herself attended St. Saviour's to hear him and he was soon offered and accepted the living of St. Andrew's, Holborn, where he dwelt till he died in 1724 as the result of an accidental fall.

The episode of Dr. Sacheverell ended an epoch. Within a few years came the Hanoverian succession and the long healing régime of Robert Walpole. The heats and torments of the seventeenth century, its vision and its bitterness, its heroism and its virulent propaganda were alike things of the past, and enthusiasm in religion and politics became the sin of which no self-respecting citizen was guilty. Only in our own day, have the clash of ideo-logies, the tension between freedom and righteousness, the conflicting sense of doom and opportunity arisen once more to challenge thinking men.

## Note on Sources

The younger William Austin (of Grey's Inn, his father being of Lincoln's Inn) wrote *Atlas under Olympus* (1664) and *The Anatomy of the Pestilence* (1666). For the dissenting churches see *Survey of London: Bankside*, p. 79 n., and Wilson, *op. cit.*, IV, 123. The state-ment made in 1644 as to the church's discomfort is in *Hist. MSS. Com: Report VI*, App., p. 40. For Christ Church Parish see *Survey of London: Bankside*, pp. 101–7; and *Commons Journals*, 1671–2. There is a printed account entitled *Narrative of the terrible fire in Southwark, 1676* in the Brit. Mus. library (16803 aa 16 (10) ); for Elizabeth Newcomen and her school see Edric Bayley: *Newcomen's Educational Foundation*, etc. (1913). For Sacheverell, see *Pious Life of Dr. H. Sacheverell* (1710) in addition to the standard histories and innumerable contemporary tracts.

# XVI

# LAISSEZ–FAIRE

WITHIN twenty years of the Sacheverell trial the select vestry of St. Saviour's had ceased to function, and the right of electing the parish officials which the thirty assistants had usurped in 1557 was at long last recovered for the parishioners as a whole. These developments in Southwark were part of a general attack made upon select vestries throughout the country; a bill had been introduced in 1696 for their "better regulation," with much consequent agitation at St. Saviour's as elsewhere, the vestry organising themselves for the "defence and maintenance of their ancient rights and constitution" and declaring that anything in the way of annual elections would be "troublesome to their parish, it being very large." This threat was averted but in 1710, the year of Sacheverell's impeachment, the attack was renewed and this time it had a specifically political flavour; the vestries in most cases were predominantly Tory and the critics militant Whigs. Certain inhabitants of St. Saviour's parish, who on this occasion petitioned the Commons against their vestry, argued that the latter chose wardens and overseers of their own political colour and, by making scot and lot men at discretion, secured too great an influence in the election of M.Ps. On this occasion, only the collapse of Godolphin's government saved the vestries.

In 1716 a third bill was introduced and St. Saviour's again contributed to the petitions and counter-petitions which flowed into the House, and someone, probably John Lade, M.P. for Southwark and a member of the vestry, proposed as an amendment that the act should "not extend to affect or change the vestry of the parish of St. Saviour's Southwark," a plea for special treatment that was firmly negatived. John Lade was one of the tellers for the "noes" when the measure was put to the vote. It passed by 135 votes to 34, yet once again the vestries escaped their inevitable end, for its promoters had made the mistake of going too far, threatening among other things the independence of the charity schools, and in the House of Lords the Archbishop spoke against the bill and secured its defeat.

The necessity for some sort of modification of parochial rule was obvious to all and became more urgent with every year. At St. Saviour's in 1703 their new minute book was redolent of good resolutions. Careful provision was made for the prompt presentation of accounts and the strict keeping of the registers while a new table of fees and church dues was submitted and "unanimously agreed to by the major part of this vestry." Yet the difficulties were all but overwhelming. The wholesale repairs in 1703 cost the wardens £2,600 and left them in debt to the tune of £800 and that winter a violent storm, the worst in living memory, destroyed church property in Axe and Battle Yard and damaged the pinnacles of the newly renovated tower. Charitable bequests increased steadily in complexity, and there were as yet no banking facilities: not till 1791 were the overseers instructed to invest the poor rate in the new bank now existing in the Borough under the names of St. James Saunderson, Harrison, Blenchley, Bloxham & Co. Until that date, one can envisage the wardens and overseer, not men of great substance, ordinary middle-class tradesmen, coping with hundreds of pounds in ready cash, housing it in their own homes, carrying it about in various bags of different shapes and sizes, borrowing and paying interest, and holding office for one year only so that there was a constant succession of inexperienced officials, and one marvels not at the occasional breath of scandal but how the work was ever done at all. Even men of integrity were likely to fail: and there was of course corruption. As far back as 1660 the Presbyterian author of *Hudibras* had defined a church warden as "a public officer entrusted to rob the church by virtue of his place, as long as he is in it," while in 1714, Daniel Defoe the Whig pamphleteer employed all his vituperative powers to slate the vestries in his tract: *Parochial tyranny or the House-keepers' complaint.* "Nothing is so profitable to these gentlemen as parish repairs," he wrote. "If the church is new beautified painted or whitewashed, whip! they come upon you with a church rate and when £200 has been expended £1200 shall be collected, for Mr. Churchwarden will strive hard, but his daughter shall be a thousand pounds the better."

Only of course in a few flagrant cases would such a criticism be justified; nor is it easy to define exactly when and to what extent genuine and honest concern for the church's welfare degenerated into jobbery and exclusiveness. Emerson and Bingham, Henslowe and Applebee were all business men and, no less than their successors, were inclined to see that their own interests did not suffer. Those who petitioned against St. Saviour's vestry in 1710 and 1716 had no doubt good grounds for their complaints, but there were not so much specific charges of corruption as a general criticism on the money spent upon the traditional feasts and the inextricable confusion in the accounts. One sore point would not be alleviated by the abolition of the assistants. The church rate levied annually by virtue of the act of 1671 fell upon all residents in the parish in due proportion, whatever their brand of Christianity might be, and thus bred a continued sense of injustice among the large number of nonconformists in the neighbourhood even after they were allowed the free exercise of their religion. As the personal relations between the nonconformists and the churchmen improved there may have been a tendency among the latter to "soft pedal" on the subject of their magnificent heritage: nor indeed did many of them appreciate it, for those of the period who possessed aesthetic taste and an appreciation of the past admired the classical and romanesque in preference to the out-moded Gothic. So as the century progressed, the deterioration of St. Saviour's progressed also and the splendid efforts of 1703 were not repeated. Instead the wardens, still in the main honest and overworked Christians, turned their attention to the problem of the poor and to building a new workhouse on the site of the old palace of the Bishops of Winchester.

For fourteen years after 1716 things went on much as before. The church's brief emergence as a place of pilgrimage while Sacheverell was chaplain had soon given place to the old sober practice of the Anglican way of worship, by a congregation composed in the main of well-to-do merchants from the Borough with a smattering of lawyers and doctors, men of the river-side trades, boys from the Grammar and charity schools and the old-folk from the almshouses. The charity school had opened its doors on St. John's day, 1706, in dark and crowded quarters in a corner of Montague Close. Two years later, Benjamin Sterry, a haberdasher, endowed it with a small legacy devoted mainly to the education of girls, and in 1711 John Collett made a gift to the church which enabled the wardens to send twenty more boys to the school and in addition to provide them with blue coats. The scholars all sat together on a Sunday morning in one of the galleries, though when Mr. Collett's twenty boys were added, the vestry wisely decided to put a door with a fastening "upon the stairs going up into that gallery." In 1718 a less pleasant entry in the minutes recorded that the late grave-digger had been conniving at some body-snatching, perhaps in the interests of St. Thomas's across the way. He was prosecuted, with the utmost severity as the law directed "for disposing of corpses to surgeons in order for dissection." In 1724 a new chaplain was elected, the first mention since 1709 of an appointment, and the fact that this was the year of Sacheverell's death and the rigorous bond of £500 which was now exacted to ensure residence makes it conceivable that Sacheverell had not relinquished the living when he went to St. Andrew's Holborn. The choice in 1724 was not satisfactory and next year Benjamin Slockock was appointed and held the cure for many years. Thomas Horne died in 1730, when Slockock asked to become forenoon chaplain and John Smith was chosen as his colleague.

This was the year of the downfall of the thirty vestry-men. It happened not by Act of Parliament but by direct action. The extra expense entailed in the erection of the new workhouse and the consequent need to raise the rate may well have been the spark which lit the train. That year the second of March fell on a Monday. On the previous Saturday, a paper was circulated summoning the parishioners to a church meeting at 9 o'clock on the Monday morning. The paper recapitulated the clause of the 1540 act, which empowered the general body of parishioners to "nominate and elect six or four able persons dwelling within the precincts of the said parish to be church-wardens," and went on to point out that, notwithstanding this act, thirty persons, calling themselves a select vestry, presumed to choose the wardens and other officials and assumed "the sole management of the parish affairs together with the disposal of the parish money and charities." At nine o'clock on the morning of March 2nd, in response to this appeal, a number of parishioners met in the church and proceeded to choose the six wardens for the ensuing year, by name Thomas Engeir, Samuel Palmer, John Corner, John Copland, Thomas Tarrant and Edward Pyke.

Later in the day, the select vestry met as usual, made their own choice, naturally of six different persons, and no doubt had their accustomed feast. On Easter Tuesday, the overseers and scavengers were elected as usual and the vestry met again to inspect the staircase and the tower which were in need of repair, and to authorise their nominees to seek legal advice and to do all that they could to maintain their position. It was, however, already too late for the parishioners had sent in to the Bishop the names of those they had chosen, and at the annual visitation, Thomas Engeir and his colleagues were the men that were sworn in to office. Very probably the political motive was not lacking, and if it were a case of a Whig majority in the parish attempting to undermine a Tory vestry, they would certainly have the Bishop behind them: Trelawney's successor at Winchester, Richard Willis, who in his early days had been one of William III's chaplains in Holland, was like most of his colleagues on the episcopal bench, a Latitudinarian in theology and a sound Whig in politics.

Throughout the summer an uneasy warfare continued at St. Saviour's. The vestry had only one effective weapon; the wardens for the year 1729–30 still had possession of the books. Among them was John Lade, a fighter to the bitter end, and he firmly refused to allow the new wardens to do more than read over the papers in his own house, so that Engeir and his friends had to carry on for some months without detailed information as to rents, pensions, salaries and the like. They retaliated by declaring that, as things were, they could not pay out the parish charities, which would "distress if not destroy ancient people who in this stage of life should have no difficulties laid upon them." At length in October, a confused and incomplete bundle of accounts and miscellaneous papers were handed over to them. Next month, the first general vestry was held, though apart from the officers only thirty-four parishioners were recorded as being present. In February 1731, a larger meeting assembled when a considered statement was presented in which the new leaders explained and justified their action.

One of their chief complaints against their predecessors was their tendency to levy a rate greater than that allowed by act of parliament and to use their powers of distraint to compel payment, "a most presumptuous attack upon the rights and liberties of the inhabitants." If well managed, the new wardens had no doubt that the £120 available after salaries had been paid would be sufficient for repairs and administration and considered that the profits of church property should be devoted to charitable purposes and so lessen the poor rate. They were no doubt overoptimistic, but they were on sound lines in insisting that the three sources of income should be kept distinct, the church rate, the rents and charitable bequests, and the fees and parish dues. By a narrow majority it was decided not to print the statement for general circulation, and this forbearance and the dying down of political animosities paved the way for a reconciliation of the conflicting parties. It was not long before the names of John Lade and others of the old clique were again to be found among those giving service to the church.

The wardens made a profit of nearly £300 in 1732, and after consulting with the Justices as to how to expend it, agreed to wipe out the workhouse debt. Later in the year they decided instead to build a new wing to house sixty poor persons, which would be "of great service to the parish." This large initial balance was not of course maintained and before long it dwindled to £60 or £70, while in 1734 church repairs, estimated at £600, were found to cost as much as £850. This large outlay had been caused by the necessary repairs to the tower and it was followed by another emergency, for in November it was reported that the tenor bell had broken but that no action had yet been taken in view of the recent expenditure. Now the parish was informed that the first four bells and the seventh bell "bore no proportion with the harmony of the fifth and sixth" and "gentlemen well skilled in music had declared that it would be difficult if not impossible to make them fall in agreeably together." The bold and most satisfactory course would be to recast them all, and by adding new metal to increase the ring from eight to twelve bells which the strengthened tower would now be able to support. This it was agreed to do and the cost was met by voluntary subscriptions. Close on £500 was raised and this united effort of the congregation must have done more than any reasoning to heal the breaches of the preceding years. The new bells were duly installed and the complaisant parishioners inscribed on one of them:

> By adding four our notes we'll raise
> And sound the good subscribers' praise.

In many ways the new régime did not differ greatly from the old for though the chaplains and the sextons were chosen by the whole parish, with a very great deal of accompanying excitement, it was found not to be feasible each year to choose the wardens and overseers in this democratic way. After 1748 it became usual to appoint a sub-committee to consult with the out-going officials and "to prepare a list of persons to present to the [general] vestry on Easter Tuesday, to serve as wardens and overseers for the ensuing year." How far this differed from election by a select vestry need not perhaps be examined too closely. The system worked and the main point at issue had been secured so that henceforth no zealous parishioner could be rightfully excluded from a vestry meeting.

Nor, after 1742, were they barred from the parish junketings. At the general vestry that year it was agreed that upon payment of 2s. 6d. all parishioners had the right to attend the famous feasts. It was also laid down how much might be spent, in addition to the half-crowns: £10 at the election of officers, now transferred in entirety to Easter Tuesday, and £5 on the occasion of levying the two rates for the church and for the poor. There were more exclusive parties on Mrs. Newcomen's birthday on November 2nd and at the annual gift of 20 cauldrons of coal to the poor, which the wardens and overseers attended perhaps with some of the "ancients." The annual visitation by the archdeacon or the bishop's officer was often held at Kingston as the importance of St. Saviour's waned, but the jolliest celebration of all remained the perambulation of the parish when white stones were set up to mark its boundaries, similar to the one still to be seen in the garden at the western end of the church.

The parish which they surveyed, the "wardens, chaplains, overseers, constables, ancient inhabitants, workmen, beadles, labourers and boys of the charity school," has left a record of itself in the pages of Strype's edition of Stow, issued in 1720, and in two later publications by John Chamberlayn in 1770 and by Concanen and Morgan in 1795. Between them they give a clear picture of eighteenth-century Southwark, in many ways the pleasantest time in which to dwell in the suburb, with the horrors of the plague gone and large-scale industry still a threat of the future. Strype described St. Saviour's parish as the largest and "best builded in the Borough and well resorted to"; a spacious churchyard still lay about the church and, westward, on the site of Winchester Park, many new roads provided an attractive setting for modern houses, built in the fashionable brick: "handsome, clean and open" are the epithets Strype applies to Red Cross Street and its fellows. Maid Lane was still "a long straggling place with ditches on each side." The better houses were on the north or river side, and paths ran up to them from the road, "over little bridges with little garden plots before them." Gravel Lane lay roughly along the line of the modern Hopton Street as it runs into Gt. Suffolk Street; in the other direction Hopton Street curves round to the old Green Walk where Christ Church built its school next to almshouses that still survive to give the passer-by a welcome glimpse of the Southwark of the past. Gravel Lane linked up the Falcon on Bankside and St. George's Fields, "by reason of which," Strype noted, "it is a great thoroughfare, especially in the summer season, by the citizens for their diversion in the Fields and entertaining houses." The traffic congestion was a constant source of anxiety to the wardens, in particular one blind corner where a house jutted out and screened pedestrians from the view of the carriages that rolled by at such a dangerous pace. Here, too, the houses had pretty gardens attached. At the other end of the parish, however, Clink Alley and Deadman's Place were still dirty and straggling streets of "no great account," and St. Mary's dock to which Clink Alley led, though "considerable for the loading and unloading of goods and likewise of account for the coal trade" was in consequence of this and the carts and cars which resorted thither "dirty, encumbered and so not well inhabited." The butchers' shambles in the lower stretches of the High Street marred the eastern approaches to St. Saviour's, but on the opposite side of the road "tradesmen of good repute" occupied the stylish houses, the flavour of which still lingers in the buildings in St. Thomas' Street.

Many of the inns had been refurbished, for it was the age of the great stage coaches, and at the Tabard and George, the White Hart and the Falcon, the old inn yards sprang to throbbing life as the coach came rumbling in from Rochester and Maidstone, from Tonbridge and Reigate and beyond, and the tired passengers gratefully sought the comfort of a warm fire while the local Sam Weller rubbed down the steaming horses. As a centre of entertainment Bankside was past its prime, but Our Lady's Fair in Southwark, held just over the parish boundary at the southern end of the High Street, remained an annual rendezvous of all those circus folk, the gypsies, strolling players, pedlars, who lived by their wits at the fairs of the countryside. It survives for all time, a compound of fun and trickery, vice and debauchery and animal high spirits on the canvas of Hogarth's great picture. How very relieved the authorities must have been when those first days of September were safely over and the boys of the Grammar School at their desks again. In 1792 the fair was at length suppressed and the gypsies and vagabonds no longer came to disturb the sobriety of the burgesses who lived in the new brick houses and tended their well-kept gardens.

Already by this date the changes were beginning which would wreck more surely the amenities of the Borough than any three days' fair. One of the first signs of the time had been the abolition in 1754 of the market held for hundreds of years at various points in the High Street on three days of the week. Always there had been resulting congestion which by the mid-eighteenth century approached to chaos. The growth of the market garden industry in Kent and Surrey led to a large increase in the goods brought up for sale in the Borough and, while it was impossible for things to continue as they were, the wardens of St. Saviour's were extremely anxious not to lose the trade. The question of the market recurred frequently after November 1753, when the City authorities first petitioned parliament for its suppression, and when an act was eventually passed it conferred upon the parish the right to set up a new market in Rochester Yard, to the south of the church. Its management was in the hands of a board of trustees, including the wardens and overseers who quashed in no uncertain way any infringement of the parish's monopoly. One such attempt was made by James Hedger, a champion of free enterprise, who had the temerity to set up a market of his own for the sale of fish and poultry in St. George's Fields. The church authorities encouraged their lessee to fight the case, which came up at the Guildford assizes where Hedger was defeated. Hereafter the Borough Market was securely entrenched, to spread like an octopus during the succeeding century and to hem in the church on the southern side as ruthlessly as the wharves and warehouses press in upon it to the north and west.

James Hedger's activities were an indication of one development that was destined to have a great effect on Southwark's future. Steadily during this century bridges were being built across the Thames: hence the rapid development of St. George's Fields and the closer inclusion of Southwark in the great wen of the metropolis. When Westminster Bridge was first mooted St. Saviour's were much perturbed and one of the first joint actions of the two parties, after the fracas of 1730, was to protest against any such development. Their objections were set aside and the first stone of the bridge between Westminster and Stangate was laid in 1739 and the bridge opened eleven years later. The light and elegant Blackfriars followed in 1779, and in 1819 the iron bridge of Southwark was erected.

The fears of St. Saviour's vestry were natural. So long as London Bridge remained the great thoroughfare between the City and the south-east of England, the Borough High Street's prosperity could not be undermined. To a certain extent their fears were groundless. As the other bridges were built, the City officials turned their minds to improving London Bridge itself and in 1754 the rickety houses were taken down and the two great gates removed. The traffic still flowed across it incessantly and Southwark still remained a point of departure. But the great growth in population and the industrial developments soon began to make it a less pleasant place in which to live. Thrale's great brewery was swallowing up Globe Alley and Deadman's Place and by the end of the century the old meeting houses had gone as the theatre had gone before them. The description in the Concanen and Morgan book of Three Crown Court, at the entrance to the Borough Market, shows alike the residents' hopes and anxieties. There were few places, "considering its situation, better calculated for an agreeable residence of the middle order of people," for its propinquity to the High Street was combined with "a trifling retirement from the busy scene." Yet it was "very unpleasant to observe the entrance from the Borough continually choked up by hawkers of garden-stuff in the day-time and too frequently by women of loose manners in an evening, the removal of these inconveniences would much increase its reputation and afford great comfort to the inhabitants." The authors went on to complain that the contiguity of the court to the market and "the idleness of servants" occasioned "much filth to be thrown before the doors" and destroyed "that air of cleanliness which all places detached from the main street should be zealous to preserve": while the fact that they possessed a pump added to the residents' difficulties as well as to their comfort, being "productive of many unpleasant visitants." How vividly these eighteenth-century accounts recall the strange mixture of characteristics that St. Saviour's parish still possessed: the merchants and the wayfarers, the market with its refuse and its filth, the residents of "the middle order" still hoping to preserve the amenities of the parish they loved, the persistent element of disreputable persons, the traffic of the docks and the stimulating bustle of the highway.

The other Southwark parishes mirrored these varied facets of St. Saviour's life, with a rather different emphasis in each case. Christ-church prospered: it was the houses on the western side of Gravel Lane that were the most elegant. St. George's, which included the High Street, south of Axe and Bottle yard (the Newcomen Street of to-day), emerged from a period of decline into a new prosperity when the right of sanctuary was abolished and the Mint cleared up. It had still more than its fair share of difficulties, so long as St. George's Fields remained the most convenient place for rioters to assemble; the comely new church, built in 1738, was still the church of the Marshalsea where Dickens spent a part of his youth, and here in his fancy little Dorrit was married. St. Olave's remained the poorest of the four Southwark parishes and the natural centre of faction and unrest, though surprisingly its school flourished better than its neighbour's. There was as always a large sprinkling of foreigners, or traders of foreign extraction, and ships, not only with coal from Newcastle but with timber from Scandinavia and from Dutch and north German ports, berthed in the wharves of Rotherhithe and Southwark and gave to these riverside parishes a character and independence all their own.

Across the High Street from St. Saviour's, St. Thomas's parish consisted almost entirely of hospital property. Here too a new church had been built in 1702, which is the Cathedral Chapter-house to-day. In this tiny parish, within a few years of Strype's description, an exciting development took place. A bookseller, Thomas Guy, decided to build a new hospital. Guy was an extra-ordinary man who combined a remarkable and rather ruthless power of making money with devotion and vision in his charit-able enterprises. He began his career selling cheap bibles and later did a less reputable trade in seamen's tickets, and he sold his investments at the crucial moment at the time of the South Sea bubble and emerged an extremely wealthy man. He was seventy-six years old and had long been a benefactor and governor at St. Thomas's. He knew how often patients were discharged for lack of room when they would have benefited by continued care. For semi-chronic cases of this kind, he decided to build a hospital, stipulating that among them there should be twenty insane persons to be treated for so long as there was hope of their recovery, a sign of enlightenment unusual at this period when the horrors of Bedlam were rampant.

A site was purchased near to St. Thomas's and in the four years intervening before Guy's death, considerable progress was made so that he had the satisfaction of seeing the first wing com-pleted. He died in 1724 and they buried him with pomp and gratitude, attended by forty coaches with six horses apiece! His hospital was richly endowed and it flourished, to become when St. Thomas's moved to Lambeth, Southwark's own hospital, famous as "Guy's" throughout the world, not only for its surgery but for a specialised department in psychiatric work that would have delighted the heart of its founder. John Lade was one of the original trustees who, upon Guy's death, brought his scheme to fruition and there were many such personal links between St. Saviour's parish and the great hospitals across the way.

The wardens' more immediate concern was with their own

schools and almshouses. To the latter was added, in 1771, eight houses in the Close, given by Alice Shaw Overman, the last not unworthy appearance of the well-known name in the annals of the parish. St. Saviour's Grammar School prospered while William Symes was head but its numbers seldom exceeded fifty and when Symes died, after close on forty years in office, his successor started the old foundation on a rapid decline, absenting himself for many days together and very frequently coming into the school "disordered with liquor." The charity school, on the other side of the church, was on the contrary flourishing. Mrs. Newcomen's gift also began to bear fruit. In 1752 the warden responsible was able to report to the parish meeting that the property had passed into his hands three years previously, that it had now been put into good condition and the profits would enable them to send six girls and six boys to the charity school and to clothe them. Eighteen months later, eighteen more children were sent and the brown clothing they wore (at one time with red caps) distinguished them from the "blue-coats." At length in 1791 with the help of voluntary subscriptions a new school was built for the boys of both foundations, not in the cramped quarters in Angel Court but further from the church at the corner of Union and Red-cross Streets in inappropriate propinquity to the single women's burying ground. The formal opening was a great occasion with a lengthy speech by John Morton, the headmaster, and though the account of it reads dully enough there were few more hopeful things occurring in the Southwark of the four Georges than this launching into life of an increasing number of boys and girls made possible by the loving kindness of such as John Collett and Mrs. Newcomen.

There was no shortage of people of goodwill yet increasingly, as the years went on, something was required on a different scale, which began with organised parochial effort, in part voluntary, in part imposed by the justices, and was not to end till the creation of the welfare state of to-day. In July 1767, for example, the justices instructed St. Saviour's to elect "five noblemen or gentlemen or the most respectable of the parish" to be the first guardians of poor children. They were to hold office for three years and were to send into the country and maintain there at the parish's expense "all poor children able to be separated from their mothers, those under two going not less than five, those under six not less than three miles away."

One of the guardians was John Levy Esq., whose name also occurs on the committee of the Surrey Dispensary, which was set up in Montague Close in 1777 on the pattern of similar bodies in the City and Westminster. Their purpose was to supplement the work of the hospitals and when possible to treat the sick poor in their own homes. The President of the Surrey Dispensary was Lord Onslow and Henry Thrale, the wealthy owner of the brewery in Deadman's Place, was among the four vice-Presidents. There were two regular physicians and a consultant, a surgeon and an apothecary constantly in residence, and "a gentleman skilled in midwifery to instruct the women employed by the charity and attend all difficult labours." Stress was laid on the risk of infection in the impure air of the hospital wards and it was observed that "many from a decent pride did not choose to be found in these public places of charity." At childbirth in particular it was not merely inconvenient but dangerous and indecent for a woman to leave her husband and family, "when their aid and consolation were most necessary." Inevitably only a fraction of those who desired help from the Dispensary could receive it and every would-be patient had first to obtain the vote of a governor; a subscription of a guinea a year entitled the donor to have one out-patient and one "lying-in" patient during the year; and if there were a ballot, "ladies, foreign ambassadors and other privileged persons" were allowed to vote by proxy. Yet hedged about though it was by such a sense of class distinction, the Surrey Dispensary and many another philanthropic endeavour in this second half of the century were the fruits of a renewal of grace, a deeper awareness of man's duty to his neighbour which sprang from the closer knowledge of God that the evangelical movement wrought in the hearts of many Christians.

One of John Wesley's earliest disciples was chaplain at St. Saviours for nine years after 1753. Thomas Jones was only twenty-four when he came to the parish, a man of delicate health and fervent spirit. A letter of his to Wesley, written when he had been for six years at St. Saviour's, asked for help and advice of which his youth and inexperience and "small stature in grace" so greatly stood in need. He went on to express his conviction that religion consisted "not in opinions but in the union of the soul with God," and ended by asking Wesley to pray for him that he might be daily more humble, *unaffectedly humble*, and he underlined the words. It was not the quality most often to be found among these new enthusiasts; it did not come easily, for instance, to Jones' neighbour at St. Olave's, William Romaine, who had suffered considerably in fashionable parishes across the river from stubborn churchwardens and well-to-do congregations who were horrified to find their pews occupied by "a ragged, unsavoury multitude come to hear the words of salvation." Romaine warned Jones that if he continued "with so much fidelity" he must be prepared to have dead dogs and cats thrown at his head, but the chaplain of St. Saviour's was of a gentler temper than his friend and he met criticism by a mixture of obedience and persistence that was disarming. "His own flock was much upon his heart," Romaine wrote of him, when he collected his friend's writings after his too-early death. "He was always studying and contriving something that might be useful to their best interest." He began to preach and read prayers to the old people of Cure's college, a duty that was often neglected, and the little congregation grew steadily as folk dropped in who would scarcely have dared to cross the respectable portals of St. Saviour's, and listened to the simple wonderful words of one who seemed to mean what he said. Whereupon, the churchwardens objected and refused Jones the use of the college chapel. He contented himself by starting a weekly lecture in the church but again the wardens would not let him continue. One summer, he succeeded in obeying the prayer book rubric and read matins and evensong daily, but even this was regarded as savouring dangerously of enthusiasm, and as soon as August came he was told that as winter was approaching he had better stop. It was against the background of these frustrations that Jones wrote to Wesley and prayed for humility. In a visitation sermon preached in 1755, in the presence of the Archdeacon, he hit out fairly hard declaring that the doctrine of salvation by faith was an integral part of the thirty-nine articles and that those who denied it were guilty of perjury. It was as well that the Bishop was not present himself, for the Bishop of Winchester was the famous Benjamin Hoadley, the champion

*par excellence* of moderation in all things. But Hoadley's worst sin
was his negligence in his episcopal duties and he probably knew
little of what went on at St. Saviour's.

Jones was happier on less controversial occasions and the
most attractive of his sermons was one he preached on a May
morning upon the text, "The time of the singing of birds is
at hand." He spoke of the beauty of the spring. Without the
Thames sparkled in the sunshine and the trees were green in the
spacious churchyard, and within young Thomas Jones spoke
of the joy which came to men, who accepted the gift of grace
and found in the beauty of the world the emblem of more
lasting felicity.

It was not always May, and within the parish bounds there were
many dark corners. To all of them, sooner or later, Jones pene-
trated. He carried with him a stock of bibles and other "good
books" which according to Romaine he took in person "to every
house in the parish; catechising the children, who came weekly to
his house for that purpose, and paying religious visits among his
parishioners when they use to talk freely of the state of their
souls." All who have known and loved a faithful parish priest will
be able to imagine Thomas Jones making his way in all weathers
along Bankside, up Deadman's Place, in Three Crown Court or the
alleyways of Montague Close, greeted by the watermen, giving a
hand to the children, cheering the tired women and asking with
sympathy and understanding of the men and their affairs. His
quiet serenity as his body wasted, his persistence in doing good
and in trying all by the touchstone of Christ, above all his love for
his people, for whom as he lay dying he prayed continally "Lord,
feed Thy sheep", these were the things that brought men to God,
be their home in Borough or in Clink. If for all her blunders, all
her blindness, the Church of England has not perished it is because in every generation she has never entirely lacked such men
as these.

The memorials in the church to the men of the eighteenth
century are a strangely varied assortment. A monument to Jones'
memory was set up by certain members of the congregation who
had appreciated his ministry. Far humbler is the stone set up to
commemorate another devoted soul who did his duty in a very

different sphere of life. Abraham Newland, born in 1730, entered the Bank of England as a clerk and rose to be chief cashier. He held the post for twenty-five years and during that time never once slept away from the Bank. No doubt he grew to be a dry old curmudgeon, an all but mythical figure to the junior clerks and office boys, a disembodied name to the public who spoke of an Abraham Newland, as we used to speak of a Bradbury. But he did his duty, and he died with a quiet mind two months after leaving his job in 1817. At the end he asked to see the papers, so that he could take the latest news to "those on the other side," and he wrote his own epitaph in the lines:

> Beneath this stone old Abraham dies
> Nobody laughs and nobody cries
> Where he has gone and how he fares,
> No one knows and nobody cares.

He left £60,000 to his housekeeper who put up a simple stone to his memory, but did not make use of his verse.

Another eighteenth century eccentric is commemorated in the window dedicated to Alexander Cruden, the author of the famous Concordance, who was subject to intermittent attacks of insanity hard to reconcile with the clarity and vigour of intellect required for such a work. Nourished on the strong meat of Scottish fundamentalism he possessed a nature so essentially simple and kindly that he could never come to terms with the cruelties and complexities of life. An unhappy love affair in Aberdeen first threw him off his balance but after a fortnight in the Tolbooth he recovered and came to London where he earned a precarious livelihood correcting proofs. For a few brief days he was engaged to read French with Lord Derby, who dismissed him because of his execrable pronunciation, and Cruden's mad ride across England from Aldermansbury to Knowsley, in an attempt to obtain reinstatement, illustrates the pertinacity of a man too regardless of circumstance to be entirely sane. Unsuccessful, he returned to his proof-reading and began his concordance, which had originated as a game on Scottish sabbath afternoons.

A dark road lay ahead of the eccentric genius. When the concordance was published he found himself famous and was invited to an audience at St. James with Queen Caroline, George II's enlightened consort. A gift of £100 was promised to defray his expenses, but within a fortnight the Queen had died and he heard no more of the money, while the immediate shock prepared the way for his second mental breakdown. It was again a love affair, the unsuccessful courtship of a rich widow, which precipitated another collapse. The widow's jealous friends upon the first signs of queer behaviour hurried him away to a private madhouse in Bethnal Green, where this mildest of men was kept in chains and a strait waistcoat for ten fearful weeks. At last he escaped and went to live with his sister, pursuing his studies undisturbed for fourteen years quietly and not too queerly. Nobody worried much that he called himself Alexander the Corrector and began to imagine that he was destined to mend the morals as well as the scholarship of his contemporaries. But in 1753 another emotional entanglement unhinged him, and one evening, after a strenuous day's work on the proofs of Spenser's *Faerie Queene* he went out with a shovel in the spirit of a medieval knight and engaged in a violent street brawl with a young man who was using evil language! A third confinement in Chelsea was the result and after his release he used gentler methods. At the end he rose to true greatness, when he heard by chance of a young sailor, condemned to death for cashing, at another's request, a pay-ticket which did not belong to him. The execution was to take place in two days, and for forty-eight hours Cruden worked feverishly, in the same mood in which he had ridden to Knowsley, writing, interviewing, making a thorough nuisance of himself until he succeeded in reaching the Home Secretary and at the very last moment obtained the reprieve. Then he entered Newgate to see the young stranger he had saved, and the horror and desolation of the scene nearly broke his heart and called forth protests and expostulations that place him among the pioneers of prison reform. In his last years he was cared for by a prostitute, who had accosted him one night and whom he had taken into his own home to be his devoted servant. It was she who found him dead one morning upon his knees in prayer. He was buried in the graveyard of the dissenting chapel in Deadman's Place. He had no particular link with the Borough and St. Saviour's knew nothing of him while he lived, yet it is fitting that he whose bones were laid to rest within the parish should be remembered in the church not only as a scholar but as one who served Christ.

Two other great men honoured to-day in the windows of the north aisle had also only a brief connection with St. Saviour's. It is none the less a link that it is good to have. In 1755, when Thomas Jones was chaplain, when the Borough Market was transferred from the High Street to Rochester Yard and when Alexander Cruden particularly enjoyed a visit to Oxford, young Oliver Goldsmith returned from his travels in Europe and settled in Southwark, where for nearly two years he practised medicine in a house on Bankside, making little money but healing and helping, in his unreliable charming Irish way, the poor and disreputable who came to him for aid. Ten years later he revisited the Borough to dine with Samuel Johnson and other literary lights at some of Hester Thrale's famous dinner parties.

In 1635 when St. Saviour's wardens were making a return of new buildings they recorded a "brewhouse and dwellinghouse," belonging to James Monger and lying between Deadman's Place and Globe Alley. (Globe Alley ran into Deadman's Place at right-angles parallel to and immediately south of Maid Lane.) Monger's successor was James Child, who died in 1696 and whose son-in-law, Edmund Halsey, inherited the property and extended it eastward. Halsey was M.P. for Southwark and a leading member of St. Saviour's congregation and his daughter married into the aristocracy, in the person of Richard Temple, Lord Cobham. A peer could scarcely be expected in the eighteenth century to run a brewery and upon Halsey's death in 1728 the business went to Ralph Thrale his nephew, whom Boswell dismisses with scorn as one who had worked "at six shillings a week for twenty years." None the less he could produce £30,000 as the estimated value of the brewery; he leased more ground from Winchester including the site of the old Globe theatre and bought back from Lord Cobham the freehold lands which Halsey had left to his son-in-law. His dwelling house stood on the west side of Deadman's Place, and a plaque on a house in the modern Park Street marks the site. The Independent meeting house and the burial ground were isolated in the midst of these developments. The land was acquired in due course in 1781 and the meeting house moved to Union Street

ST. MARY OVERIE'S DOCK TO-DAY.

The dock stands just to the west of the Cathedral.

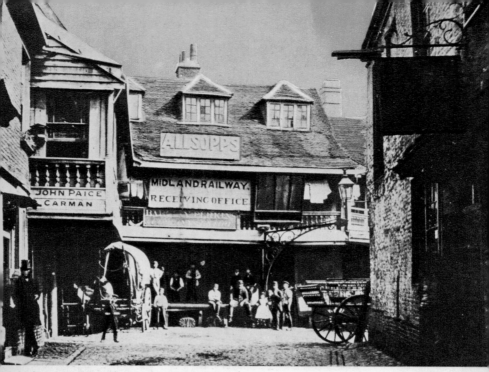

THE YARD OF THE OLD TABARD INN.    The inn was pulled down in 187

ST. THOMAS'S CHURCH, NOW THE CHAPTER HOUSE.

The Foster Memorial Hall and the eighteenth-century Treasurer's House adjoin it.

seven years afterwards; the last interment in the burial ground was in 1837.

Ralph Thrale, a trustee of St. Saviour's church and the leading man of the district, brought up his son as a gentleman, sending him to Oxford and settling £1,000 a year upon him. The result was a young man of "civil and decorous bearing" and an agreeable countenance, who possessed his fair share of the vices considered essential to an eighteenth-century gentleman. He married a young woman of Welsh extraction and extreme vivacity, represented Southwark in Parliament in the Tory interest and divided his time between his house in Deadman's Place, to which he added a delightful garden, and the villa in Streatham which his father had bought and which he enlarged and beautified. His wife enjoyed herself in making the acquaintance of men of letters and it was in October 1765 that the great Samuel Johnson received his first invitation to dinner with the "eminent and haughty brewer" and his attractive wife. Thereafter he was a constant and petted visitor both at Streatham and in the Borough, sometimes holding forth at a dinner table where Burke and Garrick and Goldsmith might be among his audience, always treated as one of the family and enjoying in Mrs. Thrale's affectionate friendship a domestic felicity he had seldom experienced. When Henry Thrale died in 1781, Johnson expected Hetty to retire into a becoming widowhood and continue to look after him. He helped her first to dispose of the brewery and Boswell has left a vivid picture of the great doctor's final visit to St. Saviour's parish on the occasion of the sale, bustling about like an excise man with an ink-pen in his button-hole and declaring with foresight that proved to be accurate: "we are not here to sell a parcel of boilers and vats but the potentiality of growing rich beyond the dreams of avarice."

The brewery was bought for £135,000 by a rich mercer, David Barclay, for his nephew Robert; "a knot of Quakers," Mrs. Thrale described them in her diary, remarking that their appearance saved her from bankruptcy. She herself, unpredictable as always, proceeded to marry her Italian charmer, the singer Piozzi, which effectively put an end to poor Johnson's hope of a pleasant and tranquil old age. He was never again to be so well-content as in the hours he spent in Streatham or in the old house in the midst of the brewery.

The Barclays had been introduced to Mrs. Thrale by the faithful John Perkins, who had worked for her husband as loyally as Ralph Thrale worked for Halsey and indeed had been for some years the mainstay of the business. It was Perkins who bought the house in Deadman's Place and in 1781 he went into partnership with the new owners. His name and that of his son, and of Charles Barclay, Robert's heir, appear frequently in the annals of the parish and of Southwark in the succeeding years, and the old house continued to welcome distinguished guests to its hospitable quarters, refugees from revolutionary France, the adorable Jenny Lind and in due time the Prince Consort himself.

On one particular occasion Perkins' shrewd courage stood the district in good stead, when Southwark experienced a night of terror more in keeping with the attacks of Tyler and Cade than the normal decency of respectable eighteenth-century life. The Gordon riots, described so vividly in the pages of *Barnaby Rudge*, grew out of a meeting in St. George's Field called to protest upon the repeal of the penal laws against the Roman Catholics. A deputation dangerous only in its numbers marshalled its thousands in orderly array and marched on Westminster where the unstable Lord George Gordon presented their case amid scenes of great excitement. Meanwhile across the river, the crowds who were left in St. George's Fields were inflamed by agitators until pandemonium broke loose and the rioters marched into the Borough, burning and destroying the old Clink prison and the Marshalsea. Then amid scenes of general havoc the mob threatened the brewery. John Perkins calmly and courteously headed them off, giving them £50 to refresh themselves at a neighbouring public house and offering them horses to transport their loot. While the baffled leaders decided how to respond to this unusual treatment the stout Mr. Perkins had surreptitiously summoned the troops and when the rioters again advanced to the attack they were firmly and successfully dispersed.

This surprising outburst of violence showed all too clearly how thin even yet was the veneer of civilisation in this unruly suburb. The Southwark of the times was a mixture of old and new. Parliamentary elections were still the occasion for incredible scenes of force and fraud combined. The steward appointed by the City still held quarterly the court leet of the three manors, the silver staff going before him that is now borne proudly in procession by the verger of the Cathedral church. The court house, rebuilt after the fire of 1676, had again fallen into decay by 1793, when the sessions were held in the Three Tuns Tavern and the statue of Charles II that had stood before the new court house was re-erected in Three Tuns Court. The relations between the City authorities and the Surrey magistrates went from bad to worse during these years and came to a head in a quarrel over the Duck and Dog, a rendezvous for prostitutes in St. George's Fields.

Amid all these varied happenings, in every change of time and circumstance and the small coin of daily living, the worship of God continued in the old church of St. Saviour's. In 1794 William Winkworth succeeded Smith, whose crabbed handwriting filled so many pages in the registers of baptisms, marriages and funerals. Winkworth died in 1804, "pious without ostentation, zealous with discretion," preaching the kingdom of God "to a very respectable and often a very numerous congregation." The good Christian of the eighteenth century lived in the spirit of the catechism: "to order myself lowly and reverently to all my betters . . . to be true and just in all my dealing . . . to learn and labour truly to get my own living and to do my duty in that state of life unto which it shall please God to call me." As the Evangelical movement spread there was an increased sense of immediacy and personal commitment in their charitable efforts. But there was not as yet a corresponding deepening of fervour in the corporate life of the church. It is not perhaps entirely chance that so much of this chapter of St. Saviour's history is the story of individuals. After the collapse of the select vestry the sense of responsibility for the well-being of the church became diffused; and the steady deterioration of the fabric is symptomatic of a changed attitude. In the first century and a half of the church's existence as St. Saviour's, Emerson or Bingham, Henslowe or Applebee or Blisse would have had their hands in their pockets and by hook or crook the decay appearing in the wooden roof would have been remedied before it was too late. They were not necessarily superior in morals to the men who came after them, but they had an active concern in the welfare of their church both as a precious possession of the past and as a

symbol of a living faith, as much a vital and compelling responsibility as their business or pleasures or duties in court or parliament. That sense of the reality of man's membership of the body
of Christ, that emphasis on worship which had been felt so
strongly by the Anglicans of the seventeenth century, had been
largely lost in the religion of the succeeding age, based often on
conduct and, after the evangelical revival, on the individual's
sense of his personal relations with his Saviour. Those very people
who were most anxious to mediate the word of God in Southwark
looked most askance at the large and cumbersome and decaying
building, which was their parish church, reminding themselves
that St. George's and St. Olave's, St. John's at Horsely Down
and their own neighbouring Christ Church all possessed new
eighteenth-century churches, more suitable to their task.

To add to their difficulties and doubts about the future, a new
age with new problems was opening for England. For a quarter
of a century the shadow of war lay upon the country as the
struggle with revolutionary France and with Napoleon shattered
for ever the idea of *laissez-faire* and, less noticeably but even more
surely, a revolution in industry made impossible any return to
what had been before. In St. Saviour's parish after the building of
the bridges, though no great manufacture was established, the
steady growth of the brewery dominated the scene and in all
the surrounding parts, as in the courts and alleys that adjoined
the High Street, large numbers of "labouring poor," who worked
across the river, came out from London each night to sleep in a
district where they had no roots. The merchants at the same time
moved out, as Thrale had done to Streatham, to Kennington or
Camberwell, to join the group of well-to-do Evangelicals at
Clapham or to occupy one of the fine new residences that were
being built around the Green at Wimbledon. How long would
the congregation at the parish church remain numerous as well as
very respectable? Would St. Saviour's soon be left with empty
pews, and with the answer yet to seek how best to proclaim the
Gospel to sordid homes and an apathetic people? Or would the
Spirit of God find a new way to pierce the hearts and understanding of men, so that the church of St. Mary Overie and St.
Saviour might be saved to glorify God in the uncertain future as
surely as in the generations that were gone?

## Note on Sources

For the various bills against select vestries, see *Commons Journals*, XVIII, 434, 438, 445, 449, and for the wider aspects of the subject cf. S. and B. Webb's *English Local Government*, vol. 1. *The Parish and the County* (1906); the struggle at St. Saviour's in 1730 is recorded in the vestry minutes. Strype's edition of Stow's *Survey* published in 1720 illustrates by the editorial additions to Stow's original the changes that were taking place in the Borough and two contemporary works give a vivid picture of Southwark at a slightly later date, H. Chamberlain, *New and Complete History of London, Westminster and Borough of Southwark* (1770) and Concanen and Morgan, *History and Antiquities of the Parish of St. Saviour's Southwark* (1795); see G. Bayley, *op. cit.*, pp. 37, 42, re John Collet's foundation.

For Thomas Jones, see W. Romaine's collection of his works; and for Cruden, Edith Olivier, *The eccentric life of Alexander Cruden* (1934). For the Thrale brewery and Samuel Johnson, see Golden *Old Bankside*, pp. 53–67, and cf. *Survey, Bankside*, pp. 78–9.

# XVII

# CHANGES AND CHANCES

BENJAMIN HOADLEY'S successors in the see of Winchester, John Thomas and the Honourable Brownlow North, were both described by their biographer as "amiable men." Sir George Pretyman Tomline, who succeeded North in 1820, was a sound theologian, a mathematician of repute and a shrewd political observer, in earlier days the friend and mentor of the younger Pitt. But neither Tomline nor his predecessors were in any close sense fathers in God to the clergy and laity of their huge unwieldy diocese, least of all to that stretch of it which lay beside the Thames, so different in its appearance and its problems from the Winchester country or the rural hinterland of Surrey.

When Tomline died in 1827 George IV seized the occasion to promote Charles Summer, Bishop of Llandaff, a young man of thirty-seven, who had been introduced to the King by a former pupil and by his charm no less than his devotion had won his sovereign's enthusiastic patronage. Summer was the son of a country parson and through his mother was connected with the Wilberforces and influenced by the Evangelical fervour of the day. He and his brother, who became Bishop of Chester, were among the first members of the episcopal bench to give their full support to the Evangelical clergy and together with Blomfield of London they were chiefly responsible for a complete change in the attitude of the bishops to their pastoral responsibilities.

Yet Summer was not a typical Evangelical and there lingered about him a certain resemblance to the great prelates of an earlier age which rendered appropriate a contemporary's salutation upon his retirement, "last of our old Prince Bishops, fare thee well." When he was a young man his sister, with excusable bias, compared him to Philip Sidney, "made to delight all eyes and win all hearts," and he possessed in youth and age alike a charm, which was in part the natural glow of good health, and a graciousness of manner that eased the path both for him and those with whom he dealt. Especially did he delight in the art of hospitality, exercised to perfection with the help of his Swiss wife, against the background of Farnham Castle. Yet all this was never allowed to play proxy for hard work and conscientious enquiry, and in spite of certain limitations in vision and in knowledge of the middle class of tradesman and artisan, which formed the backbone of the Southwark congregations, St. Saviour's owed him much as did every church in his diocese. For during a lifetime of devoted work at Winchester—forty-two years from the age of thirty-seven till he retired after a stroke in his eightieth year—he drew closer than they had been for many decades the personal relations between the bishop and his clergy. He improved the administration of the diocese, combining energy with an intelligent appreciation of the problems involved, and he met the challenge of the industrial age by building many new churches, among them St. Peter's in a new street in Southwark that was named Sumner St. He urged decent ceremonial and a more frequent administration of the sacrament, but lest externals should loom too large, exhorted his ordinands to "preach Christ, preach Him again, preach nothing but Christ."

The improvement came none too soon, for the disturbing years of revolution and war, twenty-five years of challenge and endurance and change had given men furiously to think and the reaction after 1815 had canalised criticism of an effete Church and corrupt State in such a way as to threaten not only the ecclesiastical establishment, but the faith of thinking men. Bishop Summer was no more immune than his fellows from attack, but the heightened sense of duty which characterised his administration and his encouragement of that brand of Evangelical piety which manifested itself in a concern for the abolition of social evils did much to breed in laymen and clergy alike a new sense of discipleship in the Church of England so that under God it was enabled to survive.

For the chequered history of St. Saviour's during these critical years there is a treasure-trove of information, and of inspiration if one can read the pages aright, in two bound volumes, reminiscent of the bulky photograph albums of Victorian days, housed in the library of the British Museum. They contain the papers, collected over sixty years of loving service in the parish, by Samuel Benson who came thither as curate in 1824. In the first volume is the manuscript copy of a small guide to St. Saviour's which he wrote in his old age; in the second, interleaved with many notes and illustrations, are two of the standard works on the old church, the *History and Antiquities of the Parochial church of St. Saviour's*, by Nightingale and Moss and the *Annals of St. Mary Overy*, published in 1833 by W. Taylor, one of the many antiquarians and scholars whose interest and labours contributed to the timely repair of the choir and Lady Chapel. But in addition there are magazine articles, newspaper cuttings, prints and drawings of every kind, and a host of ephemeral letters, personal keepsakes, manuscript notes, all the material remains of Benson's passionate love for everything that had to do with Southwark. With a sigh of despair, the investigator discovers that there is no pagination, no index, few references, and many an original snippet of information written in long hand with nothing to shew whether it emanated from library shelf or parish gossip. It is indeed an exasperating, unreliable and altogether irresistible collection, and there are few of the famous people whose destinies have been linked with the church's continuing life who do not appear somewhere in this glorious hotch-potch of material.

It is from these pages, supplemented by the more orthodox sources, that one can best reconstruct the story of those vivid years in the church's history between 1815 and 1843. The rush of events and the sudden rise in the spiritual and emotional barometer are refreshing after the somewhat nondescript chronicle of the preceding century. Yet it was not without growing pains that the parish emerged into the prosperous middle-years of Queen Victoria's reign, and the battles fought out in the vestry, and the surprising actions to which they sometimes led, though never dull are often hard to reconcile with the conception of a Christian congregation.

Material changes came thick and fast. Benson gives some statistics which show the parish to have grown from fifteen to eighteen thousand souls between 1811 and 1831, but this increase was in no way comparable to that of St. George's, which had a population of twenty-eight thousand in 1811 and of thirty-nine thousand in 1831, mainly in consequence of the rapid development of the area of St. George's Fields. Nor was there as yet any great change in occupation among the parishioners of St. Saviour's, though admittedly it was a far cry to the days when they had paid their dues in cartloads of hay; by 1831 only four of the ratepayers were engaged in agriculture. Of "wholesale merchants, bankers, professional persons and other educated men," there were rather more than two hundred and as yet, rather surprisingly, only one hundred and thirty-four concerned with manufacture or the making of machinery. The large majority of employers and wage earners, nearly three thousand in number, were engaged in handicrafts or the retail trade, a conclusion borne out by the baptismal registers of the period which show that leather-dressers, cheesemongers, corn chandlers, coopers, glass-blowers, hosiers, horsehairmen, brewers' servants and very occasionally gentlemen were the proud fathers of the babes welcomed at St. Saviour's into the family of Christ's Church.

Between 1820 and 1840 two major developments, within the parish, considerably accelerated the process of change. New London Bridge was built with a consequent increase in traffic and a threat to the church's very existence as the ruthless planners sited the southern approach within a few yards of St. Saviour's retro-choir. Ten years later the opening of the Greenwich railway and the building of London Bridge station gave fresh impetus to the industrial developments, and began the process which eventually drove St. Thomas's to another site and encompassed St. Saviour's with mammoth viaducts, subjecting it to a daily bombardment of noise.

It was well for the parish that there were also changes of another sort. The Evangelical revival, of which Thomas Jones had been the harbinger at St. Saviour's, had by now permeated the church as a whole and had produced in the second generation a spiritual force of so marked a character that the Evangelicals exercised an influence out of all proportion to their numbers. In Southwark, as they faced the challenge of the new industrial age, the spiritual starvation of many of the "labouring poor," the entirely inadequate provision of free seats in the churches or of opportunities for schooling became a burning question and the state of St. Saviour's began to receive a good deal of unfavourable criticism. A part of the nave was filled with "high-backed pews, in which whole resident families worshipped, many of them sitting face to face as in a room." The free seats were negligible and the "damp old monastery," as some called it in derision, was draughty, uncomfortable and owing to its bad acoustics quite unsuitable for that preaching of the Word which was the very centre of the Evangelical faith. It began to be said, though as yet very tentatively, that Christ would best be served by pulling it down and building in its place a spacious and convenient church with adequate accommodation for the poor for whom so little room could be found in the carefully locked pews of St. Saviour's.

There were however other forces at work, in the renewed interest not only in Gothic architecture but in all for which the medieval age had stood. In literature it showed itself in the romantic revival of which Keats was a supreme example, Keats, who was living in Southwark in 1815 while studying medicine at Guy's. Is it possible that his love of the medieval age which shines so clearly through the verses of St. Agnes' Eve was nourished at this time by the close neighbourhood of St. Saviour's Lady Chapel?

In 1818, W. G. Moss published his series of engravings of the old church with historical notes by the Rev. J. Nightingale. In the dedication to the Duke of Cambridge, the author claimed that few ecclesiastical buildings in the kingdom and none in the metropolis were "better calculated to display the grand and imposing character" of Gothic architecture than St. Saviour's. The book was published by subscription, to which the Bishop contributed and leading business men of Southwark and also architects and antiquarians from various other parts of London. St. Saviour's, in fact, for a few brief years was to be very much in the lime-light. For as soon as it was recognised that the church was indeed a precious heritage, and not just an unwieldy and uncomfortable parish church, the deplorable state of the fabric and the urgent need of drastic and immediate repair became the concern of many beyond the parish, and by degrees a violent divergence of opinion manifested itself between those imbued by antiquarian zeal and a love of ancient beauty and those whose watchwords were economy and more immediate efficiency in preaching the Gospel to the poor.

There were however many less worthy motives that emerged in the twenty years between 1818 and 1838 during which the antiquarians and their opponents fought out the battle over the choir, transepts, nave and Lady Chapel in turn. It would be an over-simplification to describe it as a clear-cut division between the "high" and "low" parties in the church. The Bishop, who backed up the restorers whole-heartedly at a later stage of the dispute, had evangelical sympathies as had many of those upon whom they relied for financial support. The unsavoury propaganda that poured forth at various crises in the conflict show how much of faction was involved and of personal prejudices and animosities. The vestry, consisting now not of a responsible few but of all "scot and lot" men of the parish who cared to attend, was made the occasion for promulgating anti-clerical opinions and political propaganda, and the deep distrust of popery was never absent, manifesting itself in all sorts of bitter gibes at the church's original monastic character. More sober parishioners were honestly frightened at the expenditure entailed and resented the intrusion of outsiders into parochial affairs, the visits of experts who came from Westminster or Hampstead to look at an ancient monument but took no share in the arduous business of running it as an effective parish church. St. Saviour's parish was not a rich community and the constant drain of money for repairs, particularly if it necessitated raising the church rate, bore hardly upon all sorts of persons, not least upon the dissenters whom many fair-minded people thought to be unjustly treated in this respect. But behind all these lesser causes of division, there did remain a real spiritual cleavage between the men on the one hand, whose love and knowledge of medieval lore would lead them in the next few decades into alliance with the tractarians, and those protestants who, like their puritan predecessors, tended to distrust beauty as a veil that came between the soul and its personal relationship with Christ.

In 1818 there was still apparent unanimity when action first became imperative. For the bells had struck a clear note of warning; when they sounded, the tower vibrated till it seemed in imminent danger of collapse. The work of repair was put in hand by John Crawford, warden of the great account, and George Gwilt, whose name the church must always hold in reverence and affection, set to work to strengthen the tower, renewing the vanes and rebuilding the parapets. Gwilt's father was surveyor to the Clink Paving Commissioners and to St. George's Parish. He lived in Union Street with his son and took especial delight in his private museum of local antiquities. The younger George had imbibed love of Southwark with his mother's milk and in his adult years as an architect combined knowledge and ability with a deep devotion to St. Saviour's Church. As soon as his work on the tower was completed he and a body of like enthusiasts, among whom was William Mann, the chaplain, advanced a scheme for the restoration of the thirteenth-century choir. It was now that the divergence of opinion in the vestry became apparent and the suggestion was made that the tottering old church should be demolished, but this idea was as yet only approved by a small minority and in 1821 the restoration of the choir was put in hand. It entailed a good deal of rebuilding in the clerestory and triforium and Gwilt was hampered by conflicting instructions from his committee in their urgent wish to economise. None the less, he tackled the work with care and great skill and a deep-rooted affection for the church and its glorious past, and was only driven by his love of the Gothic to one major deviation in replacing Fox's Tudor window by one of three lights, reminiscent of that in Salisbury Cathedral. In 1822 the old chapel of Mary Magdalene was removed, an alteration later architects have justified in that it admitted more light to the refurbished choir and added space that was badly needed in the approach to the church from the south-eastern side. The historian, none the less, must regret its loss.

The repair of the choir was just completed when Samuel Benson first came to Southwark. In 1823, as a young man fresh from Cambridge, he was licensed as a curate to St. John's, Horsley Down, and in the following year William Mann, who had been an old friend of his father's, invited him to transfer to St. Saviour's and paid him the not very princely salary of £80 a year. Mann and Dr. William Harrison his colleague, "highly approved and faithful ministers of the word of life," as a contemporary calls them, were both getting on in years and the figure of the hard-working young curate became very familiar and well-beloved in the highways and byways of the parish during the succeeding years. Benson was the son of a Wesleyan minister and had been born in Hull in

1799. There is a portrait of him among his papers, and it shows him to have been no weakling: one who ministered for sixty years in Southwark needed a streak of iron in his nature to survive and Benson brought with him to the task his inheritance of north-country grit. But he possessed also the gifts of sympathy and imagination, to judge by the shrewd and humorous eyes, which redeem from harshness the rather tight-lipped features and the spare, lean figure. His devotion to duty and the sincerity of his Christian discipleship was proved in many long years of unceasing and often thankless labour.

The year after his arrival in his new parish there occurred a very particular day, of which he kept every possible memento in his collection, when the foundation stone was laid of the new London Bridge. The dilapidated state of the old bridge had exercised the City authorities and the parishioners of St. Saviour's for more than half a century until at length an Act for the erection of a new bridge forced the hands of the Common Council whose reluctance to lose their ancient monument can well be understood. The designs of the famous bridge builder, James Rennie, were accepted in 1821 and the new erection was originally to be on the same site as its predecessor, but when the authorities insisted on the old bridge remaining in being till the new one was completed it was sited some yards to the westward, much to the inconvenience both of Fishmongers Hall on the north and St. Saviour's at the southern end. James Rennie died almost immediately, and his son John completed the details of his design and supervised the work. At length in June 1825 the foundation stone was laid by the then Lord Mayor, in the presence of the King's brother, the Duke of York. With them, in a splendid procession, rode fellows of the Royal Society, members of parliament, officials of the City, while those who awaited their arrival were served with fruit and wine and refreshments and entertained "by a choir of charity children and an excellent band of music." It was a perfect June day and the banks of the river swarmed with well-dressed persons while the Thames itself and the old bridge vied with each other in gaily beflagged barge and equipage. The neighbouring towers of St. Olave's and St. Saviour's were crowded with spectators. And all the while the sun shone: what a day! what an occasion!

The work took six years to complete and meanwhile one or two facts became apparent. The southern approach to the new bridge would run very near to the eastern end of the old church, and at a considerably higher level. The new road would be lined, it was hoped, by shops and houses of suitable elegance (the ones that were eventually built, John Rennie considered to be totally inadequate). The tradesmen of Southwark were eager to make the most of the new developments and more adverse than ever to wasting a large amount of money on a dilapidated building that would almost be hidden from view. The idea of a completely new church, to match the temper of the times, began rapidly to gain ground. In October 1825, tenders were invited for either the repair or rebuilding of the nave at a cost of some £13,000, and a scheme presented by George Gwilt received the proffered prize, but the vestry could not come to a clear decision whether to repair or rebuild and the work was not put in hand. Such a policy of shilly-shally was disastrous and nothing was done, while with every day's inaction the great timber roof fell further into decay.

Meanwhile the insatiable restorers turned their attention to the transepts, a smaller job which might perhaps be tackled with impunity. But when in 1828 they took advantage of a sparsely attended vestry to obtain authority to proceed, there was an immediate outcry and a flood of expostulatory leaflets. Why, asked Mr. Benjamin Blackmore of the High Street, throw away thousands of pounds on "a church ten or fifteen feet below the level of the road to the bridge; a church cold, damp, uncomfortable and unhealthy; a church so spacious that the voice of the minister is frequently inaudible except to those immediately around him, a church which at the expiration of half a century will perhaps be tumbling about your heads." Unfortunately for the cause of the restorers, the responsible committee accepted an estimate considerably higher than others that were tendered, and this of course was fatal.

Come cheer up my lads tis to profit we steer
And we'll add a new job to this impudent year,

so ran one of the leaflets, and on December 10th the parishioners voted that the work should not be continued, a decision described by Blackmore and his friends as "the glorious triumph . . . when the combination was broken up." A year later, however, the repair of the transepts was authorised and the work entrusted to Robert Wallace, a west-end architect. He was not like Gwilt soaked in the history and atmosphere of the old building and was even more hampered than Gwilt had been by his committee's insistence on the utmost economy. He did a competent piece of work, but he made an unwise choice of material, which necessitated further repairs at a later stage, and the new window he put in the south transept did not please the purists as out of keeping with the rest. It too was replaced at the end of the century.

It was at this juncture that the antiquarians suffered some bad reverses. During 1830, the bishop's chapel was removed, in part because of its dilapidated state, in part because it would leave less obscured the view of the east end from the road to the new bridge. The chapel after the 1676 fire had no great architectural merits and its removal served mainly as a warning as to the possible fate of the Lady Chapel, which lay in an equally bad condition clamouring for repair. Far more disastrous was the action taken by the omnipotent parishioners, who decided in May 1831 that the wooden roof of the nave should be taken down and the stone work and the family vaults below left open to the weather while the pews were removed to an enclosure within the choir and transepts. Some of the wooden bosses of the roof, salvaged at a later date, are preserved to-day at the west end of the church, to delight with their vitality and fine craftsmanship and to sadden the heart as a reminder of beauty that might have been preserved.

When things like this could happen it was no time for prudence, that dubitable virtue, and before the end of the year, the Don Quixotes of St. Saviour's had embarked on their greatest venture, the preservation of the Lady Chapel. In August, the bridge was officially opened by King William IV on another festive occasion, when the ceremony was succeeded by a feast of three hours' duration and unimaginable extent. When it was over and John Rennie the engineer had been duly knighted and they had put aside their fine uniforms of blue coats, white waistcoats and white pantaloons, the Bridge committee returned to the consideration of outstanding problems. Eventually they decided that the approaches to the bridge from Southwark must be widened and that St. Saviour's could only be allowed 60 ft. clearance, later extended to 70 ft. An amending bill was prepared to lay before parliament and it boded ill for the Lady Chapel, whose removal was now urged as a necessity. As if to underline its danger, in November 1831 in a letter to the Press, the antiquarian Taylor who had come to know and love every corner of the church drew attention to the dilapidated state of the chapel, "one of the most chaste and elegant specimens of early pointed architecture of the 13th century still existing in England." In fact, if it escaped the scylla of the bridge committee it was likely to perish before the charybdis of internal decay.

In January 1832 matters came to a crisis. The Bishop had averted immediate disaster by refusing his consent to the bridge committee's recommendation. He also sent a large subscription to the restoration fund, opened at a protest meeting held at the George Inn on January 21st. For the antiquarians and their friends had learnt by now what their line of approach should be. The financial burden must not be on the parish alone. They must dare to claim for the church they loved the support of all who valued it as a national treasure, worthy to be placed in the same category as its great neighbours across the Thames. It was by voluntary giving, not by mulcting the hard-pressed parishioners, that St. Saviour's would be saved.

But would it be saved? It was for the vestry to decide whether or not the Lady Chapel should go and three days after the protest meeting at the George, they passed a resolution that it should be demolished. Fortunately the decision had to be confirmed at a second vestry when the vote for the chapel's removal was carried by only three votes, and, sensing a change of feeling, the minority exercised their right of demanding a poll.

During the two days of the poll, the parish was in a state of tumult and propaganda of every sort poured forth. One "old inhabitant" complained: "even my children can now think of nothing but cupolas, arches and colums [sic] and altho' I have expended considerable sums in preparing their minds for pursuits quite different from architectural designs, yet (thanks to the great agitation of the chapel question) their attention is fixed entirely upon the Ionic, Gothic, Doric or Bore-ic order, until I have at length arrived at the happy state of having in my own dwelling

GUY'S HOSPITAL LOOKING OVER THE BOMBED SITE OF GREAT MAZE POND.

Immediately behind the hospital is the tower of St. Thomas's Church,
with the tower of the Cathedral Church to the right of it.

BANKSIDE BOYS: THE PARISHIONERS OF THE FUTURE.

no order at all." This householder objected to the disturbance of
his business, and the attitude of the average retail-trader in the
Borough is instanced in a complaint, presented to the Commons,
in which the petitioners stated that they had "already suffered great
losses in trade and rates by the removal of houses and population,
and could not afford to give up the ground requisite to provide St.
Saviour's with an adequate frontage." They even went so far as to
claim "that good houses are the greatest ornament to a commer-
cial town and therefore as a matter of taste it is desirable not to
sacrifice too large a space." Political as well as aesthetic and
economic arguments were in the forefront. The heat and diversity
of the emotions aroused can only be fully appreciated set against
the background of the times, the bitterness of class-feeling after
Peterloo, the deepening of Protestant suspectibility caused by the
Catholic relief bill, and above all in this year of 1832 the political
temper raised to fever heat by the struggle over the Reform Bill.
Among the broadsheets in Benson's collection, full play is made
with the passions of the moment; the Lady Chapel is compared
to "old Sarum" and the vestry's decision to remove it favourably
likened to the inclusion of the rotten borough for disfranchise-
ment in "schedule A" of the new Act. "You have long been
wishing Reform to the enormous expenses of job work of your
decayed Old Church and have been gulled and deceived the last
sixteen years, into a tedious expense of near £35,000."

"The anti-reform Archbishop," the diatribe continues, "Our
anti-reform Bishop, the great Tory Lords of St. Saviour's flattered
by foreign architects and surveyors, have by intrigue, great evil
and great expence prevented your Reform Bill being acted on."
The Lady Chapel had in fact been taken out of Schedule A. Other
leaflets stated that "St. Saviour's Folly was open for inspection,"
that the true aim of the Anti-Reform Association was to take away
the right and liberties of the parishioners and revert to the old
tyranny of the select vestry, that it was a case of Common Sense
v. F.S.A., L.L.D., F.L.S., F.R.S. and A.S.S. The other side asked,
for its part, "where is the spirit of Gower who thought not a
fortune too much to spend in so good a cause." But their most
cogent argument was the fact that the antiquarians and their
friends were prepared to finance the restoration, whereas the
parish itself would have to pay for the demolition. "If these

R                                        257

gentlemen like to keep up the old church at their own expense, let them do it," as one pamphlet succinctly expressed it. When the poll was taken the retention of the chapel was voted by 380 votes to 140. Victory was assured and it only remained in the course of the next two years to complete the fund, to persuade parliament to leave the clearance, as it was, at 130 ft. and to put the work of repair in hand. Charles Pott was treasurer of the appeal fund; George Gwilt added to the debt the church already owed him by supervising the restoration with scrupulous care and loving knowledge, giving freely of his services, and Thomas Saunders took charge of the wider issues. On a summer afternoon in 1835 Charles Barclay, M.P. for Southwark, presented Saunders with a piece of plate, as the man whose "enlightened and indefatigable exertions" were regarded as mainly responsible for the happy conclusion to the chapter. Later a similar presentation was made to Gwilt. It was a heartening example of a great joint effort inspired by the determination of a few and carried out by a steady application of those two favourite English weapons, a subscription list and a committee, and it has earned the gratitude of many, in these strident times, who rejoice in the quiet sanctuaries that lie behind the high altar of to-day's Cathedral church.

In 1833 when the work on the Lady Chapel was begun, the altar had also been restored to something of its original beauty. The classical screen of 1703 had been taken down during the recent repairs and Bishop Fox's reredos had been revealed. An appeal was made for money to restore it and Robert Wallace completed the task in the year Gwilt set to work on the Lady Chapel. Again Wallace did not escape criticism for he made certain alterations in the old screen, introducing new panels and adding above the original three tiers, a new pattern of angels. Yet, when the critics are silenced and the light of the candles illumines the Tudor screen, the niches filled again with the figures of men who have loved and served the church, it remains what it was in the beginning, a masterpiece in stone lifting the heart and eye to worship and to praise.

In this summer of 1833 an epidemic of cholera brought tragedy to Southwark's crowded streets. Among the victims was the younger of the two chaplains, William Harrison. While the summer heat stifled men's spirits and the pestilence still raged, the parish was plunged into the animosities and excitements of a disputed election. The natural course would have been to appoint Samuel Benson, who for eleven years had worked in the district giving devoted care to the aged and infirm, taking a personal interest in the schools and fulfilling with zeal and perseverance the multitudinous duties of the parish priest. But among the four other competitors was one very strong candidate in the person of William Curling, a brilliant young preacher from Bermondsey. Mr. Benson's committee commended their candidate's cheerful diligence on his absurdly meagre stipend, his readiness to visit the poor "by night and by day," his willing sacrifice of time and talents and energy of mind and body. Mr. Curling's committee merely urged folk to go and hear him preach.

The probationary sermons were preached on different Sundays towards the end of August, the candidates agreeing to have them published and to give the proceeds to the ever-necessitous schools. Polling took place on September 10th and 11th, and William Curling won by thirty votes. Benson's letter of thanks to his supporters was a model of discretion and for another ten years he continued to labour faithfully on a stipend of £80 a year, co-operating loyally with the new chaplain. He was not quite enough of a saint to destroy a cutting from *The Age* which remains among his papers; in it, reference is made to the election and William Curling described no doubt unfairly as "celebrated only as a preacher who minces from the pulpit pretty nothings to the weaker sex," while the Bishop is asked to investigate the circumstances of the election and "not to suffer his predilections in favour of the peculiar doctrines of the successful candidate to bias his judgment." Ten years later, when Dr. Mann died, a more subdued election took place and the main energies of the parish were directed towards securing Benson's unanimous choice; though a poll was not avoided the curate triumphed on this occasion by 119 votes to 3.

During the ten intervening years the parish continued to quarrel. Increasingly in these years of tension between the passing of the Reform Bill and the Chartist agitation of 1848, the church, conceived as the preserve of the well-to-do, was subject to continuous attacks and the opposition at St. Saviour's, becoming more virulent with the years, was now in the hands of men whose objection to the antiquarian's zeal or the imposition of the church-rate was based on principles as much political as religious. Luke Embleton the engineer, Dingle the brush-maker and Grist the plasterer were voicing the incoherent feelings of a new generation of industrial workers who suspected the Establishment, had no understanding of tradition and spoke a different language from the gentle old man, John Herd, who took office as Warden of the Great Account at an advanced age and tried in vain to keep order at the turbulent vestries. And while the extremists among the radicals attacked the whole system by refusing to levy a church rate, and the diehard antiquarians fought a rear-guard action in defence of the doomed nave, a growing body of moderate opinion pleaded for an end to strife and the provision of more adequate means of preaching the Gospel.

The crisis in regard to the nave occurred in 1836, the very year that the Greenwich railway built its viaducts, and envisaged the arches filled with houses and warehouses and shops so that on completion there would be "the novel spectacle of one even street extending from London to Greenwich, a distance of nearly four miles!" Small wonder that in such an age of progress those who loved the past fought a losing battle. In June, at a vestry held in the Lady Chapel, amid scenes of noise and violence sadly unfitted to a consecrated building, a motion to repair the nave was put to the meeting and defeated. The "Gothic antiquarian bauble," as someone termed it, was irrevocably doomed. In August a violent offensive was launched against the church rate, and the reporter of this vestry meeting is reduced to the repeated entry: "Great confusion: the confusion increased: here the confusion was very great and no one could be heard."

The rebels voted that no rate should be levied, basing their claim that the parishioners could decide on the ambiguous wording of an eighteenth-century act. The arguments went far beyond the immediate point at issue, and Dingle took occasion to attack the Establishment "where bishops were seen rolling in rich equipages with half-a-dozen powdered lacqueys in tawdry liveries at their back." As for the old church, he declared boldly that he was not interested in fine architecture, and "when he looked at the pile of building in which they were assembled he could not help saying it was a heap of rubbish (great confusion) and not a noble structure as they were told it was, which was to stand for ages (shame! shame!)." Grist was cleverer and less vituperative; he advocated not unworthily the rights of dissenters and the value of free giving in preference to compulsion. Others were content to be abusive and when at the end of a long sultry evening, Mr. Curling, the chaplain's brother, supported the rate in a lengthy platitudinous speech, a lump of mud was thrown at the speaker in complete disregard of the sanctity of the church. A poll was demanded and the contest was a close one, but at the end of the second day the anti-rate party had won by ninety-three votes.

The quarrel continued for two years and was eventually settled in favour of a rate in the courts of law. At one enquiry Luke Embleton, the engineer, gave evidence and referred to the church as "a very large and old building erected before the Reformation and used for the Roman Catholic worship and procession . . . incapable of adaptation to the worship of the present generation." There were many moderate men of both parties who by now were inclined to agree with him and on July 11th, 1838, Mr. Benson, among many others, received an invitation to attend a meeting in the Bridge House tavern, "to take into consideration the best means of promoting the erection of a new church."

The scheme then evolved which was to cost £8,000, not the £18,000 required to restore the nave, was to provide seating for two thousand persons, with ample accommodation for those unable to pay the pew rents who, it was said, were positively perishing for lack of knowledge. "It is to enable these poor," the promoters continued, "for whom our Blessed Redeemer expressly ordered his Gospel to be preached, to hear of 'the things which belong to their peace' that you are now called upon to furnish the means of erecting a new church."

When the project came before the vestry it was approved by 367 votes to 254; the opposition apparently combined the extremists of both parties, those who were opposed to any expenditure beyond the minimum, and the little group of anti-quarians who still hoped if the scheme fell through to fight again for their £18,000. This time they were worsted and the plan went ahead; the old nave was cleared away and, in June 1839, the Bishop himself laid the first stone of the new edifice. Afterwards as he returned to the vestry to partake of the "elegant collation" that had been prepared for him, he expressed his "high satisfaction" at the cordial atmosphere which appeared to be superseding the tension of the previous years. "His Lordship was then escorted to his carriage and took a most friendly leave of the company."

The new nave was completed and opened after some delay in 1841. Inspired as its builders were by a genuine concern for the welfare of the poorer brethren, it deserved better of fate than the condemnation its architectural shortcomings secured it. These strictures were severe, growing in intensity as a deeper knowledge and love of old buildings was fostered in church people by the spreading influence of the Oxford Movement. But nothing exceeded the condemnation of the younger Pugin who, writing in *The Dublin Review*, called attention to the atrocities lately perpetrated in the venerable church of St. Saviour's and continued: "In place of one of the finest specimens of ecclesiastical architecture left in London—with massive walls and pillars, deeply moulded arches, a most interesting south porch and a splendid western doorway—we have as vile a preaching-place as ever disgraced the 19th century." Pugin compared the "staircases on stilts" under the central tower to those by which the company ascended to a booth or race course, and concluded that "nothing but the preaching-house system could have brought such utter desolation on a stately church."

Between 1841, when the new nave was opened, and the date sometime in the seventies, when its inadequacy began to be unbearable to the ordinary parishioner, there intervened close on forty years of vigorous parish life. There were still occasional hot words in the vestry, about the curriculum of the Grammar School or the Bishop's prohibition of a concert of sacred music, but they were signs rather of a united parish's ebullience than of divided loyalties. It is true that St. Saviour's was no longer in the limelight, and in Worley's unnecessary depressing words," . . . beyond the parishioners and the few antiquarians who visited the church from time to time, it was scarcely known to the outside world except when the bells rang out the old year . . . or when a dismal light in the windows proclaimed the Christmas distribution of bread, coals and blankets." Yet for such a man as Benson the surrounding poverty, particularly in the hungry forties, was an opportunity for service and the burial registers bear telling witness to how incessantly he laboured among the workhouse folk. In his first probationary sermon he had proclaimed his belief that a Christian should be a living testimony to the truth he professes and he had no need of the lime-light; he was well-content to go about doing good. He was happily married, respected and beloved and in spite of his many heart-breaking duties, his papers are not bare of the record of pleasant days. After 1863, he enjoyed in particular his weekly visit to Norwood, whither St. Saviour's various almshouses had been removed, and a recurrent memento was the programme of the Grammar School's annual orations, before an examiner from Merchant Taylors school, when the young gentlemen recited passages from Livy and Euripides, Sallust and Cicero, varied by passages from Macaulay or Scott.

The Grammar School had had its vicissitudes, its numbers dwindling to twenty-three in 1794. But during the next twenty years under the headship of the Rev. W. L. Fancourt matters improved, and there were round about seventy scholars in those first turbulent days which Benson spent in Southwark. The radicals of the vestry did not always see eye to eye with the governors of the school, among whom were generally a Pott of the vinegar yard and a Barclay from the brewery, but they were less tendentious in their criticism than in the attacks they levied against the antiquarians, and there was some ground for their complaint that the school, which the founders had intended to cater for the children of the parish, had become too exclusive and the preserve of the well-to-do. They asked that a "suitable and proper education" should be provided in the English language and in reading, writing and arithmetic and other branches of useful knowledge. Neither Fancourt nor his successor would deviate one iota from a classical curriculum and as a result most of their pupils came from a distance, though a St. Saviour's boy was never refused because his parents could not afford the fees. Fancourt pointed out however that he had known parents to take their children away, when they discovered that the education was better than they expected! In 1838 it was decided to move from the comely building in Green Dragon Court, upon which the Borough Market was encroaching, to a new site given by the vinegar works. In 1839 in Sumner Street, which joined up the old Maid Lane to the new Southwark Bridge Road, the new school was erected next to the new church of St. Peter's and the juxtaposition of church and school was taken as symbolic in the year when the State's first grants to education had made men re-examine the link between religion and learning.

St. Saviour's had good reason to be proud of its schools in these years before the State shouldered the burden of the children's education. It is true that the annual report of the parochial schools in 1820 is of its age and not of ours, for it provided a minimum of schooling for the children of the poor, who were to be educated only so far as would render them "more cleanly, orderly and honest." Those who subscribed were asked to visit the school to "improve the order and decorum of the children" and perhaps the personal interest that was shewn did in practice redeem the venture from the smug complacency of the circular. The girls of the charity and Newcomen schools had, like the boys, moved to a new building in Union Street, early in the century. Although the two foundations were affiliated at this time they retained their identity and were affectionately known throughout the parish as the blue school and the brown school. In 1840 the Newcomen boys (fifty in number) moved to temporary quarters in Southwark Bridge Road, and in 1849 the brown girls, grown to a hundred, were also transferred from Union Street to a new building in Newcomen Street, at the corner of Bowling Green Alley where once their benefactress had lived. There they still remain and for a while the boys were housed on a neighbouring site, till the establishment of L.C.C. trade schools in 1905 was thought to make their continuance unnecessary.

The slant of the education at both blue and brown schools was always technical; the boys were usually apprenticed and the girls went into domestic service. A report of 1825 described the work of the girls' department which had a "ladies committee," responsible for inspecting the needle-work and the clothing of the children, and one of the pupils' main tasks was the mending and making of the boys' shirts! To-day the girls' foundation is an accredited technical school in the new educational set-up, though there is little resemblance, at least on the surface, between the present "teen-agers" who learn so adeptly, among much else, to cook and sew and sing and the girls in the long dresses and

large white aprons who once learnt the same things in so
different an atmosphere. The boys, alas, have gone, but throughout the nineteenth century they could be counted upon to be to
the fore on every parish occasion, literally as well as figuratively
for most parochial processions were led, with joy and vigour if
not always with exactitude, by the brown boys' drum and fife
band.

It was in 1839, that year when the problem of education was so
much in the air, that a young chaplain at Guy's, Frederick Denison
Maurice, gave a course of lectures on the subject in association
with Hugh Rose, the distinguished rector of St. Thomas's. To
these two men, education was something far beyond the mere
process of turning out good apprentices or maid-servants, well-
behaved children or even classical scholars. It was a complete
training of the whole man in Christian citizenship. And what he
meant by Christian citizenship, Maurice was working out, during
his years at Guy's hospital, in his book *The Kingdom of Christ*
which envisaged the church as a mystical body, above and beyond
party, in and through which Christian believers, bound together
not by opinions but by sacramental bonds, mediated the will of
God in the world about them. Maurice stayed ten years at Guy's
and found in his work among the sick-poor a happiness in
personal relationships that was often denied him; one does not
know of any close connection with the neighbouring parish, nor
is there any specific mention of St. Saviour's in his letters, but in
those ten years he must at times have worshipped there, another
of the great company of pilgrims who have prayed within these
ancient walls.

Perhaps only in our own day has Maurice's theology received
full recognition though its influence upon a minority was very
great. The Oxford Movement made a more immediate and wider
appeal and like Maurice's theology it also deepened and enriched
man's conception of the Church. No longer was the love of
medieval buildings a mere whim of the antiquarians, apt to be
travestied by Victorian architects and craftsmen who were not
equal to their inspiration; rather it was part and parcel of a new
approach to worship, recovered from the days of Laud and
Andrewes and imbued with a love of tradition and a deep sense of

history. Thus it came about as the years passed and Benson grew old in Southwark, men began to talk about rebuilding the nave, about St. Mary Overie's as once it had been, of what it might be in the South London of the future. As men interpreted again the meaning of worship, putting the altar in its true place as its centre, the "vile preaching-place," which Pugin had strictured, cried out as loudly for a drastic change within the building as the increasing unpleasantness of the Borough without called for a concerted onslaught upon ignorance and poverty and despair. Once, long ago, the canons of St. Mary Overie's had gone out to minister to Mitcham and Tooting and Footscray in Kent, in the little churches committed to their care. Might it not be that once again there should be canons at St. Mary Overie's, going out to help in a sordid neighbourhood and returning always to that prime duty of worship upon which depended the efficacy of all their other service, continuing through the years to proclaim, amid the noise and tumult and the human suffering of the south bank, the glory and the love of God?

## Note on Sources

For Bishop Sumner see G. H. Sumner: *Life of Charles Richard Sumner* (1876). The *Benson collection* referred to in the text is listed in the British Museum catalogue under *Nightingale* and *Taylor*, whose books it includes, the reference is *C.54 h.13*. The three volumes by Nightingale and Moss (1818); Taylor (1833) and F. Dollman (1881) are of interest, not only for the information they contain for all periods of the church's history, but for the dates and circumstances of their publication. Many of Moss's engravings for example are of the church as it was before the alterations of the 19th century.

The chapter on the two Pugins and the Early Gothic revival in Martin S. Biggs' *Goths and Vandals* (1952), pp. 147–69, indicates some of the wider issues involved.

A brief account of the Rev. S. Benson is prefaced to his *Guide of the Church of St. Saviour, Southwark* (1885). For the schools see *The United Parochial and Newcomen Schools for Girls* (1825) and E. Bayley, *op. cit.*

# XVIII

# THE CATHEDRAL

IN August 1877 a vital change was made in the ecclesiastical pattern to which Southwark belonged. The riverside boroughs and the greater part of East and mid-Surrey were transferred from the see of Winchester to the reconstituted diocese of Rochester. It had been clear for some time that Winchester was over large and too diverse in character for the care and control of any one bishop and, as Surrey acquired wealth and importance as a residential area, many of its inhabitants looked forward to the day when a new diocese should be founded, coterminous with its boundaries and with Guildford or Kingston as the seat of the new bishop. But difficulties of various kinds, not least the age-long affiliation of Croydon to Canterbury, made such a plan unfeasible and in 1877, in order to relieve both London and Winchester, the new see of St. Albans was created to which Rochester surrendered some of its richest and pleasantest lands north of the river and received instead the sprawling unco-ordin-ated mass of South London.

Sumner's successor at Winchester was Samuel Wilberforce, who for a few brief years in the mid-century had been Archdeacon of Surrey and was alive to the problems both of its urban and its rural districts. But a fatal fall, riding from Dorking to Abinger in 1873, put an end too soon to his devoted, vigorous life. It was his successor Harold Browne who, by sacrificing the house in St. James Square and £500 of his income, made possible the Rochester compromise. It remained, however, a compromise that pleased no one. A Surrey diocese would have possessed from the beginning a basis of local loyalties upon which the new bishop could work. In Rochester, as now reconstituted, there was no unity nor symmetry either from the geographical or spiritual point of view. So far as the towns on the south bank had a centre of unity it was to be found in the city upon whose perimeter they lay, while the parts of Surrey that now passed to Rochester regretted the severance of their county and Winchester's retention of the lovely stretches that lay on the Hampshire border. Southwark's own loyalties both to London and Surrey made it as reluctant as any to accept the new affiliation, yet if the Surrey diocese had become an accepted fact the Borough would again have been upon the fringe and the future of the old church less clearly adumbrated. As it was, it soon became apparent to men of vision that a new unity must be created with the church of St. Saviour, worthily restored, at its very centre.

Whether or not the new experiment would succeed in 1877 depended almost entirely on the choice of a bishop. Did there exist, in the ranks of the beneficed clergy of the Church of England, one so filled with zeal and wisdom and the grace of God that he could bind into a unity the diverse strands of this new diocese and make a breach in the bastion of godlessness that was South London?

Such a man was Anthony Thorold, Vicar of St. Pancras, now in his thirties and at the height of his power, one who was a glutton for work, brilliant in administration, intrepid in action and dedicated to the service of God. Thorold lacked that grace in manner and deportment which made it so easy for Bishop Sumner to charm and dominate; he lacked too the vitality and simple friendliness of his successor Bishop Talbot, who entered into his labours in Southwark, but Thorold's life was so rooted and grounded in prayer, he cared so genuinely for the people in his charge that those who got behind the seemingly aggressive and shy exterior found in him a man of God who claimed their loyal and devoted service. Zeal was the quality that dominated his own nature and that he approved in others. "It is not error which opposes the progress of truth," he wrote in a tract, characteristically called *The Gospel of Work*. "It is indolence, obstinacy, the spirit of routine, everything that favours inaction." Fervent in spirit, impatient of delay, not suffering fools gladly and slackers not at all, he had tackled impossible jobs before and he was ready to try again, knowing that he possessed in the power house of prayer what strength was needed for the task.

He had begun his service in the church as a curate in Lancashire, marrying the daughter of T. H. Greene, the local squire, who by a curious chance was already interested in St. Saviour's as Chairman of the Commons' Committee which had dealt with the problems of London Bridge and the railway. From Lancashire, Thorold came in 1852 to Marylebone and five years later to St. Giles, that wretched and turbulent parish on the edge of Holborn and Soho, where Shaftesbury founded his ragged school and Maurice's young disciples helped in the boys clubs. Thorold threw himself whole-heartedly into the work, and when the loss of his wife and small daughter left him desolate—as he was often to be left at the very moment of achievement—he turned with yet warmer sympathy and humbler faith to the task before him in which alone solace could be found. After ten years at St. Giles his health broke down and he was forced to resign, but as soon as possible he accepted another living, no country benefice where he might relax but that of St. Pancras where for eight years he laboured diligently, concentrating in particular on education but never forgetting in his duties on the first school board of 1870 the parish priest's immediate responsibility, personal contact with those committed to his charge.

In 1877 he became Bishop of Rochester and was faced at once with the twin problems that still remain the chief concern of those who have come after him. He was appalled by the "spiritual desolation" of South London, "the paralysed end of the old Winchester diocese." How to preach the gospel effectively against the obstacles of shortage of man-power, slum conditions and the resultant ignorance and sloth? This was a question that could never be absent long from the mind of any who came and went south of the river. But there was also the question of the newly-framed diocese, how was it to be given a sense of unity and common purpose, that the spiritual needs of suburbia and the countryside should also be supplied and that these more fortunate ones should come in and help in Southwark and Bermondsey and Lambeth.

Thorold's first task was to make himself known in the diocese. Since there was no natural centre of unity he must himself provide the necessary focus and he spent his first autumn visiting every corner of his see, asking for support and co-operation, and promising in return sympathy, justice and "straight-forwardness." He came to St. Saviour's, for the first time on October 19th in the morning, with the beautiful bells ringing out merrily, as he reported later. In the Lady Chapel he spoke to a number of the clergy, outlining his hopes for the diocese, but when he spoke of the need for consolidation he felt his words to be unwelcome: there was little inclination here for that spiritual unity which he desired so much. The factiousness of Southwark was not yet rooted out. Already the Bishop had experienced it in the angry protests which poured in from a certain Mr. Side and other residents of Union Street against the ritual practised at the new church of All Hallows, which had recently been founded in St. Saviour's parish as a memorial to a beloved child. The attempt of the authorities to root out Anglo-Catholic observances was at its height and the unhappy divisions between the two wings of the Anglican communion sadly hampered Bishop Thorold in his efforts to create a friendly diocese. He himself was a staunch Evangelical and erred at first on the side of severity, but his personal kindliness in most cases prevented bitterness; he would have no dealings with trouble-makers like Side and he had the courage to modify his whole attitude when he found that it was men like the maligned priest at All Hallows who helped him most zealously in the work in South London.

A part of his first pastoral letter outlined his views on ritualism and the rest set forth his immediate objectives in the diocese, among them the rehabilitation of St. Saviour's. He was far from satisfied with it as it was; at a confirmation service shortly after his first visit, he was displeased by the irreverent bearing of the congregation: "we could hardly force ourselves into the vestry through the disorderly crowd." And what could be done about that monstrous nave with its flimsy pillars and unsightly staircases? And, perhaps more urgent than anything else, there was the necessity for change in the present method of paying and choosing the chaplains by the vote of the ratepayers and the levy of a rate. It was unseemly for the merits and demerits of clerical candidates to be dragged through all the public houses in the Borough, and as to the rate, "everybody equally hates it and it is full of mischief to the church," as Thorold stated in 1880, urging that the patronage should be taken out of the hands of the parishioners and the rate abolished. The first step towards creating a local unity in South London was taken with the establishment of the Southwark Archdeaconry, covering much the same area as the presbyterian classis of the Interregnum. The second step in the campaign to make St. Saviour's a worthy centre of the work was the purchase of the patronage; while the third and most difficult step, the rebuilding of the nave, could only be attempted when the diocese as a whole was sufficiently conscious of the need to respond to an appeal for funds.

In his first vigorous years as Bishop of Rochester, Thorold worked incessantly to achieve this better state of affairs, always keeping in mind the two-fold nature of his mission, to attack the degradation in South London and to make his diocese a spiritual reality in spite of its geographical diversity. In his work for temperance, in encouraging his laymen throughout the diocese to take an active interest in all that was being done, in the improvement he sought in the calibre of his clergy through increased study and devotional retreats, Thorold went steadily on, his own life saddened by the death of his second wife and of two of his overworked and much loved colleagues, Canon Millar of Rochester and Edward Fisher, the first Archdeacon of Southwark. Two branches of the work were the Bishop's particular joy and care. The first was the Rochester Diocesan Society by whose agency mission priests were planted wherever most required, in overcrowded districts where the incumbent for some reason was unable to cope with the work or in new areas where there was no adequate provision. The second was the training of deaconesses. It was in 1884, the year in which his work in Rochester was at the flood, that the latter idea was first envisaged and Mrs. Gilmore, a sister at Guy's hospital, was asked to become Head deaconess. She hesitated as well she might. She was a sister of William Morris and as much a personality in her own way as the Bishop in his. She refused his offer at first, but he bore down her reluctance with mingled kindness and decisiveness and she agreed eventually to attempt the work with results that more than justified her own courage and the Bishop's choice. A house in Clapham was opened in April 1887 and the deaconesses have played their part in Southwark and its neighbourhood, a devoted band of women, from that day to this.

Yet not even the dedicated services of mission priest and deaconess, and the unending labours of the parish clergy and their wives could make much inroad into the apathy and mental inertia of the undernourished ill-housed masses in South London, whose indifference was supplemented by the more active opposition of the disciples of Tom Paine and Bradlaugh and the disquieting theories of Darwin. Happily it was just at this time that the schools and universities, fired by the example of Toynbee Hall, caught hold of the conception of the mission and settlement where volunteers could live and work among the people they hoped to help. In 1883 St. John's College, Cambridge, led the way with the mission at Walworth, followed in turn by Charterhouse in Tabard Street, Wellington, Cheltenham, Bradfield, and the Cambridge Colleges of Clare, Pembroke, Corpus Christi, and Trinity. In those first years the enthusiasm was genuine, and, whether they came from public school and university or from the poor homes of Southwark and Bermondsey, many hundreds of young people thus learnt far more than they realised, and a narrow rent was made in the iron curtain that hung in Victorian England between the rich and the dispossessed.

St. Saviour's was never far from the surface of Thorold's consciousness although eleven years elapsed between his first pastoral and the launching of an appeal for £50,000 to rebuild the nave and make the church a dignified and fitting quasi-cathedral for the Southwark part of the diocese. In 1883 old Mr. Benson died and his curate, William Thompson, was chosen his successor, a dark, florid, handsome man who loved the old church so much that he called one of his children Ida Marie Overie. Soon afterwards, a prerequisite of further progress, an act of parliament was obtained transferring the advowson from the people to the bishop, and Thompson, the last chaplain, became the first rector of St. Saviour's. In 1883 the Bishop had completed a whirlwind campaign for £50,000 for ten new churches and he had said when the task was accomplished, "then, after a little rest we will go to another task full of vital interest for our spiritual work in South London; the complete restoration of St. Saviour's." But the rebuilding of the nave in a manner worthy of its medieval counterpart was no easy matter and Thorold's "little rest" extended for another six years. This in part was due to a breakdown in his own health in 1885, and although he recovered sufficiently to tackle a full day's work, something was missing of his former energy. This brought home to him once again the impossible nature of the Rochester compromise. He still considered the ideal solution to be the creation of "the beautiful and opulent county of Surrey as a separate diocese with the ample resources of its gentry and men of business to back South London with its million of souls." He used these words in replying to a deputation from St. Saviour's in 1886, telling them to their disappointment that until this matter was settled he did not think it opportune to launch the appeal. By 1888 he had agreed to a compromise by which West Surrey should be transferred to Rochester and a suffragan bishop of Southwark should be appointed to assist him. The requisite bill passed the House of Lords, where nobody seemed to be interested: "it was like firing cold shot into a turf bank," Thorold commented. The measure was smothered in the Commons, and West Surrey remained in the Winchester diocese. But the creation of a suffragan bishop was made possible by the existence of a fund collected by Surrey churchmen for this purpose and by the gift of a house in Tooting presented for the bishop's residence by Alexander Macmillan, the younger of the two Macmillan brothers who had come up to London in the forties and founded the great firm of publishers. For many years the house in Tooting had been a rendezvous of the Christian Socialists and Alexander was glad for yet another opportunity to interpret his faith in terms of active friendliness. Thorold offered the newly-created post to his friend Bishop Barry, who was just about to resign his diocese of Sydney. It meant for Thorold a great lessening of the strain, and he celebrated the occasion not by relaxing but by launching the appeal for £50,000 to make St. Saviour's a worthy pro-Cathedral as a first stage towards the creation of a new diocese of Southwark.

The group of enthusiasts at St. Saviour's were delighted. A year or so previously, after fourteen years' labour, Francis Dollman had completed his architectural survey of the old church and William Drewett of the Borough High Street had printed it. Gwilt was dead, but Dr. Rendle of St. George's remained to encourage with informed zeal any scheme that boded good to his beloved Southwark. There was C. D. Field, Warden of the Great Account, in 1889, to whom the Bishop appreciatively referred as the "stroke oar." There was still a Pott and a Barclay to give their ready help as so often before, and among other laymen, humble and distinguished, Sir Frederick Wigan, most generous of benefactors. On November 3rd, 1889, Thorold preached at the evening service in support of the appeal. "How beautiful the church looked," he wrote afterwards. He had written a special prayer for the occasion. "I believe in prayer," he said.

The appeal prospered, magnificently, and in July 1890 the Prince of Wales laid the foundation stone of the new nave, which was to be as far as possible an exact reproduction of its thirteenth-century original. The work was entrusted to Sir Arthur Blomfield, and Dollman, too old to share in it himself, expressed his appreciation that it was in such able hands. His confidence was justified, for Blomfield was competent and conscientious and previous researches had supplied him with the necessary information. The few fragments of ancient stone-work that survived were scrupulously preserved, and the finished nave, which took seven years to complete, faithfully reproduced the shape and spirit of its medieval counterpart. Two years after the work was begun Thorold was made Bishop of Winchester, and was soon as absorbed in his new diocese as previously he had been in his Lancashire curacy, in the squalor of St. Giles and the challenge of Rochester. He died four years later, not many months after a final visit to St. Saviour's where he saw and admired the progress of the new nave. Choir stalls were later erected to his memory and to few of her founders and benefactors does the old church owe more than to him whose finest hours were spent in an "heroic struggle for the souls of men in the dreary streets of South London," upon which he spent all his exceptional skill, his resolution and his patience, and through the grace of God accomplished so much.

Twenty years elapsed between the date when Thorold first came to Rochester and saw the vision of what St. Saviour's might become and the February day in 1897, when the work upon the nave was finished and the church took its place as the pro-Cathedral of South London. The work went on but the people changed. Thorold's successor at Rochester was Randall Davidson, who came from the Deanery of Windsor and the close friendship of the Queen; in his five years in South London he was in continuous ill-health. He saw the importance of living "at the central hub of our great wheel," and set about building the bishop's house in Kennington. But the main architect of Southwark's fortunes in the immediate future was Huyshe Yeatman-Biggs who succeeded Barry as suffragan bishop in 1891, after twelve years as Vicar of Sydenham. He was for a time examining chaplain to the Bishop of Winchester, and he himself said once that he had been "torn from the charms of intellectual speculation and drawn into a grim application of Christianity to 19th century needs." Throughout 1896, encouraged by his new diocesan, Edward Talbot, he worked out his conception of a collegiate church as a centre of unity for the great, sprawling mass south of the river and as a power house from which salvation should come for the thousands who poured each morning over the seven bridges, "to man shops and warehouses and west end clubs, and returned wearily each night to their vast and crowded dormitory." These were the people he hoped to help. "They are mostly poor," he said; "as you approach the river from the south the poverty deepens to its darkest depth, and degradation runs it close until it finds St. Saviour's, Southwark, seated on her wretched throne, which forms the lowest depth." Yet it was this very St. Saviour's, which he hoped would become "a white hot focus whence heat would flow into the surrounding district." It would be, so the pioneers hoped and believed, as truly a missionary centre, as any of the ancient cathedrals "in the days of their first planting."

There were various difficult adjustments to be made between the new collegiate body and the parishioners, for St. Saviour's would remain a parish church and the old bogey of repairs raised its head again under the new name of "sustentation." Indeed the scheme nearly collapsed through the absence of any adequate endowment but the indomitable suffragan asked for three weeks' delay before a decision was reached, and obtained in that time promises of sufficient money to guarantee expenses for the first five years. The church of St. Thomas, abandoned when the hospital moved its quarters, was bought to serve as a Chapterhouse, and the Queen Anne house where the hospital's Treasurer had lived was also purchased as a place of residence for unmarried canons and the missioners. The chapter of the collegiate church was to have the bishop of the diocese as dean, with his suffragan as sub-dean, and four additional canons; certain laymen were also to be included so that experts in financial and business detail would be available to advise in matters of general policy and administration.

When Thorold died and Davidson succeeded him at Winchester, Edward Talbot became Bishop of Rochester, taking up his residence in the new house in Kennington. He gave Yeatman-Biggs unstinted support and when the time came to appoint the new Chapter he wrote to Samuel Mumford Taylor an old colleague in Leeds and asked him to come to Southwark as Precentor. "Have you followed our affairs enough to know what I mean by St. Saviour's," he wrote, "our magnificent Gothic church by London Bridge, full of great associations . . . which Bishop Thorold undertook to restore as a great centre for the church life of South London? . . ." "I cannot deny," he added in a later letter, "that . . . there must be something of the 'leap in the dark' which I cannot remove about St. Saviour's and of course if it be right its other name will be a 'venture of faith'." Mumford Taylor took the risk and came. There was associated with him as Chancellor the rector William Thompson, who watched with delight the insertion of windows in the new nave to commemorate famous folk who had lived in the Borough and been linked, some more, some less, with the old church. Thompson knew them all, Cruden, Bunyan, Mrs. Newcomen, Oliver Goldsmith, and wrote of them all brimming over with knowledge and affection in the book he compiled about the church in the next few years.

The other two canons were Rhodes Bristow, the missioner, and a leading evangelical, Allen Edwards, who was lecturer or catechist. Sir Frederick Wigan was the invaluable treasurer. The Rector's warden and the Warden of the Great Account were also members.

The Chapter was sworn in, early in the morning of February 27, 1897 promising to assist the Bishop with their presence and counsel and to be forward in promoting the good works of the church and diocese "unto holy and honourable living." They then took Communion together and later in the day attended a great service in the presence of the Prince of Wales and the Duke and Duchess of Teck whose daughter the late Queen Mary was so often to grace the Cathedral with her presence. The Bishop of

Winchester preached in a church that looked more lovely than ever it had done since the days of the Reformation. As the Chapter listened to the preacher, the challenge of the future humbled those who might well have been tempted to glory in the achievements of the past. For the new canons, like their brethren of the Augustinian rule, were to show forth Christ not only within the walls of the collegiate church but in the world without, where their voices should be heard upholding all that was of good report, wholesome houses, better schools, greater leisure, better working conditions, but where they were never to forget to proclaim "deliberately, avowedly distinctively the whole Christian creed."

For Southwark, the day of the church's re-opening was made festive by the presence of the royal visitors. For once in a way, the Borough made merry and even the Borough Market was smartened up for the occasion. Every narrow street and sordid thoroughfare was gay with a thousand flags. St. Saviour's magazine reported that next day Sir Frederick Wigan entertained five-hundred poor to dinner and commented, "It is an open secret that his Royal Highness the Prince of Wales expressed the opinion that it would have been better to do something for the poor than decorate the streets. It is gratifying to know that the poor were able to take part in the general rejoicing over an event of unique and historic interest to South London, for the gentlemen of St. Saviour's are not accustomed to do things by halves and so not only were the streets brilliantly decorated but the poor were also bountifully fed." This parish magazine is a constant reminder of the vigorous life of St. Saviour's going on alongside the various ecclesiastical experiments and perhaps, as an antidote to so many vague aspirations, one may quote its reports of the fine public baths recently built in Southwark, of endeavours to open museums on Sundays and provide playing grounds for children, of the schools outing to Epsom Downs and the happy day spent by the old folk of the United Almshouses at the College Warden's home at Sevenoaks (graced by the "the melodious strains of an ably conducted local band"). There was also the Poor Children's Aid Fund which in September 1895 sent a group of youngsters to Herne Bay where bathing was indulged in and passers-by astonished by "thirty-five small forms and two large ones in scarlet and white (St. Saviour's colours) skipping, jumping, rolling, plunging, floating and swimming in the water to the merry accompaniment of screaming, shouting and singing."

A dominant influence in the transition years between 1897 and 1905 was the personality of Edward Talbot, a man as different as possible but as devoted in his own way as Bishop Thorold had been. Talbot was a High Churchman and his first post had been that of Warden of Keble. He differed from Thorold not only in his brand of churchmanship but in the whole temper of his mind. Both men lived to an exceptional degree in the presence of God but the fruits of the spirit seemed in Talbot to spring without effort from the qualities with which nature had endowed him. The sore trials that beset Anthony Thorold, the loss of wife and child, the frequent loneliness, the ill-health against which he fought so bravely had no part or lot in the life of Edward Talbot. His own ideally happy marriage with his cousin lasted for more than fifty years and his connection with the Gladstones and Lytteltons linked him with some of the most interesting and cultured families of the day. Yet he remained sensitive, humble and, in spite of his whole-hearted enjoyment of it, unspotted from the world, able to meet on their own terms the men and women to whom he ministered. From Keble he went as Vicar to Leeds for seven years and when he left in 1894 to succeed Thorold at Rochester, one of his Leeds stalwarts is said to have commented, "Nay it's a bad business is this o' t'owd Vicar goin. He's gotten a hold o' this place, sure enough." So it was to be in South London, in his seventeen years of living there. For in one most essential point, he and Thorold were alike. They were both pastors; they both cared. For both of them, "no person was a 'type'; no situation was a 'case'."

In the years before 1905, when the work which Thorold had begun was completed with the creation of the diocese of Southwark, Talbot was already a familiar figure at the collegiate church. He wrote in Easter 1903 of a "beautiful Good Friday at St. Saviour's" and next year it was the scene of his elder daughter's marriage. Meanwhile he worked assiduously to secure the consummation of Thorold's work which necessitated the collection of funds, in the absence of an endowment, and an act of parliament establishing the new see. By degrees the various obstacles were surmounted. Money was of course the main problem, though the bishop wrote to Taylor from the Tyrol, that he was not cast down. "My holiday has inspired me with the zeal of a Dick Turpin and all his recklessness, I wish you could come out here and pour out your St. Saviour's anxieties. They would not last an hour." Talbot's optimism was justified even when the Tyrol gave place to Kennington again. The descendants of Bingham and his fellow-bargainers rallied to the task. There were voluntary subscriptions of every kind from every corner of the old Rochester diocese and a shilling fund started by the Vicar of Malden eventually produced over £2,000! More than £100,000 was raised by the time the Letters Patents had been issued in May 1905, appointing Talbot the first Bishop of Southwark. Yeatman-Biggs was translated to Worcester, leaving behind him a community deeply indebted to him for his vision and determination.

The requisite act of parliament had not proved easy to obtain, for Talbot's tractarian background led to one of those unreasoning and violent outbursts of Protestantism apt to irrupt in the House of Commons at any suspicion of undue High Church influence. Eventually the measure was tacked on to a bill creating the diocese of Birmingham which was sponsored by Balfour the Prime Minister. On June 29, 1905 Talbot was enthroned as the first Bishop of Southwark and four days later, at a solemn service, the Cathedral was inaugurated. The new diocese was unwieldy in shape, "a couple of small continents joined together by a sort of isthmus," as Worley described it. It stretched southwards for twenty-five miles from the riverside boroughs through the suburban hinterland, narrowing about Banstead where Winchester encroached on the west and Canterbury, with the Croydon intake, on the east. South of this it widened again to include the villages of the north downs and Reigate, which had been the Kirkesfeld of William de Warennes' gift. Talbot remained as bishop for the first six years assisted by two suffragans, J. C. Leeke of Woolwich and Cecil Hook of Kingston. Taylor had become Archdeacon of Southwark in 1904 and soon afterwards succeeded Thompson as Rector of St. Saviour's. Gradually the somewhat heterogeneous collection of places and people became a diocese with a unity and a character of its own. By the time Talbot left them they had become in a sense a family, united by their loyalty to him and by their shared adventure of the spirit. The atmosphere of the diocesan conference changed from one of distrust and dissension to one of understanding. If disputes arose the bishop's one criterion was loyalty to that *via media Anglicana*, whose historical framework and wide tolerance appealed alike to his mental habits and instinct of behaviour. His wide sympathies and the fairness with which he struggled to see every point of view enabled him to win the confidence and trust of many whose slants on politics or religion were different from his own. The influence of the happy home in Kennington contributed not a little to the steady growth of friendliness, and Mrs. Talbot was equal to most occasions, though she did once write, "we are in a rather maddening state here with half the house in a mess over electric lighting work and Edward calmly having gatherings of lay readers, deacons, seven bishops to luncheon and so on."

Mrs. Talbot's secretary, Miss Wilmot, left a vivid sketch of Bishop Talbot as he was in 1911, as a man of sixty-seven, a vital determined person, who peered at her eagerly through a pair of enormous spectacles and overcame her diffidence in face of a new job with an: "Oh you can *do* it all right." This faith in the capacity of his young colleagues was characteristic of him though none, according to Miss Wilmot, "could make you feel more extraordinarily foolish, even if he only pushed his spectacles up on his forehead, rubbed his short-sighted eyes and remarked cheerfully, 'how silly!' "

Talbot counted for more in the general counsels of the church than Thorold had done and his friendship with Gore and Scott-Holland connected him with that group of thinkers who linked the Christian Socialists of the past with Temple and the challenge of C.O.P.E.C. His own intellectual life was vital rather than profound, but it kept him fresh and alert in the wearisome day-to-day administration of his diocese. The greatness of the man lay less in any specific gift but in the wholeness of his happy and sensitive personality. Whether in his dealings with his clergy or with the young people of the settlements or with the deaconesses and the companion sisterhood of Greyladies founded

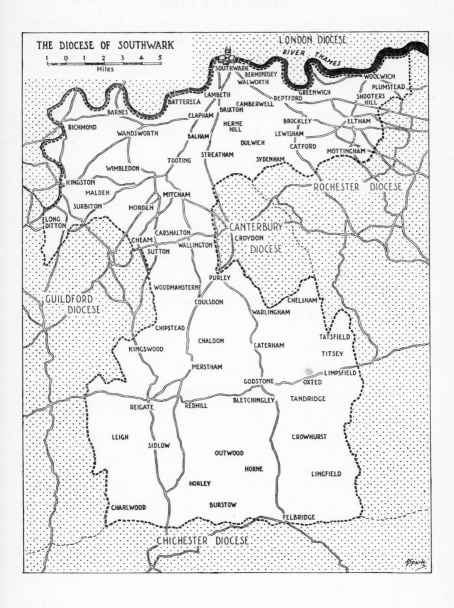

by Yeatman-Biggs, he remained pre-eminently a friend, quick to sympathise, ready to advise, eager to understand.

In 1911 he became Bishop of Winchester, moving not without some hesitation from Kennington to Farnham. There he grew old in tranquillity, bearing one great sorrow in the loss of his youngest son, Gilbert, in the first world war. Yet even from this loss, and the service of Neville his second son as chaplain, something of light and beauty has survived, for Talbot was the name linked with the foundation of Toc H, which has brought so much of strength and comfort into so many lonely lives.

Talbot resigned his bishopric at the age of eighty in 1924, but lived on in London for another nine years. On January 25, 1934, he visited Southwark for the last time and attended a great service at the Cathedral, to give thanks for the successful conclusion of the campaign for twenty-five new churches. He stood proudly between Bishop Garbett, who like him had served in turn in Southwark and Winchester, and Parsons, newly come to Southwark from the north. A few days later he had a slight seizure and died on January 30, praying with his son beside him, at peace and without fear.

## Note on Sources

See C. H. Simkinson, *Life and Work of Bishop Thorold* (1896), G. K. A. Bell, *Randall Davidson* (1952), and Mrs. G. Stephenson, *Edward Stuart Talbot* (1936).

For the creation of the diocese see Mrs. Jas. A. Heaton, *Origins of the Diocese of Southwark 1877–1905* (1950), *The diocese of Southwark* . . . intro E. S. Talbot (1906).

For the parish, Baines and Langston: *The Corporation of Wardens of the Parish of St. Saviour, Southwark*, see also *The properties and charities of the Parish* (1887).

# XIX

## POSTSCRIPT

FIFTY years have passed since Southwark became a diocese. In 1905 the Bishop of London said of the Cathedral: "Nothing has been too old for it to touch in the past: nothing will be too new for it to welcome in the future." Yet those who started so hopefully then on their twentieth-century journey could not conceive of the size and complexity of the tasks that lay ahead, nor can the succeeding generation still at work easily compute to what extent they have used, or failed to use, the opportunities of fifty years. A great improvement has been made in the material conditions of the people, and in the cause of social betterment the Church has played its part, in the work of the schools and clubs and settlements and the devoted service of individual Christians. But did the Cathedral become, as some had hoped, a "white hot focus," to proclaim the gospel of Christ "and through the power of God to change, uplift and transform men and women"? Are the people of the Borough conscious of the church in their midst and the way of life for which it stands? Are Kingston and Rotherhithe, Wimbledon and Bermondsey conscious, for their part, of a common purpose and a common discipleship in the diocese of Southwark? What of the continuing life of the parish of St. Saviour?

The first six years, until Talbot moved to Winchester, were for the Cathedral church as for the country at large, years of serene if fallacious optimism. The Bishop's sagacity and sympathy fostered in the diocese a deepening sense of community, and the rancours stirred by the conflict of "high" and "low" gradually subsided. In Southwark, Talbot's old friend Archdeacon Taylor worked with him in close co-operation as precentor of the Cathedral and after Thompson's death, as rector of the Parish. As precentor, he laid the foundations of Southwark's reputation for fine music. Sir Frederick Wigan had made a bequest to the collegiate church in 1899 whereby twelve "singing boys," known as the Wigan Chanters, were maintained at the local Grammar School for the service of the church. Taylor was an expert in liturgical worship; and the fine traditions which he established with the help of Madeley Richardson, the first organist and choirmaster, were carried on by Edgar Cook after 1909 until his death in 1952 robbed music and Southwark of a loyal friend and servant. Sir Frederick Wigan, the head of a firm of hop-merchants which continues in the Borough, died two years after the creation of the diocese he had done so much to secure. His modesty and quiet faith had matched his generosity; as Talbot said of him, when he died, "the heart that is empty of self has room for others and their needs."

The parochial life went on quietly at St. Saviour's during these years. Services were held in the Lady Chapel and the rector was usually the precentor of the Cathedral. The existence of a sub-dean in addition might mean on occasion a certain disunity of direction, but though the informal nature of the arrangements made between chapter and parish left plenty of scope for friction, Archdeacon Taylor's attractive personality, his charm and sense of fun, obviated most of the difficulties. The creation of Southwark as a municipal borough in 1899 relieved the Corporation of Wardens of many duties that had survived from an earlier day, including the nomination of the parish's representatives among the governors of Dulwich College and the Grammar School. The Corporation of Wardens still administer the parish charities and control its property but the ecclesiastical duties are now vested in two wardens, one appointed by the rector. In 1899, when its numbers had dwindled to a mere handful, the Grammar School had united with St. Olave's School and moved over the boundary into Bermondsey, to begin a new chapter of scholastic success and wide usefulness as St. Olave's and St. Saviour's Grammar School. From the school's endowments in 1903 a new girls school was founded and St. Saviour's and St. Olave's Grammar School for girls flourished throughout the fifty years and continues to maintain those same traditions of sound learning and good citizenship so dear to the hearts of John Bingham and his colleagues three centuries ago. Within the parish's more immediate sphere of action are the Newcomen school, a continued source of pride and interest, and the parochial schools in Union Street.

When Talbot became Bishop of Winchester in 1911, Hubert Burge followed him to Southwark after nine successful years as headmaster of Winchester. It cannot have been for him an easy transition, the more so as his health was not robust, for he came to Southwark just when industrial unrest and the growing hysterical temper of the country were manifested in the unhappy dock strike of 1912. Burge combined a sure faith with an intellectual ability to balance all arguments and the desire to apprehend with sympathy all points of view that differed from his own. He was thus, in Archbishop Temple's words, able "in the most remarkable degree to interpret people to one another." Unhappily in the Southwark of 1912 there was no wish on either side to be interpreted and the Bishop's suggestion of compromise as the wretched strike dragged on only earned him criticism for having interfered. Scarcely were these dark days over than the war began, and between 1914 and 1919 under conditions of increasing strain and deteriorating health, Burge worked incessantly and lived austerely in the large unwieldy house in Kennington; at the conclusion of peace he was translated to the see of Oxford to serve for a few tranquil years in an atmosphere more suited to his scholarly bent of mind. His associate at the Cathedral was Canon Woodward, who became Precentor and Rector when Archdeacon Taylor was made Bishop of Kingston in 1914. Woodward was a man of energy and enthusiasm who tried during his few years in Southwark to make the mission church of St. Peter's a real centre of evangelism among the slum property which surrounded it. He was well liked in the parish not only by his own people but by the business men and the public officials of the borough at a time when friction was all too frequent.

Among Bishop Burge's published writings is a charge he delivered in Southwark Cathedral in 1915, at a time when the "shock and bewilderment" caused by the war had led to a weakening of effort in some of the parishes. Characteristically even in 1915, the Bishop urged the need of continued study and disciplined thinking, that minds as well as hearts might be disposed to receive that "right judgment in all things" which was one of the gifts of the Spirit. He warned his listeners that peace, when it came, would bring not tranquillity but more exacting problems, which could only be met if the narrow individualism that infected the whole country was replaced by a true sense of community based not on the assertion of rights but on a recognition of mutual obligation.

Through twenty years of deepening disillusion that truth was brought home to men. They are not years which churchmen, any more than humanists or statesmen, can regard with equanimity, and perhaps the error of judgment, as it seems, with which they began at St. Saviour's was symptomatic of the exhaustion of mind and body which made clear thought and bold action difficult. In 1919, partly for reasons of financial stringency, the Cathedral authorities sold to the railway company the Treasurer's house that lay beyond the chapter house in St. Thomas Street. Here had been the home of the college, as envisaged by Yeatman-Biggs, the centre which was to provide lodging and refreshment and a common meeting place for the mission priests, who went out to preach the gospel in the hard-pressed parishes or the hospital wards or wherever the need was greatest. There were certain arguments beyond the financial in favour of the sale; for there were still many in the diocese to whom, as they complained, their cathedral meant so little "because it was so far off" and, by removing the headquarters of the missioners to a more rural part of Surrey and combining it with a retreat house for all parts of the diocese, diocesan unity might be enhanced. Yet to all who had the work of South London at heart, the sale of the college was a matter of real regret, a set-back which the passing years have emphasised, for thereby the Cathedral lost not only an asset in its spiritual warfare, but a row of seemly buildings in a quiet street to which as the stridency of the years increased there still clung something of the dignity of the Close.

In these years also there was a change of personnel in Southwark. Woodward was succeeded as precentor and rector by J. B. Haldane, formerly priest of St. John's, Earlsfield, a man who devoted himself until his death in 1938 to the interests of the parish but did not find the more general relationships as easy as did his predecessors. He had a wide experience of social welfare work, and happily for the witness of the church in South London, Burge's successor as bishop was Cyril Forster Garbett, formerly vicar of Portsea, later to become in turn Bishop of Winchester and Archbishop of York. One other man in particular was associated, in the thoughts and the affections of all sorts of persons in Southwark's crowded streets, with the church's social witness. This was William Hough, whose devotion to South London began at the Cambridge mission in the Old Kent Road. From 1918-32, after eleven years as Vicar of Lewisham, he was the much-loved Bishop of Woolwich. Such men as he and Bishop Garbett would see to it that the church in Southwark played its part in this first essential task of achieving a real measure of social justice, a task which must be at least attempted before a spiritual revival could take place. Garbett's whole career has witnessed to his knowledge and zeal in this field of Christian service. A small book he wrote in 1931 about the work in South London shewed how alive he was both to what had been accomplished in the improvement in health, the care of children and the work of the clubs and settlements and in regard to the yet unconquered evil of overcrowding. Yet though he gave credit for the quiet and per-sistent ministrations of the clergy and of such agencies as the Church Army and gave credit to the Ecclesiastical Commissioners in their role as property owners, he added a proviso which the developments of the succeeding years were to underline; the work would only have value if the people themselves grew in spiritual stature, ". . . it is fruitless to build better houses unless there are men and women who know how to make the best use of them." The cure of souls remained the prime task of the church at the southern end of London Bridge no less in the twentieth century than in the years that had gone before.

And so the Bishop went on to describe the Cathedral, as he would have it be, the only building that still linked modern Southwark with the past. He did not regret its humble site among the crowded streets. "While some Cathedrals," he wrote, "by their majesty witness to the glory of God, while others high set on hills speak of Him as the Sovereign ruling from His throne, Southwark Cathedral, hidden away low down amidst the homes of poverty and the warehouses of modern com-merce, witnesses to One who in His love came and dwelt among ordinary men and women for the redemption of their souls and bodies."

In 1932 Garbett was translated to Winchester. His successor in Southwark was Richard Parsons who came from the Manchester church of Birch-in-Rusholme to serve as Bishop through ten anxious years, shadowed by economic stress and unemployment and ending amid the ravages of war. It was however during these years, while men of different ways of thought were fighting, sometimes in unison, sometimes in rivalry, the evils of poverty and ignorance, that a sense of goodwill and common purpose was growing in the diocese. Much was due to the work and personality of successive suffragan bishops. For twenty-five years after 1927 Frederick Hawkes was Bishop of Kingston; and Leslie Hamilton Lang was for eleven years at Woolwich after 1936. They gave unsparingly of themselves and their work and personality contributed much to the life of the diocese. In the thirties, a great effort was made to build twenty-five churches in the new housing estates, which sometimes were as bare of centres for worship or community life as the old slums had been of light and air. The necessary money was raised, and the great achievement brought to all who had a part in it a deepened sense of unity. It was, however, those who worked together on the various diocesan boards who became most aware of the reality of their fellowship as they shared a common interest and compared their difficulties and their hopes, while the efficacy of all that was done was maintained by the day-to-day work of the South London Church Fund which ably co-ordinated the diocesan finances and with money contributed by every parish assisted the work of those who were most hard-pressed.

Increasingly the Cathedral supplied a fitting background, owing to Haldane's high standards of dignity in worship and the additions he made to the church's beauty. Meanwhile its constitution as a Cathedral was clarified by law and in 1937 the creation of the office of provost, who should also be rector, gave unity to the direction of parish and chapter. In 1938 Haldane died and was succeeded as Provost by F. D. Narborough who went on to St. Martin-in-the-Fields and later became Bishop of Colchester. In 1944 Cuthbert Bardsley was appointed to face the strenuous tasks and accept the challenge of the post-war years. He was succeeded in 1948 by H. E. Ashdown, the present Provost and Rector.

In the midst of the anxious war-years when Parsons went to Hereford, Bertram Simpson, then Bishop of Kensington, became the fifth and present Bishop of Southwark; his suffragans to-day are Robert Stannard, Bishop of Woolwich since 1947 and William Gilpin, Bishop of Kingston since 1952. To all these as to many others who have not been named who have served the diocese in the fifty years since its inception, the Cathedral Church on the south bank owes honour and gratitude.

During the war years, Southwark was in the front line, once the enemy had begun the air attack. In February 1941 a bomb fell close to the church, shattering the glass of the memorial windows and causing tragic damage in the vicinity. On other occasions, St. Peter's was destroyed, All Hallows burnt out and large areas demolished. Where once in the past had been the gardens of Winchester House, there was open ground again, a wilderness of bombed sites. When the war ended, the church was battered and the Borough devastated but by God's grace in the years of reconstruction the Cathedral was again blessed in those who served it. As the children came back to the schools and the bomb-sites were slowly cleared, the church was restored to the seemly dignity of a building where God is worshipped and the work of the parish went on with renewed zeal. At West Norwood where the almshouses had suffered, a wing was rebuilt and the gardens planted again to the delight of the old people. In the diocese, there was scarcely a parish in the metropolitan area where church and schools had stood unhurt, and the Bishop's appeal for half a million pounds in part to finance the necessary repairs, recognised again the need for sharing one another's burdens. The other purposes for which the money was intended, an increase in the stipends of the clergy and the preservation of the church day schools, stressed the urgency in the post-war world of maintaining an active priesthood, and of linking the children of a society, often ignorant of Christian teaching, with the life and worship of their parish church.

In the world without, as the next chapter begins in the Southwark story, there is a challenge for the church to face as great as any in the past. The shock of two world wars and all that lay between of industrial hardship and unrest changed not only the theological stress, as a new awareness of sin coloured Christian thinking, but brought home to all the increasing secularisation, the ignorance, the insecurity of those whom the Church had failed to reach and who so often regarded her as unconcerned in their welfare. Many of the best brains and warmest hearts of the day sought to help their weaker brethren in a myriad humanitarian ways and in a better organisation of industry without reference to the Christianity which so obviously seemed to have fallen short. Yet as the ideological stresses increase and the threats of atomic power pose questions no secularist can answer, new opportunities are arising for men of vision and faith. At the Cathedral in recent years, a centre of study and Christian learning is steadily growing in scope and vitality, while a brave attempt has been made in the work of the industrial missioner to reach by personal contacts the hearts and minds of those who work in the Borough and its neighbourhood.

In 1950, the appointment of an advisory council to the bishop on industrial relations recognised the value of the work that had been done, and by the provision of further staff made expansion possible. But of necessity progress must be slow in a task rendered well-nigh impossible by weight of numbers and the limitations of time. Yet although by making friends steadily and selflessly with men and women in the riverside offices and in the streets littered with the refuse of market stalls no spectacular results may be achieved: in such a way and perhaps in no other can the people of Southwark be assured that those who serve Christ in this place truly care for them and that this is the Gospel for which their Cathedral stands.

Thus from the old church of St. Saviour and St. Mary Overie the work goes on, rooted and grounded in worship. Limited by the straitened means of to-day the work of restoration has continued, greatly assisted by the zeal and generosity of the Fellowship of Friends of Southwark Cathedral. Some of the tombs have been restored by the artist Janet Becker who was at work on the Gower monument when she died, while the East and West windows and those on the Northern side have gradually been replaced. To-day on every hand there is evidence of the continuing love and care of those upon whom the maintenance of the ancient church depends, while in less tangible ways the atmosphere of worship persists, to be experienced each year by a greater number of persons from every corner of the diocese. The great Cathedral services touch every aspect of life to-day: the world of the theatre gives thanks on Shakespeare's birthday, nurses and doctors from Guy's and St. Thomas's pray for the work of healing, or at a harvest festival for the borough, artisans and employers, apprentices and craftsmen lay upon the altar their gifts of leather goods or electric fittings. Perhaps most moving of them all is the yearly service of thanksgiving for founders and benefactors. Then as the procession makes it way beneath the arches of the Lady Chapel, by the spot, where Rogers and his friends were tried, to Lancelot Andrewes' tomb, there to pray for all who in this place have "strengthened the church of God and upheld the light of truth," the chancel for a while stands empty and the spirits of the past draw very near. The eye passes from the stonework of Fox's altar screen to the lights of Dorothy Applebee's candelabrum, below which the clergy and borough officials halt to pray for all who have "enriched our worship and our common life," from John Gower to Thomas Guy, from Prior Martin to Elizabeth Newcomen.

Thus in the Cathedral on great occasions as in the humbler offerings of every day the worship of God continues. Outwardly much has changed. On the scarred wilderness of the bombed sites great blocks of flats are arising, housing a new generation of Southwark folk, their material well-being greater than of old, their chances of mental development enhanced by the educational reform and scientific discoveries of the century. Of their spiritual starvation they are only vaguely aware, and to the indifference of the majority is added the energetic hostility of a few and the questing, insecure faith of an increasing number asking the puzzled question: what does it all mean? What is the key that gives significance to the round of days and the bustle of the market place? Is there something that unites as nothing else can do, the barrow-boys of the station approach, the stevedores of St. Mary's dock, the executive who goes home each evening to the suburbs, the teachers who labour so assiduously in the schools; and when the end comes and darkness falls, what is the sure hope that alone can conquer death? Where everything else has changed, the church still stands, the same in outward form as in inner meaning, the one building that has outlasted the assaults of time and circumstance. It believes it holds the answer to the questions, the same answer that it has given through the centuries to man's abiding need. Every day since it was built there has been offered to God in this place the worship of praise and thanksgiving. Outside, the warehouses and crowded streets, the brewery and the borough market, the traffic of the bridge and the thunder of the trains have blotted out the beauty that once there was. But still the church stands, and within its quiet walls people pause to pray and go out to help their fellows; still the ancient bells are sounded and the Gospel of Christ is preached, the same yesterday, to-day and forever.

## Note on Sources

See *Discourses and Letters of Hubert Murray Burge*: edited with memoir by Lord Charnwood (1930); C. Garbett, *The Heart of South London* (1932), and cf. for a general outline, Roger Lloyd, *The Church of England in the 20th century* (2 vol. 1946, 1949), in particular the chapter on *The witness of the Cathedrals* (vol. II, p. 231 *seq.*). The Annual Reports and statements of accounts of the *South London Church Fund and Southwark diocesan board of finance* give facts and figures which illustrate the activities of the various boards and committees whereby the work of the diocese is carried out.

# NOTE ON THE CATHEDRAL WINDOWS

THERE is no medieval glass in the Cathedral Church to-day. Drawings of various coats of arms, previously inserted in some of the windows, were made by the Lancaster Herald, Nicholas Charles, in 1610 (Brit. Mus. Lansdowne MS. 874). They belong in many cases to families connected with the Warennes, though Gower's coat of arms is also included. There is also in this collection a drawing of a window in the south transept, which depicted three knights in armour, one of whom is a Warenne. Taylor in his *Annals of St. Mary Overies* (p. 92) believes him to have been Reginald de Warenne and the other two knights to represent a Marshal (Earl of Pembroke) and a de Lacy (Earl of Lincoln).

The only old glass in the church to-day is the Tudor panel inserted in a single-light lancet in the north choir aisle. After the restoration and rebuilding, in the late nineteenth century and early in the present century, new windows were given by generous donors, the majority being the work of C. E. Kempe, of whose developing talent they formed an interesting record. One of the best, still in existence, is the window of three lights in the north wall of the Lady Chapel, depicting Thomas Becket, Laud and Charles I.

Nearly all the windows in the church were damaged or completely destroyed in the last war. The memorial windows on the north side of the nave have been repaired; they represent literary figures connected with the Borough, from Chaucer to Goldsmith. Those on the south side, which represented figures connected with the theatre on Bankside, have been replaced by clear-glass, except in the case of the Shakespeare memorial window. Here a new window has been erected, designed by Christopher Webb and unveiled by Dame Sybil Thorndike on April 23rd, 1954. In it are shewn the great Shakespearean characters in a design of much grace and beauty of colouring.

The 'tree of Jesse' window in the south transept and the East window, both by Kempe, were destroyed, but a new East window by Sir Ninian Comper, depicting the risen Christ, was inserted in 1950. The West window, a fine example of Henry Holliday's work, survived the war.

Two of the windows in the Lady Chapel are war memorials, one in St. Christopher's Chapel given by Oxo Ltd., that in St. Mary's chapel commemorating the men of the South Metropolitan Gas Company. (A war memorial to the men of Southwark stands behind the high alter on the western side of the Lady Chapel.)

The Harvard window, in the former St. John's Chapel, originally inserted in 1905, was restored in 1948 "through the generosity of Harvard alumni in the United States of America."

Further details of the windows, with particulars of the donors and the persons commemorated, have been collected by Mr. George Young, Secretary to the Friends of the Cathedral.

# Note on Sources

A detailed description of the architecture and memorials of Southwark Cathedral is included in the volume of the *Royal Commission on Historical Monuments: East London* (1930), pp. 58–66. Cf. the *Victoria County History, Surrey* (1905), II, 1–46 for the ecclesiastical history of the county; II, 107–12, for the Priory of Southwark; II, 172–87 for the Grammar School and IV, 125–62, for a detailed history of Southwark and the Church; see also *Survey of London: Vol. XXII Bankside: parishes of St. Saviour and Christchurch* (1951); to which constant reference has been made, as to the following general histories of the church:

W. G. Moss. *The history and antiquities of the parochial Church of St. Saviour, Southwark,* illustrated by Rev. J. Nightingale (1818).

W. Taylor. *Annals of St. Mary Overy* (1833).

F. T. Dollman. *Priory of St. Mary Overie* (1881).

W. Thompson. *History of St. Saviour's, Southwark* (1904).

G. Worley. *Southwark: The Cathedral and See* (1905).

T. P. Stevens. *Story of Southwark Cathedral* (1922 and later revised editions).

H. Monroe. *Cathedral church of St. Saviour at Southwark: a Pilgrimage* (1932).

For Southwark in general, see, in addition:

Manning and Bray. *The History and Antiquities of the County of Surrey* (1814), Vol. III, pp. 530 seq.

W. Rendle. *Old Southwark and its people* (1878).

Mrs. E. Boger. *Bygone Southwark* (1895).

Grace Golden. *Old Bankside* (1951).

For the Bishops of Winchester, in addition to specific biographies, reference has been made to S. H. Cassan. *Lives of the Bishops of Winchester*, 2 vol. (1827).

The *Survey* is invaluable for topographical detail and throws light on the identity and property of many leading parishioners of the 16th and 17th centuries. Dollman's massive tome includes 44 plates of considerable architectural interest while Canon Thompson's history deals mainly with the various memorials in the church, and is an exhaustive and scholarly if rather chaotic goldmine of biographical information.

The manuscript sources for the medieval period, are restricted to various charters and formal deeds in the British Museum and to scattered references in the Close and Patent rolls and the Papal Registers. After the Reformation, the documents in possession of the Corporation of Wardens of St. Saviour throw invaluable light on the day to day management of parochial affairs. They are housed at the London County Record Office, and the Southwark Central Library. An account of the ecclesiastical records and their whereabouts is contained in the Pilgrim Trust Report of Church of England archives, a copy of which is in the British Museum library (Ref. C. 120 h 7/8).

A brief note of other writings to which reference has been made is appended to the relevant chapters.

# INDEX

ABBEY WHARF, 57
Adelold, 25
Aelfheah, Archbishop of Canterbury, 24
*Age, The*, 259
Agincourt, Battle of, 81
Albemarle, George Monck, First Duke of, 202
Aldgate Priory, 60
Aldgood, Prior, 32
Alfred, King, 22
All Hallows Church, Southwark, 270; destruction of, 289
Alleyn, Edward, 17, 124, 144, 145-7, 148-9, 149-50, 158, 164, 167
Alleyn, Joan, 165. *See also* Woodward, Joan
Almoner, function of in priory, 37
Almshouses, 136; removal of to Norwood, 263; reconstruction of after World War II, 289
Anabaptist groups and assemblies, 184, 185, 205
Andrewes, Lancelot, Bishop of Winchester, 128, 168-71, 173, 174, 180, 186, 216, 265; *Preces Privatae*, 175; his tomb, 291
Angel, Matthew, 172
Angell, William, 197, 198, 206
Anglican rites, suppression of, 186, 199-200
*Anglo-Saxon Chronicle* (quoted), 22
Anne, Queen, 217, 219, 221
Anne of Cleves, 105
Anselm, Archbishop of Canterbury, 29
Anti-clericalism, after the Black Death, 62

Applebee, Dorothy, 58, 211-12, 291
Applebee, John, 208-9, 224
Archbishop's Liberty, 52
Archer, James, 160, 161, 174, 179, 189, 196
Archer, Sergeant, 155
Armada, the, 137-8
Arundel, Thomas, Archbishop of Canterbury, 81
Ashdown, H. E., Provost and Rector of Southwark, 288
Assumption, Guild of, Southwark, 89, 103
Aubrey, John: *Brief Lives*, 100, 173
Audley, Baron, 115
Augustine, St., landing of, 19
Augustine, St., of Hippo, 34
Augustinian Order, 16; Rule, 34-7, 48; diversity in observances, 95; need for reform, 95-6
Austin, Joyce, 178
Austin, William, 164, 170, 174, 175-7, 188; his poems, 177-8
Austin, William (the younger), 188, 200, 202
Austin family, the, 206
Austin Canons, the, 28, 57, 86, 87. *See also* Augustinian Order
Axe and Bottle Yard, 178, 210, 223, 232

BACON, FRANCIS, LORD CHANCELLOR, 164
Bakers: sentenced for giving light weight, 111; lease of Lady Chapel by, 128

Ball, John, 66, 67, 70

Bankside, 16, 17, 47, 56; brothels in, 53, 111-12; taverns in, 53; the theatre in, 124; inhabitants attending St. Saviour's, 112; in the seventeenth century, 156-7; nonconformist Chapels in, 202

Banstead: endowment from, to St. Mary Overie Priory, 31

Barclay, Charles, 242, 258

Barclay, David, 241

Barclay, Robert, 241

Barclay family, the, 242, 263, 273

Barclay's brewery, Southwark, 148

Bardsley, Cuthbert, Provost and Rector of Southwark (later Bishop of Croydon), 288

Barford, Jonathan, 188

Barford, Susannah, 196

Barking, nunnery at, 20

Barnwell Priory, 33, 34-5

Barry, A., Archbishop of Sydney, later Suffragan Bishop of Southwark, 273, 275

Bartholomew Fair, 93

Barton, Dr. Samuel, 216-17, 218

Bastwick, Dr., 185, 186

Baths, public, building of in Southwark, 277

Battle Abbey: town house, 57; Sussex, 100

Battle's Inn, Abbot of, 55

Baxter, Richard, 215

Bear-baiting, 133, 149, 196, 197, 202

Bear Garden, 57, 147

Bear Tavern, 202

Beaufort, Henry, Bishop of Winchester, 78, 81-6, 92; rivalry with Duke of Gloucester, 81-2, 83; niece's marriage to James I of Scotland, 82-3; unpopularity in City, 83; accepts position of Cardinal, 84; Pope's legate in

Germany, Bohemia and Hungary, 84; further crusades, 84-5; supports Regent in French Wars, 85; death, 85-6

Beaufort, Joan, 82-3

Beaumont, Francis, 150, 167

Becker, Janet, 290

Becket, Thomas à, 40, 293

Beddington: Saxon settlement at, 18

Bedford, Duke of (John of Lancaster), 85

Bedlam, 233

Bell Tavern, Bishopsgate, 142

Bell and Cross Keys, Gracechurch Street, 142

Benefield, Richard, 167, 168

Benson, Samuel, 252-3, 257, 259, 261, 262-3, 266, 272; collection of papers, 248ff.

Bermondsey: parish of, 194; Grammar School moves to, 284

Bermondsey Abbey, 92, 99, 101, 110

Bermondsey Manor, 28

Bermondsey Priory, 27, 50, 68

Bible, The: English translation of, 106; Authorised Version of, 168

Bilson, Thomas, Bishop of Winchester, 154, 157, 162, 168, 169

Bingham, Anne, 175, 177

Bingham, John, 123, 140, 150, 154, 158, 161, 162, 164, 170, 174, 177, 224, 284

Birmingham: diocese created, 279

Bishop, boy, choosing of, 59

Black Death, the, 50, 62

Blackfriars Bridge, 231

Blackheath: Jack Cade at, 90

Blackmore, Benjamin, 254, 255

Black Prince, the, 57, 64, 65, 80

Blisse, Richard, 214

Blomfield, Sir Arthur, 274

Blomfield, Charles, Bishop of London, 246

Bloxsom, Barnabas, 205
Boadicea: attack on London, 18
Bolton, Samuel, 194
Bonner, Edmund, Bishop of London, 116, 120
Borough High Street, 16, 23, 32, 52, 53, 54, 90, 148, 178, 210, 229, 231, 232
Borough Market, 15, 56, 130, 230, 231-2
Boston (a parish clerk), 161
Boswell, James, 240
Bosworth, Battle of, 94, 97
Bowling Green Alley, 264
Bradfield College mission, 272
Bradford, John, 117, 119
Bradlaugh, Charles, 272
Bretigny, Peace of, 63, 64
Breweries, in Southwark, 112, 166. *See also* Barclay's Brewery, Thrale's Brewery
Bridge House Tavern, 261
Bridge Ward Without: Southwark constituted as, 111
Briskett, Elizabeth, 210, 211
Bristow, Canon Rhodes, 276
*British Magazine, the*, 88
Bromfield, Sir Edward, 178, 186, 199
Bromfield, Edward (the younger), 206
Bromfield, Sir John, 178, 202
Bromfield, Robert, 168
Bromfield family, the, 164, 188, 200
Browker, Hugh, 162, 166-7, 188
Browker, William, 131
Browne, Sir Anthony, 100, 105
Browne, Harold, Bishop of Winchester, 267
Browne, Robert, 139
Buckeridge, John, Bishop of Rochester, 174, 175
Bunyan, John, 215, 276
Burbage, James, 140, 144, 145, 146, 147, 149, 167

Burge, Hubert, Bishop of Southwark, 285
Burgh, Hubert de, 43
Burghley, William Cecil, Baron, 139
Burke, Edmund, 241
Burnet, Gilbert, Bishop of Salisbury, 217
Burton, Prior Henry, 49, 93, 94, 104
Butler, Samuel: *Hudibras*, 223

Cade, Jack, 58, 90-1, 114
Cambridge: Corpus Christi College, 272; Emmanuel, 170, 173; Pembroke, 272; St. John's, 272; Trinity, 272; University mission, Old Kent Road, 287
Cambridge Platonists, 216
Campeggio, Cardinal, Italian legate, 98
Candlemas processions, 59, 102, 107
Canne, John, 184
Canute, King, 23-4
Cardinal's Cap Tavern, The, 57, 213
Cardmaker, John, 117
Caroline, Queen, 239
Carpenter, Stephen, 69
Cathedral Street, 56
Catherine of Aragon, Queen, 80, 81, 95
Catherine Wheel Inn, Southwark, 123
Catholic Relief Bill, 257
Cecil, Robert (First Earl of Salisbury), 122
Cellarer, function of in priory, 36
Chamberlain, John, 164
Chamberlayn, John, 229
Chambers, Mrs., 180-1
Chapman, Edward, 144
Chapter of Augustinian Canons, 48
Chapter-house, 233, 275

Charity schools, Southwark, 234, 264-5

Charles I, King, 168, 178, 182, 188, 293

Charles II, King, 200, 202, 203

Charles, Nicholas, 293

Charterhouse: Tabard Street Mission, 272

Chartist agitation (1848), 259

Chaucer, Geoffrey, 70, 293; (quoted), 60; and anti-clericalism, 62; *Canterbury Tales*, 72-3; *Troilus and Chresyde*, 71

Cheltenham College mission, 272

Chequer Alley, 133, 272

Chertsey Minister, founding of, 20

Chester, John, 205

Chesterton, G. K. (quoted), 62

Chichester: Civil War in, 190

Child, Alwyn, 27

Child, James, 240

Children's festival, 59

Chillingworth, William, 193

Cholera, 258-9

Christ Church, Southwark, 218, 244; building of (1671), 206; rebuilding (1738), 206; gutted by incendiaries (1941), 206-7

Christ Church, parish of: created, 207; in the eighteenth century, 232

Christian Socialists, 280

Christ's Hospital, 112

Chrodegang, Bishop, of Metz, 34

Church Army, 287

Church rate, 207, 224, 260-1

Cistercian Order, characteristics of, 32

Clarence, Lionel Duke of, 70

Clarendon, Edward Hyde, First Earl of, 203

Clark, John, 159

Claybrooke (a baker), 128

Clerke, Lady, 164, 170, 175, 186

Clink Liberty, the, 49, 53, 111, 124, 125, 148, 190, 197, 202

Clink Paving Commissioners, 252

Clink prison, the, 110, 242

Clink Street, 57, 197, 229

Cluny: eleventh-century reform movement from, 27, 33

Coal ships, 233. *See also* Sea coal

Cobham, Joan, Lady, 58, 60

Cock-fighting, 196

Coiners, caught in Southwark, 111

Collett, John, 225, 234

Collier, J. Payne, 88

Collingbourne, Prior Henry, 49, 67-8, 96

Collyer, Joseph, 188

Comper, Sir Ninian, 294

Compter prison, the, 110, 118, 124, 126, 208

Concanen and Morgan: *History*, 56, 229, 231

Cook, Edgar, 284

Copland, John, 226

Corner, John, 226

Corpus Christi processions, 59-60

Covent Garden Theatre, 202

Coverdale, Miles, 106

Cranmer, Thomas, Archbishop of Canterbury, 107

Crawford, John, 251

Cristehall, William de, 47

Crodacott, John, 193, 194, 195, 196, 204

Cromwell, Oliver, 191, 192, 196, 198, 200

Cromwell, Mrs. Oliver, 192

Cromwell, Thomas, 49, 98, 99, 105

Cruden, Alexander, 238-40, 276

Cure, Thomas, 112, 123, 129, 131, 135-7; his Will, 136-9

Cure's College, 168, 211

Curle, Walter, Bishop of Winchester, 180, 184

Curling, William, 259

INDEX

Curtain Theatre, Shoreditch, 143
Curtis, Robert, 129

DANES, INVASION BY, 22
Dauncey, William, 28
Darwin, Charles, 272
Davidson, Randall, Archbishop of Canterbury, 274, 276
Deaconesses of Southwark, 271, 280
Deadman's Place, 184, 185, 197, 205, 211, 229, 231, 235, 240; chapel in, 215, 239
Dekker, Thomas: *The Shoemaker's Holiday*, 148
Despenser, Constance le, 80
Dickens, Charles: *Barnaby Rudge*, 242
Digby, Kenelm, 190-1
Dingle (a brush-maker), 260-1
Dissent. *See* Nonconformity
Dollman, Francis, 214, 273
Domesday Book, 24
Donne, John, Dean of St. Paul's, 146, 165, 185; (quoted), 53
Dover Castle, 185
Drewett, William, 273
Drury Lane Theatre, 202
*Dublin Review*, 262
Duck and Dog, Southwark, 243
Dulwich College, 17, 146, 164-5, 213, 284
Duppa, Brian, Bishop of Winchester, 203
Dyeing works in Southwark, 166
Dyer, Sir Edward, 152-3

EDGEHILL, BATTLE OF, 188
Edington, William, Bishop of Winchester, 63
Edward the Confessor, King, 24
Edward I, King, 47, 49
Edward III, King, 49, 63; anti-French feeling during his reign, 50

Edward IV, King, 49, 93, 94
Edward VI, King, 100, 110, 111, 112, 113, 127, 128, 129
Edward VII, King, 274, 276, 277
Edwards, Canon Allen, 276
Edwards (a vintner), 181
Edwin of Northumbria, 19
Eliot, John, 179
Elizabeth I, Queen, 109, 122, 128, 138; visit to Southwark, 135
Elphinstone, John, 155
Embleton, Luke, 260, 261
Emerson, Humphrey, 157
Emerson, Thomas, 172, 177, 224
Emerson, William, 102, 110, 129, 131, 135
Engeir, Thomas, 226
Episcopacy: attacks on, 186; protests against attacks, 187; restoration of, 204
Erasmus (quoted), 106
Erconwald, Bishop of London, 20
Ethelred the Unready, 22
Eton College, founding of, 92
Evangelical movement, 243, 244; nineteenth-century revival, 249

FAIRFAX, GENERAL THOMAS, 191, 192
Falcon Inn, Bankside, 123-4, 229, 230
Fancourt, W. L., headmaster of St. Saviour's Grammar School, 263
Farnham Castle, 247
Fastolf, Sir John, 90, 91
Fauconberg, Thomas, 94
Fawcett, Christopher: report on vagabonds, 171
Fermerer, function of in priory, 36
Ferrar, John, Bishop of St. David's, 118-19
Ferthing, Aleyn, M.P. for Southwark, 49-50, 55, 60

301

Feudalism, 27

Fichett, John, 89

Field, C.D., 273

Field, Nat, 150, 161

Fire: damage done to Cathedral by, 16, 40, 207-8

Fisher, Edward, Archdeacon of Southwark, 271

Fisher, William, 47, 48

FitzAlan family, the, 49

Fitzgerald, Alexander, 32

Fitzgerald family: gifts to St. Mary Overie Priory, 32

Flemish weavers in Southwark, 66

Fletcher, John, 150, 167, 173; *The Faithful Shepherdess*, 167

Fletcher, Lawrence, 148

Footscray, land from, granted to St. Mary Overie, 30

Fortune Theatre, Clerkenwell, 149

Fountains Abbey, 101

Fox, Richard, Bishop of Winchester, 44, 96-7, 213, 229, 252, 291

Francis, Chaplain, 160

Franklyn, Gregory, 162

French, the: feeling against, during Edward III's reign, 50

French invasion (1216), 43

French Wars (Fourteenth-century), prosperity due to, 48, 55-6

Froissart (quoted), 63

Fuller: *Church History* (quoted), 19-20

GALEAZZO, GIAN, 79

Garbett, Cyril, Bishop of Southwark (later Bishop of Winchester and Archbishop of York), 282, 286-7, 288; (quoted), 287

Gardiner, Stephen, Bishop of Winchester, 97, 100, 102, 105-9, 115-16, 119-20, 124; consistory court of, 116-17

Garland, Thomas, 140, 154

Garter, Order of the, 63, 84

Garrick, David, 241

Gataker, Thomas, 194

Gaunt, John of, 64, 65, 70, 78

George IV, King, 246

George Inn, Southwark, 54, 124, 230; destruction by fire (1676), 207; rebuilding of, 209

Giffard, Walter, Archbishop of York, 46

Giffard, William, Bishop of Winchester, 28-9, 30, 33

Gilbert of Merton, 33

Gilmore, Mrs., Head deaconess, 271

Gladstone family, the, 278

Glastonbury, Abbot of, 100

Globe Alley, 204, 231, 240; chapel in, 205

Globe Theatre, Southwark, 124, 149, 163, 167; demolition by fire, 149; rebuilding and re-opening of, 150; destruction of, 197

Gloucester, 118

Gloucester, Humphrey Duke of, 81, 83, 84

Godolphin, Sidney, First Earl of, 219, 222

Godstone: St. Saviour's property at, 213

Godwin, Earl, 24

Goldsmith, Oliver, 240, 241, 276, 293

Goodwin, William, 99

Gordon, Lord George, 242

Gordon riots, the, 242

Gore, Bishop Charles, 280

Gothic architecture: nineteenth century interest in, 250

Gower, John, 70, 71-6, 112, 290; *Speculum Meditantis*, 71; *Vox Clamantis*, 71-2, 74; *Confessio Amantis*, 72-3, 75
Grand Remonstrance, 188
Grapes Inn, Southwark, 124
Gravel Lane, 175, 229, 232
Gray, John de, Bishop of Norwich, 41
Great Fire (1666): problems as result of, 206
Great Liberty, the, 52, 111
Great Suffolk Street, 229
Green Dragon Court, 263
Green Walk, 229
Greene, T. H., 268-9
Greenwich Railway, 260; opening of, 249
Gregory, Saint, 19
Greville, Fulk, 153
Greyfriars, 112
Greyhound Inn, Southwark, 123
Greyladies, sisterhood of, 280
Grist (a plasterer), 260, 261
Groundolf, Alice, 75
Guardians: first election of (1767), 234-5
Gunpowder Plot, 152
Guy, Thomas, 233, 291
Guy's Hospital, 233
Guyot de Provence (quoted), 34
Gwilt, George, 251-2, 254, 255, 258, 273

HADLEIGH, 119
Haldane, J. B., Precentor and Rector of Southwark, 286, 288
Hales, Treasurer, execution of, 66
Halsey, Edmund, 240
Hansonne, Chaplain, 132-3
Hardwick, Colonel John, 198
Harington, Sir John, 154
Harman, Chaplain, 132
Harold, King, 24, 25
Harris, Richard, 169, 211

Harrison, Dr. William, 252, 258
Harvard, John, 173
Harvard, Robert, 164, 173
Harvard, Thomas, 188
Harvard University, 173
Hawkes, Frederick, Bishop of Kingston, 288
Hayman, John, 188
Hedger, James, 231
Henden, Thomas, 99
Henry I, King, 28, 30
Henry II, King, 31
Henry III, King, 43
Henry IV, King, 69, 74, 78, 79-80, 81, 82
Henry V, King, 79, 81, 82, 84
Henry VI, King, 79, 92, 94
Henry VII, King, 97
Henry VIII, King, 95, 98-9, 100, 124
Henry of Blois, Bishop of Winchester, 31
Henslowe, Philip, 124, 140, 143-7, 149-51, 158, 162, 163, 167, 213, 224
Herd, John, 260
Herne Bay: poor children's outing to, 277
High Churchmen, 216
Hoadley, Benjamin, Bishop of Winchester, 296-7
Hoare, William, 205, 216
Hogarth, William, 230
Hoke, Simon, 69
Hokering: endowment from to St. Mary Overie Priory, 31
Holland, Susan, 167
Hollar, Wenceslaus, 125
Holliday, Henry, 294
Holyland, James, 132
Holy Trinity-the-less Church, 106
Hook, Cecil, Bishop of Kingston, 279
Hooker, Richard, 154
Hooper, John, Bishop of Gloucester, 112, 116-18, 119

Hope Theatre, Southwark, 149-50, 167, 196
Hopton Street, 229
Horne, Robert, Bishop of Winchester, 129-30
Horne, Thomas, 218, 220, 225
Hough, William, Bishop of Woolwich, 287
How, Sir Richard, 200, 202, 206, 208-9
Howard of Effingham, First Baron, 138
Howard, Catherine, Queen, 105
Humble, Peter, 163
Humble, Richard, 138-9, 157, 158, 163, 174, 184
Humphreys, John, 188
Huntingdon Priory, 33
Hussites, the, 84
Hyde, Abbot of, 55
Hyland, Samuel, 198-9, 206

INTERREGNUM, THE, 184ff.
Ireton, Henry, 193
Isaac, Bartholomew, 214
Isle of Dogs, 147
Ivo of Chartres, 34

JACKSON, REBECCA, 212
Jacob, Henry, 184, 212
James I, of Scotland, King, 82-3
James I, of England, King, 149, 154, 155, 168
James II, of England, King, 217
Jansen, Gerard, 174-5
Jenkins, David, 211
Jessey, Henry, 184, 189, 196
Jesuit schools, 182
Joan of Arc, 85
John, King, 41
Johnson, Dr. Samuel, 240, 241
Jones, Inigo, 149
Jones, Philip, 216
Jones, Thomas, 235-7, 249

Jonson, Ben, 146, 147, 149; Bartholomew Fair, 150
Justus, Archbishop of Canterbury, 19, 21

KATHERENS, GILBERT, 149, 159
Keats, John, 250
Kelle, Chaplain, 131-2
Kempe, C. E., 293, 294
Ken, Thomas, Bishop of Bath and Wells, 203
Kennett, White, Bishop of Peterborough, 220
Kent, Edmund Earl of, 79, 80
Kent, Joan of, 80
Kidbrooke (Kedebroke): church appropriated by St. Mary Overie Priory, 86
King's Bench prison, 52, 54, 91
King's College Chapel, Cambridge, 88
King's Game, Mastership of, 149
King's Head Inn, Southwark, 124
Kirkesfeld (Crechesfeld) Church, given to St. Mary Overie Priory, 31
Knight of the Burning Pestle, 167
Knowles, Professor (quoted), 50
Kyngeston, Prior John, 68-9

LACY, DE, FAMILY, 293
Lade, John, 222, 226, 227, 233
Lady Fair. See Our Lady's Fair
Lambert, Major-General John, 197
Lambeth Palace, the burning of, 66
Lanfranc, Archbishop of Canterbury, 27, 34
Lang, Leslie Hamilton, Bishop of Woolwich, 288
Langley, Francis, 140, 147, 166
Lannoy, Peter, 198
Lant, Thomas, 210

Latimer, Hugh, Bishop of Worcester, 113
Latitudinarians, 216, 226
Laud, William, Bishop of London (later Archbishop of Canterbury), 128, 170, 180, 181, 182, 186, 265, 293
Lawrence (a sexton), 126
Lectures, given by seventeenth-century clergy, 180
Leeke, Henry, 131
Leeke, J. C., Bishop of Woolwich, 279
Leicester: Chapter of Austin Canons at (1518), 95
Leland, John, 105
Lenthall, Sir John, 185
Levy, John, 235
Lewes: foundation of Cluniac cell at, 27
Lewes Castle, 27
Lewes, Robert, 134
Lilburne, John, 191
Lind, Jenny, 242
Linsted, Prior Bartholomew, 20, 49, 96, 98, 99, 100
Little Rose, the, 143
Lock Street, lepers in, 76
Locke, John: influence of his philosophy, 216
Lollardry, 81
Lombards, in Southwark, 66
Londinium, 18
London Bridge, 32, 37, 39, 43, 50, 57, 231; fall of (1014), 22-3; fire on (1212 or 1213), 40; Wat Tyler's rebels cross, 66; Jack Cade crosses, 90-1; fighting on, under Fauconberg, 94; Sir Thomas Wyatt's rebels come to, 113-14; less use of in Elizabeth I's reign, 122; re-building of (1825-31), 249, 253-4, 255
London Bridge Station, building of, 249

London, City of: Charters to, giving extended rights over Southwark—(1462), 93; (1550), 111; relations of, with Surrey magistrates, 243
London County Council trade schools, establishment of, 264
Long Parliament, 185, 186
Long Southwark, 83, 93
Longe, Richard, 102
Love (a bailiff), 152
Lyttelton family, the, 278

Macaulay, G. C., 71
Macmillan, Alexander, 273
Magna Carta, 41, 43
Maid Lane, 112, 144, 148, 229, 264
Manchester: Grammar School, 119; Civil War in, 190
Mann, Dr. William, 252, 259
Marberry, Mr., 160
Marlborough, John Churchill, First Duke of, 217
Marlborough, Duchess of, 219
Marlowe, Christopher, 163; Tamburlaine the Great, 144; The Jew of Malta, 144
Marshall, John, 159, 178, 188, 200
Marshall, John (the younger), 178, 179, 206
Marshall family, the, 172, 178, 293
Marprelate, Martin: tracts, 133
Marshalsea, the, 52, 54, 66, 91, 118, 124, 138, 147, 179, 242
Marston Moor, Battle of, 200
Martin, Prior, 41, 42, 49, 104, 291
Martin, Dr. Richard, 205, 217
Mary I, Queen, 113-14, 116, 129
Mary, Queen (wife of King George V), 276
Masham, Mrs., 219
Massinger, Philip, 167, 173-4

Matthew, Thomas, 107
Maurice, Frederick Denison, 265;
　*The Kingdom of Christ*, 265
Mayhew, Mr., 159
Maynard, Mr., 159
Meade, Jacob, 140, 147, 150
Medwall, John, 89
Mellitus, Bishop of London, 19
Merbecke, John, 108-9
Merchant Taylors School, 190, 263
Merton Priory, 101
Mews, Peter, Bishop of Winchester, 217
Michell, Prior, 99
Mickelthwaite, Chaplain, 169, 170
Milan, Bernabo Duke of, 79
Milan, Lucia of, 79-81
Milan Cathedral, 81
Millar, Canon, of Rochester, 271
Miller, George, 183
Mint, the, 197, 232
Missionaries, landing of in England, 19
Mitcham: Saxon settlement at, 18; advowson of, granted to St. Mary Overie Priory, 31
Mitre Tavern, Fenchurch Street, 218
Monasteries, dissolution of, 97, 98ff.
Monger, James, 240
Monmouth, Duke of, 217
Montague, Anthony Browne, First Viscount, 100, 110, 114, 116, 120, 136, 138
Montague, Anthony Mary Browne, Second Viscount, 152
Montague Close, 100, 122, 138, 166, 190, 204, 208, 224-5, 235
Montague, Edward, Bishop of Winchester, 168
Montfort, Simon de, 58
Moore, Mary, 172
Morals, seventeenth-century surveillance of, 181

Morley, John, Bishop of Winchester, 203
Morris, William, 271
Morton, John, 234
Morton, Nicholas, 170, 173, 175, 179, 180-1, 189, 196
Moss, W. G., 248, 250

Napoleon; war with, 244
Narborough, F. D. V., Provost and Rector of Southwark (later Bishop of Colchester), 288
Naseby, Battle of, 191, 200
Nash, Thomas, 144, 147
Neal, William, 214
Neile, Richard, Archbishop of York, 180
Newcomen, Elizabeth, 58, 209-11, 234, 276, 291
Newcomen family, the, 200
Newcomen schools, 264, 284-5
Newcomen Street, 178, 211, 232, 264
Newdigate, advowson of, granted to St. Mary Overie Priory, 31
Newington: parish of, 194
Newington Butts: playhouse at, 143
Newland, Abraham, 238
Nicholson, James, 106
Nightingale, J.: historical notes by, 248, 250
Nightingale and Moss: *History and Antiquities of the Parochial Church of St. Saviour's*, 248, 250
Nonconformity, 202, 218; seventeenth-century growth of, 184ff.; persecution of, 215
North, The Hon. Brownlow, Bishop of Winchester, 246
Northampton, Battle of, 92
Norton, Philip, 134
Nottingham: Royal Standard raised at, 188

ODO OF BAYEUX, 25
Olaf of Norway, 22, 23
Old Kent Road, 122
Onger, Nicholas, 190
Onslow, George, First Earl of, 235
Our Lady's Fair, Southwark, 93, 162, 202, 230
Overman, Alice Shaw, 209, 234
Overman, Thomas, 168, 178, 186, 191-2, 200
Overman, William, 209
Overman family, the, 152, 178
Overs, Mary, 20, 58
Owen, Robert, 193
Oxford, Sixteenth Earl of (John De Vere), 142
Oxford University: Keble College, 278; Magdalen College, 218; the founding of, 92; New College, 129; the founding of, 68
Oxford Movement, 262, 265-6
Oxo Ltd., 294

PAINE, TOM, 272
Palaces, mediaeval, in Southwark, 55
Palmer, Samuel, 226
Paris Garden, 49, 52, 124, 140, 149, 167, 197, 202
Park Street, 136, 144, 240
Parliamentary party: politics and religion of, 191
Parsons, Richard, Bishop of Southwark (later Bishop of Hereford), 282, 288, 289
Paston, John, 90
Pattinson, Brian, 134, 140
Paulinus, Bishop of Rochester, 19
Payn, John, 90
Payne, John, 158, 178
Peacock (a baker), 128
Peasants' Revolt, 66-7, 68
Pecham, John, Archbishop of Canterbury, 46-7, 69

Pembroke, Second Earl of (Henry Herbert), 147, 167
Pepys, Samuel, 202
Perambulation of parish bounds, 156, 159, 228
Perkins, John, 242
Perrers, Alice, 64, 65
Pestilence. See Plague
Peter (builder of first stone London Bridge), 39-40
Peterloo, 257
Philip, of Spain, King, 113, 114-15
Philips, Edward, 133, 140, 160
Phillips, Augustine, 148
Piers Plowman, 62
Pilgrim Church, Great Dover Street, 205
Pimlico Path, 197
Pious Life of Dr. Sacheverell, 218
Piozzi, Gabriel, 241
Plague, the: (1467), 93; (1592), 144-5; (1576), 147; (1625), 173-4; (1665), 205
Playhouses. See Theatre
Plumstead, hermitage of, granted to St. Mary Overie Priory, 31
Poitiers, Battle of, 57
Politics and religion: late seventeenth-century intermingling of, 215-17
Poll-tax, 65-6
Pont de l'Arche, William, 28
Poor Children's Aid Fund, 277
Pope, Sir Thomas, 110
Pott, Charles, 258
Pott family, the, 263, 273
Powell, Thomas: The Mystery of Lending and Borrowing, 166
Poynet, John, Bishop of Winchester, 110
Pratt, Henry, 212
Precentor, function of in priory, 36
Presbyterians, 191, 192, 193-4
Pride, Colonel Thomas, 198, 199
Prince Consort, Albert, 242

Prior: function of, 36; importance of character of, 48-9; his house, 56
Prior, Thomas, 181
Prynne, William, 185
Pudding Mill, 30
Pugin, A. W. N. (the younger), 262, 266
Puritans: control in London, 189
Putney: troops in, during Civil War, 193
Pyke, Edward, 226
Pyke Gardens, 197

QUARLES, THOMAS (QUOTED), 163
Queen's Head Inn, Southwark, 124, 211; as endowment to St. Saviour's School, 162

RAHERE (KING'S JESTER AND FOUNDER OF ST. BARTHOLO- MEW'S HOSPITAL), 33
Rainsborough, Thomas, 192, 193
Ralegh, William de, 45
Ranelagh Gardens, 202
Ratclyffe, Chaplain, 132, 133
Red Cross Street, 229
Red Lion Inn: as endowment to St. Saviour's School, 162
Reform Bill (1832), 257, 259
Reformation: effect of on great houses of Southwark, 112
Reigate (Kirkesfeld), 279
Rendle, William, 273
Rennie, James, 253
Rennie, Sir John, 253, 254, 255
Richard I, King, 41
Richard II, King, 57, 65, 67, 70, 74, 78, 96
Richardson, Madeley, 284
Richardson family, the, 178
Ridley, Nicholas, Bishop of London, 113, 119
Rievaulx Abbey, 101
Robinson, Lawrence, 131
Roches, Peter des, Bishop of Winchester, 41-3, 44, 45

Rochester, 19: Southwark trans- ferred to diocese of, 267
Rochester Diocesan Society, 271
Rochester House, 55, 56
Rockett, Gilbert, 162
Rogers, Elizabeth, 172
Rogers, John, 106, 117-18, 119, 291
Romaine, William, 236, 237
Roman settlement in Southwark, 18
Roman Catholics: in the seven- teenth-century, 205; repeal of penal laws against, 242
Rose Alley, 57
Rose, Hugh, 265
Rose Theatre, Bankside, 144, 145, 146, 163, 167
Rose, William de, 31
Roses, Wars of the, 92
Rotherhithe, parish of, 194
Rump Parliament, dissolution of, 198

SACHEVERELL, DR. HENRY, 218- 21, 222, 224, 225
Sacrist, the, function of in priory, 36
Sadler, John, 126
St. Albans; new see created, 267
St. Andrew's, Holborn, 221, 225
St. Augustine's, Canterbury, Abbot of, 55
St. Bartholomew's Hospital, 60
St. Bartholomew's Priory, Smith- field, 33, 60
St. Benet Sherehog, Church of, 31
St. George's Church, Southwark, 54, 98, 189, 244, 273; dis- turbances at, 187; Presbyter- ianism in, 194
St. George's parish, 112, 172; during Great Plague, 205; during eighteenth-century, 232; nineteenth-century growth of, 248-9

St. George's Fields, 229, 231, 232, 242, 243, 249; burnings in, 120

St. Giles Cripplegate, 164, 168

St. Hilda's Nunnery, Barking, 20

St. Hilda's Priory, Aldgate, 33, 60

St. John's, Horsely Down, 244, 252

St. Lawrence, Old Jewry, 188

St. Lucy's Day celebrations, 89

St. Margaret's Church, Southwark: bestowed on canons of St. Mary Overie Priory, 31, 32; fifteenth-century Church accounts, 87, 88; expenses, 88; foundation of Guild, 89; absorbed into new parish, 102, 103

St. Margaret's Day celebrations, 89

St. Margaret's Hill, 171

St. Margaret's parish, 54, 59

St. Mary Abchurch, 31; advowson of, granted to Duke of Suffolk, 86

St. Mary's dock, 56, 167-8, 229

St. Mary Magdalene Church, Southwark, 44, 76, 101; becomes part of St. Saviour's Church, 102, 103

St. Mary Magdalene's parish, 54, 59

St. Mary Overie, Priory of: possible early nunnery dedicated to, 20; old legend of, 20-1; new church built, 29; reconstruction of Observances, 34-6; destruction by fire (1212 or 1213), 40; during the baronial wars, 46; rebuilding of, 44; Great Door, 58-9; fire in southern transept (Richard II's reign), 67; scandal at, 69; rebuilding (c. 1400), 75; scene of royal weddings (1406), 79, 82; fifteenth century, great prosperity during first half of, 86; recasting of bells, 87; collapse of stone roof of nave (1469), 93; erection of new wooden roof, 93-4; surrendered to Henry VIII (1539), 99; becomes parish church, 102-3; election of wardens, 103. See also St. Saviour's Church and Southwark Cathedral

St. Mildred, Bread Street, Church of, 31, 86, 144

St. Mildred, Poultry, Church of, 31

St. Nicholas's Day, children's festival on, 59

St. Olave's Church, Southwark, 23, 28, 244; disturbances at, 187; Presbyterianism in, 194

St. Olave's parish, 52, 54, 92, 112, 185, 232-3

St. Olave's School, 131

St. Olave's and St. Saviour's Grammar School, 284

St. Paul's Cathedral, founding of, 19

St. Paul's School, 190

St. Peter's, Sumner Street, 247, 264; destruction of, 289

St. Saviour's Church, 16; tessellated pavement in churchyard, 18; naming of, 104; expense of upkeep, 104; sixteenth-century repairs and alterations, 112-13; consecration of six bishops in (1554), 115; first century of, 123; rules governing conduct of church and officials (1557), 125-6; election of Church wardens, 125; vestryman's job, 126; Minute books: (1557), 126-7, 134; (1582), 135; (to 1627), 175ff.; (1627-60, missing book), 179, (1703), 223; wardens' new lease (1558-9), 127; establishment of grammar school, 127; sale of parish ornaments, 127, 128; letting of Lady Chapel, 128; Thursday

St. Saviour's Church—*cont.*
lectures, 133; music, 134; parish registers, 134; legal position of vestry men challenged, 155-6; purchase of rectory from Crown, 158-9; choice of clergy, 160; wardens' care for fabric, in seventeenth-century, 179-80; attack on Communion rails (1641), 186-7; contribution to Parliamentary loan (1642), 188; Presbyterianism in, mid-seventeenth century, 193, 194; after Restoration, 205; authorisation of wardens' rate (1671), 207; financial difficulties, 207; fire of 1676, 208; end of select vestry, early eighteenth century 222, 225-6; financial difficulties, 223; prosecution of grave-digger for body-snatching, 225; complaints of new wardens against predecessors (1730), 227; new method of electing wardens, 228; parish parties, 228; deterioration of fabric, early nineteenth century, 243; nineteenth century: unfavourable criticisms of church, 249-50; proposed restoration, 250-1; controversy over, 254; criticisms of restoration, 262; becomes pro-Cathedral of South London (1897), 274-6; Chapter sworn in, 276; parish magazine, 277

St. Saviour's parish: petition to put down play-houses, 148; seventeenth century: 166-8, 171-3; plague, 173-4; benefactions, 211-12; wardens' difficulties, 212-13; eighteenth century: 229-32; nineteenth century: early difficulties in, 244; growth during, 248; quarrels (1832-48), 256-61; offensive against Church rate, 260-1; pride in schools, 264; grimness and poverty in later years of century, 275; parochial life since formation of diocese, 284

St. Saviour's Grammar school, 127, 130-1, 161-2, 168, 190, 234, 263, 284; Bingham scholars, 190; fire of 1676, 208; re-building of, 209; legacy from Elizabeth Newcomen, 210

St. Saviour and St. Mary Overie, Cathedral and Collegiate Church of. *See* Southwark Cathedral

St. Saviour's and St. Olave's Grammar School for Girls, 294

St. Stephen, Coleman Street, 188

St. Stephen, Walbrook, 188

St. Swithun's, monks of, 55, 85, 112

St. Thomas's Almshouse, 42

St. Thomas's Church, 275; re-building of (1702), 233

St. Thomas's Hospital, 40-1, 56, 171, 190, 225, 249; foundation of, 16; printing press of, 106; refounding and new dedication of, 112; and fire of 1676, 208

St. Thomas's parish: in the eighteenth century, 233

St. Thomas's Priory, 68, 76, 99

St. Thomas' Street, 230

Salcot, John, Bishop of Salisbury, 108

Sanctuary, right of, 56, 166, 202, 232

Sanders, Lawrence, 118

Sandwich, French attacks on, 118

Santon (Sawton), Daniel, 194

Saunders, Thomas, 258

Saxon invasion, 18-19; conversion to Christianity, 19-20

Saye, Baron, 91, 92

Scales family: gifts to St. Mary Overie Priory, 31-2

Scott-Holland, Canon Henry, 280
Sea coal, 166; complaints about, 54-5; blockade on in Civil War, 190
Sectaries, growth of, 184ff.
Sedgemoor, Battle of, 217
Shakespeare, Edmund, 148
Shakespeare, William, 146, 148, 163, 167; *Henry VI*, 144; *Henry VIII*, 149; *Titus Andronicus*, 144
Shaw, James, 209
Shere: St. Saviour's property at, 213
Shorter, Sir John, 215
Side, Mr., 270
Sidney, Sir Philip, 153
Simpson, Bertram, Bishop of Southwark, 289
Six Articles, Act of (1539), 98, 108
Skelton, John, 73
Slockock, Benjamin, 225
Smith, John, 225, 243
Smith, Matthew, 130
Snape, Chaplain, 160
Soap industry, in Southwark, 112, 166, 199
South Metropolitan Gas Company, 294
South Sea bubble, 233
Southwark: as "Sudewerke", 21; as "Suthvirki", 22; scene of fighting against Danes, 22-3; burning of by William I, 24-5; suitability of for twelfth-century ecclesiastical residences 29-30; parliamentary representation from, 49; Manor of, 52; importance of geographical position of, 54; sixteenth-century improvements in, 111-12; Sir Thomas Wyatt's rebels encamp in, 113-14; character altering during Elizabeth I's reign, 122-3; fortified against

approach of Charles I, 188; radical faction in mid-seventeenth century, 192; fire of 1676 in, 207-8; Lord Mayor's court of record in, seventeenth-century, 208-9; eighteenth century in, 229ff.; archdeaconry established in, 271; appointment of first suffragan bishop, 273; appointment of first bishop, 279; made municipal borough (1899), 284; dock strike (1912), 285; sale of Treasurer's house to railway company (1919), 286; World War II in, 289; Bishop's appeal for funds, 289; post-war Christian work in the diocese, 289-90
Southwark Bridge, 231, 264
Southwark Cathedral (*see also* St. Mary Overie Priory, *and* St. Saviour's Church):
Aisles, 28, 49
Altar screen, 97, 129, 213, 214, 258, 291
Atmosphere of, 16
Bells, 87, 148, 205; new (1734), 227-8
Bishop's Chapel: removal of (1830), 255
Cathedral Plate, 23
Choir: nineteenth-century repair of, 248, 252
Clerestory, 44; rebuilding in, 252
Cloisters, 28
Coffin of Prior, 49
Crusader, effigy of, 49
East Window, 294
Fellowship of Friends of, 290
Harvard Chapel, 28
Harvard Window, 294
Lady Chapel, 15, 44, 49, 112-13, 116, 284, 293; letting of, 128, 170, 255-8; nineteenth-century repairs of, 248

Mary Magdalene Chapel: removal of, 252
Memorials, 16, 174-5, 211, 214, 215, 237-8
Nave, 15, 28; bosses on roof of, 93-4; taken down, 255; new nave, 260-2, 271, 272, 274
Norman remains, 28
Organ, 214
Prior's entrance, 28
Pulpit, 214
Reredos, 288
Rood loft, removal of, 129
St. Christopher's Chapel, 294
St. John's Chapel, 28, 75, 173, 179, 294
Saxon traces, 28
Shakespeare window, 148, 293
Tower, 213; repairs to, 227, 251-2
Transepts, 28, 44, 84; repairs to, 254-5
Triforium: rebuilding in, 252
Windows, 293-4
Southwark Place, 122, 178
Spencer, Benjamin, 189, 191-2
Spenser, Gabriel, 147
Stacy, John, 69
Stane Street, 18, 33, 122
Star Chamber sentences: revocation of, 185
Starch industry in Southwark, 123
Stephen, King, 31
Sterry, Benjamin, 225
Stoke Poges Church: given to St. Mary Overie Priory, 31
Stokes, Hugh de, 31
Stokes, Reginald de, 31
Stow, John: *A Survey of London*, 20, 21, 74, 153, 206, 229; (quoted), 54
Stoney Street, 136, 197
Strafford, First Earl of (Thomas Wentworth), 185
Strange, Baron (later Earl of Derby), Ferdinando Stanley, 144, 145

Street markets, 54
Strype, John, 206, 229
Sturlason, Snorre: Icelandic sagas of, 22-3
Sudbury, Simon, Archbishop of Canterbury, 66
Suffolk, Duke of (Charles Brandon), 95, 98, 110-11
Suffolk, Duchess of (Mary Tudor), 95
Sumner, Charles, Bishop of Winchester, 246-7, 267, 268
Sumner, John Bird, Archbishop of Canterbury, 246
Sumner Street, 263-4
Supremacy, Act of (1534), 98
Surrey: early history of, 18-19; Dispensary, 235; nineteenth-century wish for diocese of, 267; suggested transfer of West Surrey to Rochester, 273
Surveys, annual, of clerical property, 156-7
Sussex, Fourth Earl of, 139
Sutton, Dr. Thomas, 161, 169, 184
Swan Theatre, 140, 147, 167
Sweyn: capture of London by, 22
Swithun, St., Bishop of Winchester, 21-2
Swynford, Katherine, 70, 78
Symes, William, 234
Symonds, Dr., 160, 161

Tabard Inn, Southwark, 54, 55, 60, 124, 207, 230
Tachau, Battle of, 84
Talbot, Edward, Bishop of Rochester, Southwark, Winchester, 268, 272, 275, 276, 278-82, 283, 284
Talbot, Hon. Mrs. Edward, 278, 280
Talbot, Gilbert, 282
Talbot, Bishop Neville, 282

Talbot Inn: *see under* Tabard Inn, Southwark
Tarrant, Thomas, 226
Taylor, Jeremy, 193
Taylor, Rowland, 119
Taylor, Samuel Mumford, Archdeacon of Southwark, Bishop of Kingston, 276, 279, 283-4, 285
Taylor, W.: *Annals of St. Mary Overie*, 248, 256, 293
Teck, Duke and Duchess of, 276
Temple, William, Archbishop of Canterbury (quoted), 285
Temple, Richard (Lord Cobham), 240
Tenements: evolving from Southwark's great houses, 112, 124; profits from, given to St. Saviour's School, 162
Test Act, 218
Testwood, Robert, 108
Tewkesbury, Battle of, 94
Thames, River: blockade of by royalist fleet, 190
Theatre, The, Shoreditch, 142-3
Theatre, the, in Southwark, 140, 142
Thirlby, Thomas, Bishop of Ely, 116
Thomas, John, Bishop of Winchester, 246
Thompson, Ida Mary Overie, 272
Thompson, William, Chancellor of Southwark, 272, 276
Thorndyke, Dame Sybil, 293
Thorold, Anthony, Bishop of Rochester (later Winchester), 268ff., 276, 278; *The Gospel of Work*, 268; views on ritualism, 270; rehabilitation of St. Saviour's, 270; Church rate, 270; vigorous work as Bishop, 271; training of deaconesses, 271
Thrale, Henry, 235, 241
Thrale, Hester, 240, 241, 242

Thrale, Ralph, 240
Thrale's Brewery, 231
Three Crowns Court, 231-2
Three Tuns, Bankside: as endowment to St. Saviour's School, 162
Tickner, Chaplain, 160
Timber ships, 233
Tintern Abbey, 101
Tiptree, Prior of, 57
Toclyve, Richard, Bishop of Winchester, 32
Tolbooth, the, 238
Tolls, disputes over, 25
Tomline, Sir George Pretyman, 246
Tooting: endowment from to St. Mary Overie Priory, 31; Christian Socialist rendezvous in, 273
Tories, the, 216, 217, 219
Tower of London, 57, 122
Toynbee Hall, 272
Tractarians, 279
Transport trade in Southwark, 123, 166
Trehearne, John, 154, 158, 163
Trelawney, Jonathan, Bishop of Winchester, 217
Trinity-the-Less, Church of, 31
Tryggvason, Olaf, 22
Tudor destruction of mediaeval records, 15, 129
Tyler, Wat, 58, 62, 66-7, 70, 90, 114
Tyndale, William, 106

UNIFORMITY, ACT OF, 138
Union Street, 252; chapel moved to, 240-1; schools, parochial, in, 264, 285

VAGABONDS, REPORT ON (1622), 171
Valence, Aymer de, Bishop-elect of Winchester, 45-6

Valerianus, Prior, 32
Vauxhall Gardens, 202
Vindication, the (1649), 195, 204
Visitations, annual, 156, 236

WADSWORTH, THOMAS, 196, 205
Wandle, River, 18
Wainfleet, William, Bishop of Winchester, 91, 92, 94
Walker, Thomas, 197, 198
Wallys, Prior William, 46, 47-8, 49, 60
Walpole, Sir Robert, 221
Walton, Isaac, 203
Walton, Margery, 181
Warcopp, Robert, 198
Warcopp, Samuel, 188
Ward, William, 164
Ware, Mrs., 182
Warenne, Hamelin de, 31
Warenne, John de, 46, 49
Warenne, John de (the younger), 49, 52, 60
Warenne, Reginald de, 293
Warenne, William de (First Earl of Surrey), 25, 27-8, 43, 279
Warenne, William de (Second Earl of Surrey), 29, 30-1
Warenne, de, family, 31, 293
Warwick the King-maker, 92
Waterman, George, 214
Watkins, John, 195
Watkins, Stephen, 193, 194, 195, 196, 204, 210
Watkins, Susan, 210-11
Watkins daughters, the, 195
Watling Street, 18
Waverley Abbey, 33, 101; Abbot, 55
Waverley House, 55, 112, 136
Webb, Christopher, 293
Wellington College mission, 272
Wells, Canons of: disobedience to Pope, 86

Wendover: endowment from to St. Mary Overie Priory, 31
Wengham, Henry de, Bishop of London, 46
Werkworth, Henry, Prior, 49, 86, 89
Wesley, John, 235-6
Westminster Assembly (1645), 193
Westminster Bridge, 231
Westminster School, 168
West Norwood: almshouses in, 289
Weston, Prior Robert, 49, 69, 75
Whigs, the, 216, 217, 226
White, John, Bishop of Winchester, 125, 129
Whitehall Palace, 122
White Hart Inn, Southwark, 90, 91, 124, 230; destroyed by fire (1676), 207
White Lion Inn, Southwark, 138
Whittaker, Jeremy, 194
Wickham, William (the younger), Bishop of Winchester, 153-4
Wigan Chanters, the, 284
Wigan, Sir Frederick, 274, 276, 277, 283-4
Wilberforce, Samuel, Bishop of Winchester, 267
Wilberforce family, the, 246
William I, King, 24-5, 27
William II, King, 28
William IV, King, 255
William of Oxford, Prior, 32
William of Savoy, Bishop of Winchester, 45
Willis, Richard, Bishop of Winchester, 226
Wilmot, Miss, 280
Wilson (a baker), 128, 170
Winchelsea, French attacks on, 64
Winchester: Civil War in, 190
Winchester Cathedral, 129
Winchester College, 125; founding of, 68

Winchester House, Southwark, 30, 32, 55, 56, 63, 68, 79, 83, 86, 105, 110, 112, 113, 152-3, 168, 190, 191, 197, 202-3; tearing up of books in, 114; Queen Mary I entertained at, after her wedding, 115; new workhouse built on site of, 224
Windsor: Civil War in, 190
Windsor Castle, 63
Winkworth, William, 243
Winnington-Ingram, Arthur F., Bishop of London (quoted), 283
Wolsey, Thomas, Cardinal, 95, 96, 97
Women stew-holders, 53
Wood, Anthony, 154
Woodward, Canon C. S. (later Bishop of Bristol and Gloucester), 285
Woodward, Hezekiah, 190
Woodward, Joan, 145, 150. See also Alleyn, Joan
World War II: damage in Southwark during, 289

Worley (quoted), 262, 279
Worrall, Thomas, 212
Wren, Matthew, 174, 175
Wright, Richard, 181
Wriothesley, Charles, 97-8
Wyatt, Sir Thomas, 113-14
Wyatt (a baker), 128
Wycliffe, 62
Wydfleete, the, 30
Wykeham, William of, Chancellor of England, Bishop of Winchester, 62-5, 67-8, 69-70, 75, 79, 92
Wyngaerde, Anthonie van den, 125


YEATMAN-BIGGS, HUYSHE, BISHOP OF WORCESTER, SUFFRAGAN BISHOP OF SOUTHWARK, 275, 276, 279, 280, 286
York: Civil War in, 190
York, Frederick, Duke of, 253
Young, George, 294
Young, Henry, 212
Younger, Margaret, 172

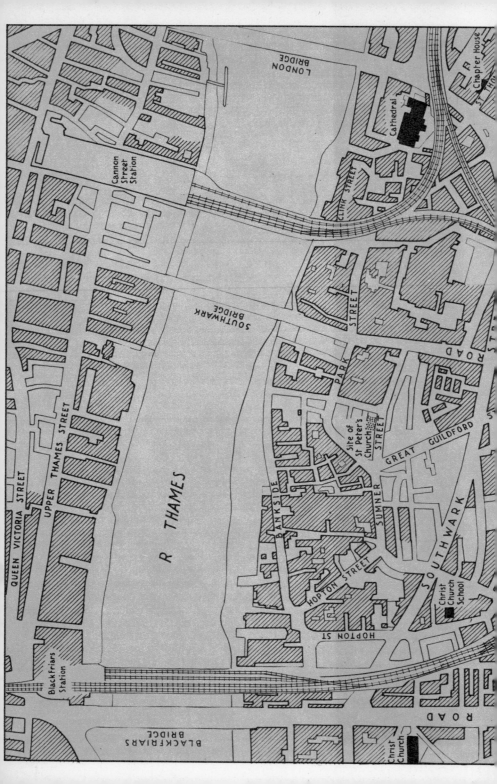